The Hiker's Guide

to UTAH

By Dave Hall
Revised by Ann Seifert

Falcon Press is continually expanding its list of recreational guidebooks using the same general format as this book. All books include detailed descriptions, accurate maps, and all information necessary for enjoyable trips. You can order extra copies of this book and get information and prices for the books listed above by writing Falcon Press, P.O. Box 1718, Helena, MT 59624. Also, please ask for a free copy of our current catalog listing all Falcon Press books.

Copyright © 1991 by Falcon Press Publishing Co., Inc.
Helena and Billings, Montana
Second Edition.

Library of Congress Catalog Card Number: 91-072794
ISBN: 1-56044-062-7

Printed in the United States of America.

Falcon Press Publishing Co., Inc.
P.O. Box 1718, Helena, MT 59624

Photos by the author except as noted.
Cover Photo: Mark Muench, Capitol Reef National Park.

 Text pages printed on recycled paper.

Acknowledgments

The author of a favorite book said it best: Although it's a little book, it took a lot of help to become a book at all.

The *Hiker's Guide To* Utah would not have gotten past the planning stages had it not been for Dick Carter and the Utah Wilderness Association. UWA members did most of the hikes in this guide, often publicizing favorite areas in the hopes that more hikers will mean more support for wilderness designation. To Dick and Association members go heartfelt thanks.

Of course, thanks go to all the writers and photographers—too numerous to mention here—who contributed their time to this project. You will find their names throughout the guide. If you run into these folks on a mountaintop sometime, you might also thank them. Their passion is to save small pieces of wild Utah for you and future hikers.

Employees of several federal and state agencies were immensely helpful. They hiked some of the trails, offered advice on backcountry problems and ethics and reviewed many of the chapters and all the hikes. I am indeed grateful to these employees of the U.S. Forest Service, Bureau of Land Management, U.S. Geological Survey, National Park Service, Utah State Divisions of Wildlife Resources and Parks and Recreation, and the Utah Travel Council.

Many thanks go to Jim Ure, Steve Alder and Lee Kapaloski who offered valuable editorial advice and to top-notch photographers John Telford, Jim Kay and John George for their various contributions.

Besides contributing two hikes to the guide, Alexis Kelner also consulted on the maps and provided considerable background on the history of the conservation movement in Utah. He, like many members of the Wasatch Mountain Club—Utah's first real conservation organization—has led dogged battles in support of Utah's backcountry.

I would be remiss if I did not thank personally Ann Mason and Melody Fairbourne in the Wasatch National Forest Information Office as well and Wendy Hassibe, Clem Heagren, Susan Farnsworth and Cheryl Johnson in the U.S. Geological Survey map office. Also thanks to Kris Richardson and Sylvia Jorgenson who did an admirable job with all the typing.

The fine maps in The Hiker's Guide To Utah come from the steady hands of Margaret Pettis and my father, Vern Hall. Besides doing several of the hikes for the guide and contributing the sketch found in the Afterword, Margaret also spent a considerable amount of time dealing with a fussy editor in planning the maps and doing the pen and ink work. All the lettering comes from my father in Princeton, Massachusetts, who refused payment but insisted on the opportunity to have a drink with his son in celebration of the guide's publication. He has never hiked in Utah, but admits that he's intrigued now.

Finally, I want to thank Becky, my wife and favorite hiking companion, who did many of the hikes in the guide and has become a fine copy editor. She did none of the typing.—*Dave Hall*

CONTENTS

CENTRAL UTAH — *The Great Basin, Fish Lake National Forest, Wasatch Plateau, San Rafael River, and the Book Cliffs*

SOUTHERN UTAH — *The National Parks, Pine Valley Mountains, BLM Wilderness, The Escalante River, Henry Hountains, and Grand Gulch area*

LOCATION OF HIKES

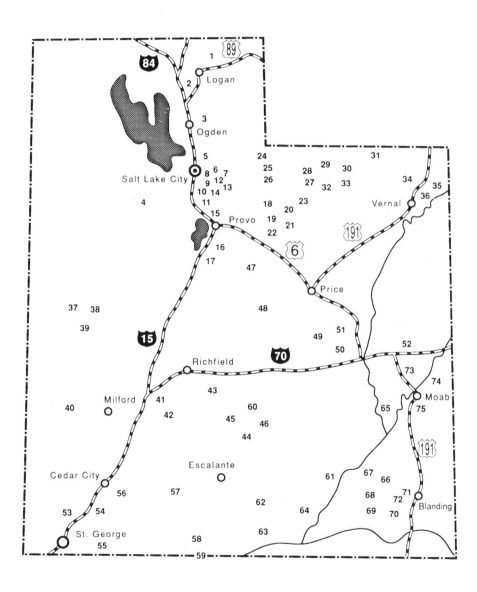

Arches National Park—Bob Bauer.

HIKING IN UTAH

Who says the whole family can't make the trip? Dave Hall photo

Hiking is for everybody

Although we occasionally hear claims that only the young , rich, and elite use wilderness, quite the reverse is true. Families spend many pleasurable nights camping far from vehicles. And day hiking (or "walking for pleasure," as agencies sometimes call it) is undoubtedly one of the most popular forms of outdoor recreation.

The people who make such statements must do little, if any, hiking or they surely would see young, old, large, small, rich and poor—all thoroughly enjoying the backcountry trails. Hiking and backpacking are available to all ages, sexes, and sizes. They only require a small amount of physical conditioning and a minimal amount of equipment.

That's right—a minimal investment. Hiking and backpacking can be expensive like any other pastime if one chooses to make them so. On the other hand, they can be one of the most economical forms of outdoor recreation—especially with day hiking which requires nothing except a pair of hiking shoes that may already be in the closet.

1

The Utah backcountry is unmatched in its variety.

Fire rings and trash are becoming an all-too-common sight in many of Utah's backcountry areas.—Dave Hall photo

For overnight trips, more expense is required. But even this can be a small investment. The cost of a two-week vacation, staying in motels and eating in restaurants, would be sufficient to outfit an entire family for backpacking. And this equipment can be used year after year. Once a small initial investment is made, hikers can see millions of acres of spectacular, roadless country without spending another penny on equipment. They only need a few dollars for food and for transportation to the trailhead. After the trailhead, it's free.

Not only is hiking free in the economic sense, but it is also free of the stress and regulation of modern America. Once on the trail, hikers can forget (albeit only temporarily) the tension of their work, the Internal Revenue Service, the unpaid bills, the noise and pollution—it's all behind them for a few hours or days. They can't even hear the bad news on the radio.

Hiking provides an escape—a chance to inhale the pungent aroma of a wildflower meadow, to hear a bugling elk or the wind whistling through mature pines, to hook a native trout instead of a hatchery-raised catchable, to see the sunset across a mountain lake or a mountain goat race over cliffs man would need climbing gear to negotiate, to drink from a gin-clear stream, and to study vegetation that evolved without man's influence.

All this is here for the taking. Fortunately, Utah offers plenty of opportunity to do so.

Hikers can, of course, plan their own trips by talking to local hikers or agency personnel and searching through topographic maps. But to make it easier, we published this guide. It contains enough hikes for a lifetime of backcountry thrills.

We've included hikes from almost every roadless portion of Utah—from the alpine splendor of the Uintas to the deep canyons of the slickrock country and the ranges and valleys of the Great Basin.

We've also included hikes for all kinds of hikers—beginners, families, experienced backpackers. In fact, most of the hikes are short day hikes—usually well-suited for families or inexperienced hikers. Since we've picked hikes from throughout Utah, one of the trailheads is likely only a short drive away.

Also, we feel the way this guide is written makes it particularly valuable. Instead of relying on the experience of one or a small group of hikers, we've listed the favorite hikes of veteran Utah hikers—people who wish to share their experience with others, hoping new users will appreciate these areas and fight to preserve them.

The maps included with each hike add a final touch to the already detailed and accurate descriptions. In addition, there are several chapters of interest to all hikers on subjects from backcountry ethics to hiking with children. With this guide, hikers shouldn't have any trouble discovering and enjoying wild Utah.

Writing a hiking guide for any state is a challenge. But for Utah—with thousands of hikes in the Wasatch, Uintas, Great Basin, Book Cliffs, canyon country, national parks and elsewhere—the chore becomes more difficult. Utah is unique among western states in that it offers exciting alpine hiking typical of the northern Rockies as well as some of the most breathtaking canyon hiking in the world.

Obviously, this guide does not cover every hike from every backcountry area of the state. Rather, our philosophy in assembling The Hiker's Guide to Utah has been to offer beginning and veteran hikers, long-time residents, and newcomers an introduction to Utah's spectacular wild lands. There are hikers who know every peak and lake in the Uintas, yet know nothing of the Pine Valley Mountains, Mt. Naomi, the San Rafael River, the Wah Wahs and Grand Gulch.

In addition to getting the hiker to the trailhead, it is also our intention to relate the importance of responsible wilderness use. With more people in the backcountry and increasing demands on public lands each year, some of our "pristine" areas are beginning to look like city parks. Hikers, along with other backcountry users and land management agencies, will have to assume the responsibility of maintaining the opportunity for quality outdoor experiences in the future.

Hence, this guide stresses outdoor ethics. You will find sections on walking softly, the preservation of archaeological resources, and wilderness in Utah. The names and addresses of state and federal land management agencies and local conservation organizations are provided in the appendix in the event you wish to ask a question, voice an opinion, or take a more active role in management issues. And where appropriate, suggestions are made throughout The Hiker's Guide to Utah to make your trip a safe one and lessen your impact on the land.

Happy hiking.

Touching the land lightly

Compare your favorite hiking area with your living room.

You don't mind visitors. Often, you invite them. But you want them to treat your home with respect.

If you have six obnoxious visitors who put their cigarettes out on the floor, spill drinks, and use foul language, your living room has, in your mind, exceeded its carrying capacity. And these visitors will leave lasting marks.

On the other hand, if you have a dozen quiet, polite, neat guests, the thought that your living room is being overused never enters your mind. And after they've gone home, there is no sign of their presence.

Using wilderness can follow the same theme. There is a large capacity as long as everybody behaves. But a few thoughtless or uninformed hikers can ruin it for others. An important item on every hiker's checklist should be proper wilderness manners. Don't leave home without them.

Most hikers treat wilderness gently, but some aren't aware that they have poor manners. Often, their actions are dictated by outdated remnants of a past generation of wilderness campers who cut green boughs for evening shelters and beds, set up camp close to alpine lakes, built fire rings, and dug trenches around tents. Twenty years ago, these "camping rules" may have been okay. Today, they leave unacceptable, long-lasting scars.

The wilderness is shrinking, and the number of hikers is mushrooming. In fact, use has increased by more than 300 percent in some western wilderness areas in past years. In some national parks, it has increased even more. Without question, some camping areas show unsightly signs of this craze.

Thus, a new code of ethics is growing out of necessity to cope with unending waves of hikers—all wanting a perfect wilderness experience. Indeed, they should have it and probably can have it if all hikers educate themselves on proper and courteous use of fragile country.

• As a general rule, touch the land as lightly as possible. Canoeists can look behind them and see no sign of their passing. The next canoe party has no idea another canoe is around the next bend. It should be the same with hiking and backpacking. Leave only memories and good times behind.

• Nowadays, nobody dares litter—in or out of the wilderness. This means everything, including orange peels, flip tops, cigarette butts and gum wrappers. Leave nothing, regardless of how small it is, along the trail or at the campsite.

• Try to camp below timberline. Alpine areas are delicate and require special care. Often, it's only a short hike to a good campsite below timberline.

• Also, keep your camp off the shoreline or stream bank. Take alternate

Escalante country.—Utah Travel Council photo

routes to water to avoid leaving a beaten path.

• Hikers seek solitude and silence, so avoid making loud noises that may disturb others. This is only common courtesy.

• Be careful with food wastes to prevent unsightly messes and bad odors. If fires are allowed, burn food wastes. Throw cans and foil into the fire to burn off food scraps and odors. Then before breaking camp, dig them out of the ashes and pack them out.

• Likewise, burn fish viscera if fires are allowed. If fires aren't allowed, wrap fish viscera and leftover food in plastic bags and carry them out or at least to the next fire area. Avoid throwing fish viscera into mountain streams and lakes. (Technically, the State Wildlife Code permits fish viscera to be deposited in streams as long as the air bladder has been broken. However, this is not recommended in small alpine streams. In the case of lakes, it is illegal to throw viscera into the water closer than 100 feet from shore.)

• Waste water from boiling foods should be poured around the perimeter of the fire to keep it from spreading. This also protects natural vegetation. Wash dishes and clothing well away from streams and lakes and carefully discard dish water, such as in a small sump hole that can be covered with soil later. Never wash dishes in a mountain stream or lake; a glob of instant oatmeal is almost as ugly as an aluminum can on the bottom of a crystal-clear lake or stream. If you use soap, make sure it's biodegradable.

• As with food wastes, be careful with human wastes. If toilet paper is used, bury it or burn it. Thoroughly bury human wastes to avoid any chance of bad odor. This is an excellent reason to carry a lightweight trowel. Obviously, waste must be kept away from lakes and streams.

• Perhaps fires cause more damage than any part of backcountry camping. In many areas, avoid fires completely. (Sometimes regulations prohibit fires.) This goes double for alpine areas where wood is scarce and topsoil is sparse.

• If a fire is allowed and appropriate for the campsite, dig out the native vegetation and topsoil and set it aside. Don't build a fire ring with rocks. When breaking camp, douse the fire thoroughly, scattering or burying the cold ashes. Replace the native soil and vegetation.

• Another acceptable method is spreading several inches of mineral soil on a flat rock to avoid fire-scarring the rock. Later, scatter or bury the ashes and expose the rock—which should still look natural.

• Build fires away from trees to prevent damage to root systems. Keep them small. And widely disperse any partly burned wood.

• Don't make a mess tearing apart trees to get firewood. Don't use a saw or ax on a tree and leave a lasting scar. And never build a fire ring or light a fire near a reflector rock which will be permanently scarred.

• Whenever possible, consider using your backpacking stove.

• Take a bath by jumping in water, then moving away from the water to lather yourself. Rinse off by pouring cans of water over your body. This allows soap to biodegrade quickly as it filters through the soil. Of course, use only biodegradable soap.

• Avoid cutting switchbacks. And leave "souvenirs" for the next hiker to see; don't carry them out. See page 9 for a discussion of state and federal laws which protect archaeolgical resources.

• Finally, follow the pack-in, pack-out rule. If you carry it in, you must consume it, burn it, or carry it out.

Hiking with the kids

Watching a two-year-old's eyes as he listens to his first echo at Arches National Park is a rare and wonderful experience. So is watching confidence swell in a five-year-old as he enjoys his first backpacking adventure in the High Uintas. And observing a three-month-old's eyes as she sees the outdoors from her dad's back is something a new parent will never forget.

In fact, seeing a national park, state reserve, or local hiking trail from your child's perspective is like rediscovering a favorite spot.

Kids see things from a different angle. They can spend hours watching a bug walk across the sand. They take great delight in running from one number to the next on a guided trail. And flnding the next rock cairn on the trail can be the highlight of a hike.

Children are impressed by the little things in the outdoors, often more so than adults. They enjoy studying a spider web hidden beneath a log. They can spend hours playing make-believe on a hill near your camp. And they gain confidence by climbing a steep hill.

But many parents make the mistake of postponing backpacking trips until their children get old enough to take care of themselves. These parents miss some rare treasures.

Sure, there are hassles involved in hiking, camping and exploring with young children. The kids cry in the car. They get hot and tired. They get scared of the dark. And with young children, there are diapers to worry about.

But many of these problems can be avoided with careful planning and some common sense.

First of all, plan your camping vacation with your kids in mind. Obviously, a five-year-old isn't going to be able to handle a two-week, sixty-mile trek through the Escalante Wilderness. While he might be capable of an overnight or two-night trip in the Uintas, he's going to need plenty of rest and encouragement to get him to your destination.

So, plan your initial vacations with children under six at places where the hikes are short, where there are plenty of interesting things to feel, see and listen to, and where your camp is close enough so afternoon rests are easy to enjoy. Places like Goblin Valley near Hanksville, Kodachrome Basin near Cannonville, Coral Pink Sand Dunes near Kanab, and Arches National Park near Moab are all excellent spots to take young children camping.

You should try to plan your trips so that when your children hike hard one day, they can relax around the camp the next. That may sound dull to adventure-minded adults, but this method will help you relax a bit on your vacation as well.

Don't always expect to reach the final destination of a hike with your children. Sometimes, kids will spot something along the trail that really fascinates them. They won't want to reach that special lake or arch at the end of the trail. It's better at times to give in to their wishes and put off that goal for another time.

It's a good idea to take some "treats" along the trail with you. Give them to your children when they appear to be getting tired. Let your older children carry their own small day pack with water, candy and lunch.

Finally, try to be a step ahead of your children when hiking. Anticipate what's ahead and see if you can get your kids to look forward to learning many things on the trail. Is there a waterfall around the next bend? Do you know the name of the plant? What did Indians use that plant for? Is that a squirrel up ahead? Questions like these will encourage your children to stay interested and keep walking.

When hiking with very young children under eighteen months, carry them on your back with a child carrier as much as possible. But as soon as they learn to walk, allow them to toddle a bit on the trail. This serves two important purposes. It will expand their growing awareness of the world around them and it will tire them out so they'll sleep better in the tent later.

In many ways, expanding a young child's world is the best of all reasons to take them on hikes and camping trips as early as possible, even when they are two and three weeks old. Much of a child's intellect is formed in the first five years of life. Children who have seen geysers at Yellowstone, buffalo in the Black Hills, taken a river boat ride on the Mississippi River, and walked through a cave have a head start on their peers when school begins.

Besides, hiking, camping and enjoying the outdoors as a family can provide you with some of the best vacation memories and most enjoyable times imaginable. — *Tom Wharton.*

Archaeological resources, the law and you

"Of approximately 25,000 recorded archaeological sites in Utah, over ninety percent of them show effects of vandalism." — Richard Fike, Archaeologist, Bureau of Land Management.

While hiking in almost any part of Utah, it is common to find archaeological sites and artifacts—dwellings, pottery, arrowheads, grinding stones and woven sandles. These discoveries are an intriguing, exciting part of Utah hiking. They give us a glimpse of former cultures, of farming, architecture, recreation, food gathering, art and religion many hundreds of years old. When we hike these areas, we leave the twentieth century behind—if only for a weekend.

Unfortunately, artifacts are becoming less common, dwellings are crumbling under the weight of hikers scrambling over them, and rock art is being crowded by the likes of "Jim loves Sue."

The largest wholesale removal of artifacts occurred during the last century, when scientific parties shipped thousands of pieces to eastern and foreign museums. Federal and state laws have since put controls on these activities, and research designs now must accompany any proposals to remove artifacts. However, unauthorized pilfering continues.

Pocketing an arrowhead on federal or state land is illegal and it leaves one less treasure for tomorrow's hiker to see. Artifacts should be left in place. They're of much more value where they are than they possibly could be in your bureau drawer.

Two federal laws, the Antiquities Act of 1906 and the Archaeological Resources Protection Act of 1979, forbid removal or destruction of archaeological resources on Utah's federal lands. The acts' intentions are to protect and preserve the resources for the future — for the scientific community *and* for other hikers who will follow after you. The more recent act updates and improves the earlier Antiquities Act. It's purpose "is to secure, for the present and future benefit of the American people, the protection of archaeological resources and sites which are on public lands and Indian lands, . . . " Stiff fines and imprisonment can result from failure to follow these guidelines.

The Utah State Antiquities Act, enacted in 1973, provides similar protection on state lands.

What can you do to help protect this splendid resource? First, recognize that you and several other hikers bringing home "just one small arrowhead"

Vandalized ruins and kiva in Grand Gulch.—Kent Miller photo

can in time be just as damaging as large-scale and purposeful vandalism. It takes a little longer, but the result is the same. So, enjoy and study what you find, but leave these pieces where you find them. Second, report any vandalism to the nearest federal or state resource office. In some cases, rewards are offered.

Helping to find Utah's rare mammals

The Utah Division of Wildlife Resources is asking hikers to help inventory populations of some of Utah's rarest mammals.

In 1978, the state wildlife agency began a program to survey and inventory populations of the black-footed ferret, Canada lynx, wolverine, river otter and wolf. Historically, these five species had stable populations here. But due to alteration of habitat, persecution, and value as furbearers, they are now extremely rare in the state. Some may no longer exist here or are documented only by occasional sitings or wanderings.

If Wildlife Resources finds that one or more of these species is indeed present, then decisions will be made for their management. Before plans can be made, however, current populations and distributions must be determined.

The black-footed ferret (*Mustela nigripes*) was last seen in San Juan County in 1952. A member of the weasel family, its most conspicuous markings are a black-tipped tail and feet and a black mask across the face. The rest of the body is a pale buff.

The lynx (*Lynx canadensis*) is slightly larger than a bobcat and once roamed throughout the Uintas and Utah's central mountains as far south as Iron County. Now, you'd be most likely to see a lynx in the forested areas of the Uintas.

Wolverines (*Gulo gulo*) were last seen in the high Wasatch and Uintas. One shot near Vernal in 1979 was probably introduced to the state. The wolverine could now be extinct in Utah, but possible sitings in recent years keep biologists wondering.

The same is true of the wolf (*Canis lupus*). This misunderstood and maligned animal was once found statewide, except in the western desert regions. It is probably extinct here now. However, the wolf may make occasional wanderings through the state's more remote sections.

The river otter (*Lutra canadensis*) has been seen along streams and lake borders in the Raft River Mountains, the Wasatch and Uintas. Historically, it was also present in the Colorado and Green rivers.

You can help with the Division of Wildlife Resources' research. If you think you have spotted one of these rare mammals or have seen tracks or other signs, contact the Rare Mammal Specialist at the Division of Wildlife Resources, 1596 West North Temple, Salt Lake City, Utah 84116, (801) 538-4700.

For more information on these species, consult two guides—A Field Guide To The Mammals and A Field Guide To Animal Tracks, both in the Peterson Field Guide Series. These offer complete information on the species as well as sketches and discussions of various signs. Division of Wildlife Resources biologists are also available to answer any questions.

About the maps

The maps which accompany each of the hikes have been prepared from United States Geological Survey (USGS) quads and from Forest Service and Bureau of Land Management maps. While the maps in the guide are up-to-date renditions, you should also take along the appropriate USGS map(s) on your hike. These will provide more detailed information on the area. They are available at several locations around the state (see Appendix 111).

The appropriate maps for each hike are mentioned in the introductory information prior to the hike description.

Each map is accompanied by a small map of Utah indicating the location of the hike in the state. There is also a north-south directional indicator, and the scale.

North is toward the top of the page on most maps, but to avoid confusion, consult the directional marker on the maps before orienting yourself. On several maps, north is slightly to the left or right of the top of the page.

Consult the scale carefully on each map. Obviously, hiking distances will vary on maps with considerably different scales—even though the maps are the same size on the page.

Although the maps have been reproduced from the most up-to-date maps available, there may have been changes—natural or otherwise—since publication. This is why sources of current information have been provided for each hike. It is wise to consult the appropriate land management agency before making your hike, especially on those hikes which require a long trip to the trailhead on low-grade roads.

MAP LEGEND

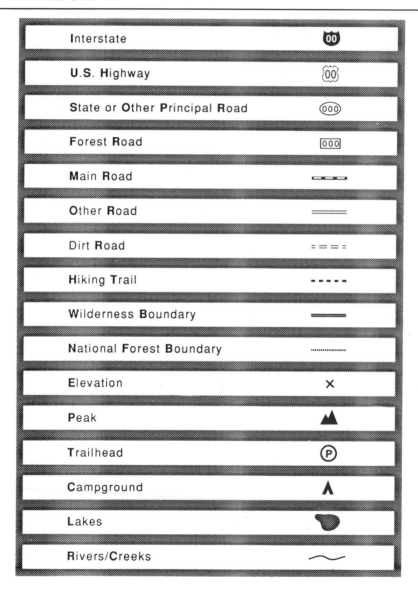

Interstate	00
U.S. Highway	00
State or Other Principal Road	000
Forest Road	000
Main Road	
Other Road	
Dirt Road	
Hiking Trail	
Wilderness Boundary	
National Forest Boundary	
Elevation	X
Peak	▲
Trailhead	Ⓟ
Campground	Λ
Lakes	
Rivers/Creeks	

MAKING IT A SAFE TRIP

Backcountry safety

Perhaps the best safety advice has guided scouts for many decades—be prepared. For starters, this means carrying survival and first aid equipment, compass, and topographic map—and knowing how to use them.

Perhaps the second best advice is to tell somebody where you're going and when you plan to return. Pilots must file flight plans before every trip, an excellent safety rule that can be used by hikers. Leave your plan with a friend or relative before taking off.

After those two points, safety advice can go on and on. There are probably other tips besides those listed here, but if hikers adhere to the following suggestions, they should have a safe trip.

• Be especially careful with fires.

• Watch weather carefully, being especially careful not to get caught in a deep canyon during a rain storm, on a ridge during a lightning storm, or at high altitude by a snow storm.

• Check the long-term forecast to avoid extended periods of stormy weather.

• Consult the appropriate land management agency to get the latest update on road conditions, water levels, and/or snow depths.

• Don't hike at night.

• Never split up in the backcountry; always keep your party together.

• Avoid temptations to swim across cold alpine lakes.

• Stay on the trail unless you are a very experienced hiker.

• Don't slide down snowbanks with cliffs or rocks at the bottom.

• Know the symptoms and treatment of hypothermia, the silent killer (see page 21).

• Be aware of the consequences of drinking contaminated water. Become familiar with Giardia and the illness it causes—giardiasis (see page 16).

• Study basic survival and first aid before leaving home.

• Don't eat wild mushrooms or other plants in the backcountry unless you are positive of the identification.

• Find out as much as you can about the hike, especially any potential hazards, before you leave.

• Avoid hiking alone.

• Don't exhaust yourself or weaken members of your party by trying to travel too far, too fast.

• Don't wait until you're confused to open your topo map. Follow it as you go along, starting from the moment your hike begins.

• If you get lost, don't panic. Sit down and relax for a few minutes while you carefully check out the topo map and take readings with the compass. Confidently plan your next move. Thousands of hikers have spent unplanned nights in the woods and survived. A few—usually those who panicked and

Whether you're hiking in stark "wastelands" or along lush river bottoms, desert hiking requires special planning.—James Kay photo

wandered about without a plan—didn't survive. If you've followed the rules and left your "flight plan" with somebody, they will be looking for you in the morning.

• In general, don't take any chances while in the backcountry such as climbing cliffs, jumping ravines or canyons, or challenging shaky tree "bridges" over streams.

• Finally, stay clear of all wild animals. A healthy respect can prevent potentially dangerous confrontations.

Although well publicized when they occur, rattlesnake bites are not common in Utah. Only about five bites are reported annually, and only one person has died from a bite in Utah since 1900. Complications from bee stings are much more common. However, if a member of your party is bitten by a snake, the best treatment is to get medical attention as soon as possible, keeping the victim calm in the process. Both tourniquets and cutting are controversial and are not recommended unless you know exactly what you are going.

Hiking the desert

Many beginning hikers and newcomers to the state are awed—indeed, per-plexed—by the prospects of hiking the desert. Undoubtedly, there are visions of unending salt flats, heat waves dancing on the horizon, and a lone cactus breaking the monotony. Why would anyone want to hike there?

Actually, the "desert", as Utah hikers like to call it—possibly to weed out the tenderfeet—is a diverse country of deep canyons, shady, often lush river bottoms, high plateaus, bizarre rock formations, and rich archaeological his-tory. Hiking here inspires superlatives.

Conditions can be harsh, but the desert does not have to be an inhospitable place to travel. Follow the general advice below and you can have a safe and enjoyable trip.

• Get a general idea of the kind of hiking you will be doing. Call the appro-priate management agency or a person familiar with the hike.

• Get a report on road conditions leading to the trailhead.

• Avoid mid-summer hikes. In most cases, spring and fall hikes are preferable.

• Know what the water conditions are. If water quality is poor or if no water exists along the trail, you must carry all water in with you. Generally, one gallon per day per person is required.

• Some river water may be too silty to drink. Carrying in a collapsible plas-tic container permits the water to "settle out" while you are making camp. (Treatment may still be necessary.)

• When drinking untreated water, make sure it is from springs or canyon seeps.

• Prepare for the sun. Carry a good sun screen or lotion. A cap with a vi-sor is also recommended. Legs can be particularly susceptible when hiking along rivers.

• Deer flies can be bothersome in some areas. A good brand of insect repel-lent helps to solve the problem.

• Watch the weather carefully. Flash flooding can be very dangerous. When hiking long distances in deep canyons, be sure to get a reliable long-term fore-cast. Remember that it does not have to be raining where you are hiking. A storm miles up the canyon can mean trouble.

• Canyon hiking does not require the heavy boots necessary elsewhere. In fact, they become a burden when hiking long distances through water. Light canvas boots or old running shoes are recommended. (Incidentally, if you do wear your leather boots and they get soaked, let them dry in the open air. Drying them next to fire breaks down the cells in the leather.)

• When river crossings are required, line your pack with heavy-duty plastic bags. Seal the bags well, and the pack will float across. Some hikers bring along an inflatable air mattress to use for ferrying packs.

• Above all, prepare for your trip and use common sense.

Hypothermia: The silent killer

Be aware of the danger of hypothermia—subnormal temperature of the body. Lowering of internal temperature leads to mental and physical collapse.

Hypothermia is caused by exposure to cold and is aggravated by wetness, wind and exhaustion. It is the number one killer of outdoor recreationists.

The first step is exposure followed by exhaustion. The moment you begin to lose heat faster than your body produces it, you are undergoing exposure. Two things happen. You voluntarily exercise to stay warm, and your body makes involuntary adjustments to preserve normal temperature in the vital organs. Both responses drain your energy reserves. The only way to stop the drain is to reduce the degree of exposure.

The second step is hypothermia. If exposure continues until your energy reserves are exhausted, cold reaches the brain, depriving you of judgment and reasoning power. You will not be aware that this is happening. You will lose control of your hands. This is hypothermia. Your internal temperature is sliding downward. Without treatment, this slide leads to stupor, collapse and death.

To defend against hypothermia stay dry. When clothes get wet, they lose about ninety percent of their insulating value. Wool loses less heat; cotton, down and some synthetics lose more.

Choose rain clothes that cover the head, neck, body and legs and provide good protection against wind-driven rain.

Understand cold, wind-chill factor and humidity. Most hypothermia cases develop in air temperatures between thirty and fifty degrees Fahrenheit.

If your party is exposed to wind, cold and wet, think hypothermia. Watch yourself and others for these symptoms: vague, slow and slurred speech; memory lapses, incoherence; uncontrollable fits of shivering; immobile, fumbling hands; frequent stumbling and lurching gait; drowsiness (to sleep is to die); apparent exhaustion; and inability to get up after a rest.

When a member of your party has hypothermia, he/she may deny any problem. Believe the symptoms, not the victim. Even mild symptoms demand treatment.

- Get the victim out of the wind and rain.
- Start a fire or get the victim to another heat source.
- If the victim is only mildly impaired, give warm drinks (never give alcohol). Strip off all wet clothes and get the person into warm clothes and/or a warm sleeping bag. Well-wrapped, warm (not hot) rocks or canteens will help.
- If the victim is badly impaired, attempt to keep him/her awake. Put the victim in a sleeping bag with another person—both stripped. If you have a double bag, put the victim between two warm people.—*U.S. Forest Service*

Giardia lamblia (*Should I drink the water?*)

There are few backpacking pleasures that can top a cool drink from a high country lake or stream. Whether on a day hike close to a large metropolitan area or miles into the backcountry, the refreshing sip along the trail is tradition.

The Utah Department of Health (UDH), however, points out that even crystal clear streams in low-use areas can carry waterborne parasites. The most common is Giardia lamblia, an invisible protozoan which can have far from inconsequential results when ingested. The UDH reported more than 650 cases from across the state in 1980, up four times over 1977.

The illness (called giardiasis or sometimes "beaver fever") is characterized by severe diarrhea, weight loss, gas, "rotten egg" belches, fatigue, and possible cramps. The symptoms occur a week to three weeks after drinking the water, so backpackers may dismiss the illness as "something I ate yesterday." See your doctor if these symptoms arise soon after a backpacking trip. Giardiasis is treated effectively with various drugs but can last indefinitely if untreated.

The spread of the protozoan through the United States (there seem to be particularly high concentrations in the West) is partly the result of an influx of persons into backcountry areas in recent years. Specifically, control of the disease is hampered by the sloppy sanitary habits of some backcountry users.

Giardia is carried by wild and domestic mammals and humans. When carriers defecate near or in a stream, tiny cysts are introduced. These cysts, a dormant and hardy phase of *Giardia*, can withstand climatic extremes for months. The stream or lake may be contaminated in no other way and can appear "pristine."

When cysts are ingested (just a few picked up while brushing your teeth can be enough), they attach to the wall of the upper small intestine. Increased temperatures activate the cysts into a reproductive trophozoite stage, causing the sickness several days later. Wildlife and humans pass both the trophozoite and cyst stages in their feces, and the "bug" can be carried into uninfected drainages.

What can you do to steer clear of *Giardia*? First, the UDH suggests you assume that *no* water source is immune from the parasite. With this in mind, boiling your water is the recommended treatment prior to use. Iodine, while not foolproof, is probably better than Halazone. Neither, however, has been shown to be consistently effective in penetrating the hard shell of the cyst.

Also, sanitary practices in the backcountry are essential. Burying feces more than 200 feet from a water source is advised. This practice all but precludes the possibility of cysts being washed into the water if you are a carrier. It also contributes to a neater camp.

Survival Kit

Compass, whistle, matches in waterproof container, candle, surgical tubing, emergency fishing gear, sixty feet of six-pound line, six hooks, six lead shot and six trout flies, safety pins, copper wire, signal mirror, fire starter, aluminum foil, water purification tablets, space blanket and flare.

First Aid Kit

Sewing needle, snake bite kit, twelve aspirin, antibacterial ointment, two antiseptic swabs, two butterfly bandages, adhesive tape, four adhesive strips, four gauze pads, two triangular bandages, twelve codeine tablets, two inflatable splints, moleskin, one roll of three-inch gauze and lightweight first aid instructions.

HIKE 1 *BIRCH CANYON*

General description: A day hike introducing the land forms and animal and plant life of the Mt. Naomi Wilderness, or the first day of a trip traversing the entire region.

General location: Five miles east of Smithfield.

Maps: Northern Utah Multipurpose Map and USGS Smithfield, Mt. Elmer, and Naomi Peak Quads.

Special attractions: Diverse habitat, from riparian to the high, open ridges of the divide.

Best season for hike: Late spring through fall.

For more information: Logan Ranger District, Wasatch-Cache National Forest, 860 N. 1200 E., Logan, UT 84321; (801) 753-2772.

The hike: Birch Canyon heads east from Smithfleld, curving southeast to meet the main divide of the Bear River Range in a series of high, green subalpine bowls, surrounded by a line of cliffs unequaled in the range. This little-visited canyon has a perennial stream and good campsites in the lower portion, limited camping in the upper portion.

The twelve-mile round trip from the trailhead to the summit of 9,566-foot Mt. Jardine at the head of Birch Canyon makes a good stout hike. You gain about 4,100 feet. Figure on eight hours walking time for the round trip. Alternatively, you can make camp high on Birch Creek, take the next day to travel past 9,676-foot Mt. Elmer to upper Cottonwood Canyon and Cottonwood Spring, and the next to reach the Mt. Naomi and White Pine Lake area. For summer backpacking, you have to carry water between these places, and the going will be slow, but the rewards of seeing the many hidden wonders of the Mt. Naomi Wilderness are great.

From Smithfleld (about six miles north of Logan on U.S. 91), turn east on 100 North. Go two blocks east, then a half block south to Canyon Road. Follow Canyon Road east and northeast about a mile. Turn right onto the Birch Canyon Road, which is marked. Follow this dirt road (narrow, winding, potentially dangerous at blind curves) a mile to the mouth of Birch Canyon and a locked gate. There is no parking here except off the side of the road; groups will need to park three miles farther down the canyon and hike up the road.

The land is private from the gate .25 mile to the national forest. Please be conscious of this situation and respect the private landowner's rights.

About .5 mile beyond the forest boundary at 5,400 feet, the jeep road becomes a trail, and stream crossings are numerous. The stream is beautiful, bordered with stately cottonwoods and, in the wet streamside area, with yellow monkeyflower. In season, you'll hear warbling vireos, yellow warblers, hermit thrushes and Swainson's thrushes as you ascend. Openings in the forest allow views of dramatic cliffs and broken country on both sides of the canyon.

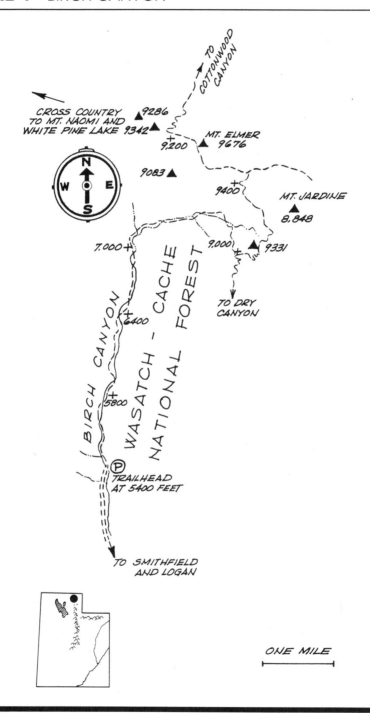

TO COTTONWOOD CANYON

CROSS COUNTRY
TO MT. NAOMI AND
WHITE PINE LAKE 9342 ▲

▲ 9286

+ 9,200

MT. ELMER
9676 ▲

9083 ▲

+ 9400

MT. JARDINE
▲
8,848

7,000 +

9,000 +

▲ 9331

BIRCH CANYON

WASATCH – CACHE NATIONAL FOREST

TO DRY CANYON

6400 +

5800 +

Ⓟ TRAILHEAD
AT 5400 FEET

TO SMITHFIELD
AND LOGAN

ONE MILE

Gradually gaining elevation, the trail passes through maple and aspen woods, Douglas fir and subalpine fir, and finally emerges in a series of lush meadows. At the first opening to the east, the great headwall between Mt. Elmer and Mt. Jardine comes into view, and the country takes on a montane feeling. The stream here drops swiftly through the steepening meadows, edged by mossy rocks and columbines. The going gets steeper as the trail ascends into subalpine bowls covered by lupine, columbine, alpine, buttercup and pentstemon, among others.

You'll see (or hear) rock wrens, whitecrowned sparrows, and Clark's nutcrackers. About five miles from the trailhead, the trail tops out at a 9,000-foot saddle dividing Birch Canyon from Smithfield Dry Canyon, dropping away to the south and west. Take the obvious ridge southeast to Mt. Jardine. Along the way, you'll pick up the Smithfield Dry Canyon trail. From Mt. Jardine, you have excellent views of Cache Valley to the west, the wild, forested north slope of 9,713-foot Logan Peak to the south, Logan Canyon to the south and east, and the Bear River Range stretching to the north. For most day hikers, this is the turnaround point.

There are a number of backpacking possibilities from this point—each requiring a car shuttle. You can descend Green Canyon, which is directly below you to the east and south. Or, you can follow the main ridge and trail north for 1.5 miles to Mt. Elmer (at 9,676 feet, the next prominent peak), then continue north into Cottonwood Canyon, and descend to Logan Canyon, reaching it at a point about fifteen miles from Logan.

Another possibility is to continue north about six miles from Mt. Elmer on the main divide (off-trail but open) to Mt. Naomi (9,979 feet). One-and-one-half miles beyond Naomi, a descent to White Pine Lake is feasible. Alternatively from Naomi, take the trail (.25 mile to the north) southeast 2.5 miles to Tony Grove Lake trailhead.

There are many possibilities in this splendid country. Most of the routes have trails which are shown on the appropriate USGS maps, and from the crest of the ridge, the rugged and mixed-terrain beauties of this area are laid out before you.

The 44,964-acre Mt. Naomi Wilderness was designated under the Utah Wilderness Act of 1984. — *Tom Lyon*

HIKE 2 *WELLSVILLE MOUNTAINS*

General description: A loop hike to the crest of the Wellsvilles.
General location: Ten miles southwest of Logan.
Maps: Northern Utah Multipurpose Map and USGS Wellsville Quad.
Special attractions: Views of Cache Valley extending north into Idaho, west past the Promontory and Raft River ranges, and south to the Great Salt Lake. Fall raptor migrations offer exciting hawk watching.

Meanders of the Bear River from the Wellsville crest.—Dave Hall photo

Best season for hike: Late spring through fall.
For more information: Logan Ranger District, Wasatch-Cache National Forest, 860 N. 1200 E., Logan, UT 84321; (801) 753-2772.

The hike: The Wellsville Mountains have been called the steepest mountains in the world. After climbing the precipitous east side and gazing down the rugged west side to the oxbow bends of the Bear River, you'll agree. However, the hike is worth it, as this northern Utah range offers some splendid views from the ridge.

A loop hike over the Deep Canyon and Coldwater Lake trails necessitates a car shuttle. Both trailheads, however, offer good access to the ridge if you choose an "in and out" hike rather than the loop.

Expect a strenuous 2,700-foot climb to the ridge and more elevation gain as you continue along the ridge line. However, distances are not excessive, so an early start and a leisurely pace make the trip possible. Overnight camping is not recommended due to a lack of water and protected campsites on the ridge. The windchill factor on the exposed ridge may be substantial, so be prepared. Don't be misled by warm temperatures in the valley.

Trails ascend the eastern slopes of the Wellsvilles from Cache Valley. To

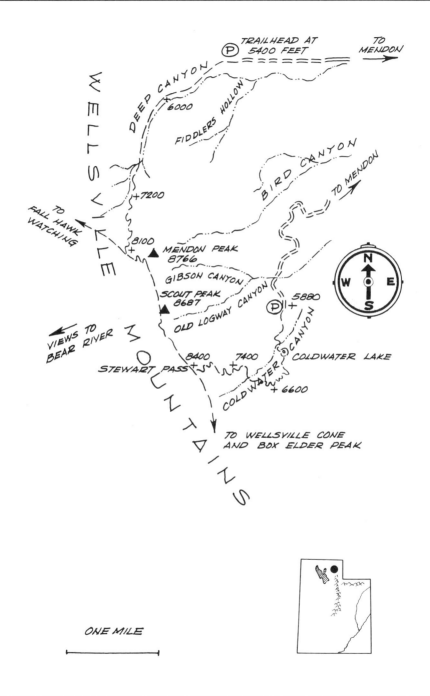

TRAILHEAD AT 5400 FEET

TO MENDON

DEEP CANYON

WELLSVILLE

+6000

FIDDLERS HOLLOW

BIRD CANYON

TO MENDON

+7200

TO FALL HAWK WATCHING

8100 +

MENDON PEAK 8766

GIBSON CANYON

SCOUT PEAK 8687

OLD LOGWAY CANYON

+5880

VIEWS TO BEAR RIVER

MOUNTAINS

STEWART PASS

8400 +

7400 +

COLDWATER CANYON

COLDWATER LAKE

COLDWATER

+6600

TO WELLSVILLE CONE AND BOX ELDER PEAK

N W E S

ONE MILE

reach the Deep Canyon trailhead (the recommended starting point), turn off State Highway 23 in Mendon and drive west two miles on Third North to the trailhead/parking area.

To reach the Coldwater Lake trailhead, drive south on Main Street in Mendon as it diagonally crosses Highway 23, then follow the "To National Forest" signs as the road zigzags west and south. The distance from Mendon to the trailhead is about 3.5 miles.

The Deep Canyon Trail begins at 5,400 feet in scrub maple and continues through aspen and mountain ash for three miles before reaching the ridge in a saddle at 8,100 feet. You get a good workout; this section of the hike is steadily uphill.

An option upon reaching the saddle is to continue along the ridge .75 mile to the northwest. The tallest peak (8,585 feet) is a popular hawk-watching spot during fall raptor migrations. It's one of the better places in the state to view raptors "face to face" as they ride up-drafts along the mountain. No other location has as many birds passing close to the ridge. The Logan Ranger District or the Division of Wildlife Resources (see the Appendix) can give you more information.

The views in all directions are spectacular. Of particular interest are the oxbow bends of the Bear River nearly 4,000 feet below.

Not only does the Wellsville ridge offer an outstanding view of the northern portion of the state, it also has a showy display of wildflowers. Old and determined stands of limber pine are scattered along the ridge, interspersed with clumps of Indian paintbrush. In the spring and early summer, leopard and glacier lilies, bluebells, spring beauty, stinging nettle, and mountain lover are visible along the trail.

To continue the loop hike from the saddle at the top of Deep Canyon, turn left (southeast) along the ridge. Stay directly atop the ridge as the trail ascends 8,766-foot Mendon Peak. As you approach the summit, the trail skirts it and continues south.

Scout Peak (8,687 feet) is about .5 mile south. Continue contouring near the ridge another mile to Stewart Pass at 8,400 feet. Watch carefully for the Coldwater Lake Trail descending to the left (east). This is your route off the ridge. The ridge trail, incidentally, continues south to other attractions, among them 9,372-foot Box Elder Peak—the highest point in the Wellsvilles. Box Elder Peak is about 2 miles from Stewart Pass.

The descent from Stewart Pass is steep, dropping about 2,100 feet in 1.5 miles to tiny Coldwater Lake. Avoid the temptation to use the shortcuts between switchbacks. It is easier to stay on the established trail, preventing destructive erosion. A gentle .75-mile hike can be made from the lake down to the Coldwater trailhead.

Early in this century, overgrazing and uncontrolled burning left the Wellsvilles vulnerable to erosion. Although conditions were not as serious as they were farther south along the Wasatch Front, floods did pour out of the range onto the Wellsville-Mendon road and into the Beaver Dam and Petersboro areas. Concerned citizens, desiring to return the mountain to its original condition, formed the Wellsville Area Project Corporation in 1941. They obtained contributions, bought land, and deeded it to the Forest Service for protection. The Wellsville Mountains have now recovered to the point where a few gullies are the only readily visible evidence of past abuse.

The 23,556-acre Wellesville Mountain Wilderness was designated under the Utah Wilderness Act of 1984. — *Steue Flint and Eric Rechel*

HIKE 3 *MALANS PEAK*

General description: A moderately demanding hike and scramble above Ogden.

General location: Immediately east of Ogden in the Wasatch Mountains.

Maps: Northern Utah Multipurpose Map and USGS Ogden Quad.

Special attractions: Spectacular views of Ogden, the Salt Lake Valley, and a 400-foot waterfall.

Best season for hike: Late spring through fall.

For more information: Ogden Ranger District, Wasatch-Cache National Forest, 507 25th St., Suite 103, Ogden, UT 84402; (801) 625-5110.

The hike: Presently, the entire Malans Peak loop trail system is on private land and not maintained for public use by the forest service. Hikers should obtain permission from the private landowner prior to hiking. Contact the Ogden Ranger District for more information on the status of this area.

Beginning just east of Ogden, the 5.5-mile round trip follows Waterfall Canyon to the Malans Basin high country. A gradual climb from there brings you to Malans Peak overlooking Ogden and the Great Salt Lake. Finally, a well-developed trail on the north side of the peak leads to within a few blocks of the trailhead.

You gain plenty of elevation—more than 2,300 feet from the trailhead to Malans Peak.

The loop is an ideal day hike, but overnighters are also popular in the area. Campsites abound in the Malans Basin area. Hike from south to north—up Waterfall Canyon, over the peak and down Taylor Canyon. A steep scree slope at the top of Waterfall Canyon can make the hike dangerous and more difficult in the other direction.

Water is plentiful in Waterfall Canyon. But Taylor Canyon is dry in mid-summer, so plan accordingly.

Begin your hike at the east end of 29th Street in Ogden. Park just east of a high-rise apartment building. Hike south on a dirt road just east of the apartments. Take the first road heading to the left (east) up through the oak brush. It is easy to get sidetracked on one of the many roads not shown on maps, but if you continue generally to the south for .5 mile toward the obvious mouth of Waterfall Canyon, you will have no trouble. Just before entering the canyon,

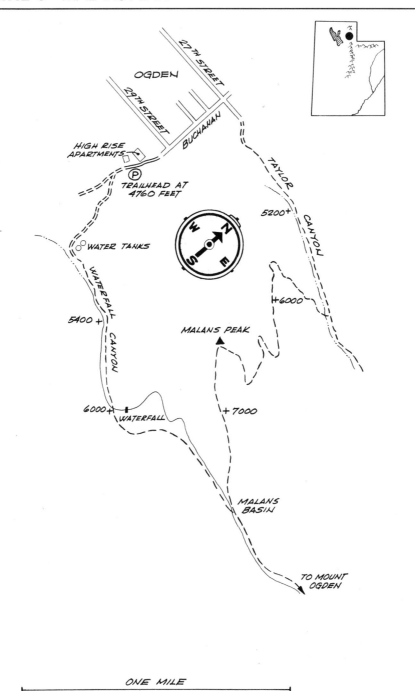

ONE MILE

the road swings left (east) above two large water tanks and becomes the trail.

Entering the canyon is a relief after the short but dusty hike up from your car. Water flows year-round in Waterfall Canyon, and the overhanging vegetation offers plenty of shade on a hot summer day.

Hike and occasionally scramble along the trail beside the tumbling stream. White arrows placed strategically on rocks indicate the way. After a .5-mile, 800-foot climb past the mouth of the canyon, you arrive at a spectacular waterfall. Not much water falls by mid-summer, but you'll want to pause in the amphitheater. There are some nice lunch rocks here, and the spray of the falls keeps the temperature very comfortable.

When you are ready to continue to Malans Basin, look for the canyon continuing east up the gulch to the right of the falls. A few ledges warrant caution, but they are not dangerous, and no technical equipment is required.

Above the ledges there is a fairly steep scree slope. Stay together in the area since rocks are easily jarred loose and can tumble down the slope. Views behind you along this section are worth the pause.

After a few hundred yards, the couloir curves to the left (north). Follow the slope north above the waterfall. The trail becomes indistinct here, but if you contour northeast for .25 mile and drop into the stream drainage, the trail appears again.

Malans Basin is .5 mile upstream to the east. There are campsites and relics of an old hotel. Signs of wildlife abound, and eagles and deer are commonly sighted.

From Malans Basin the terrain to the east toward 9,572-foot Mount Ogden can be explored before beginning the gently rising traverse for .75 mile to Malans Peak. A well-beaten trail heads northwest from Malans Basin. The peak presents a splended panoramic view of Ogden and the Great Salt Lake.

The route down the north side of Malans Peak switches back several times in 1.25 miles before meeting the trail and stream bed in Taylor Canyon—about 1,600 feet below.

An excellent example of cutting off switchbacks can be observed on this slope. Hikers have made an unsightly shortcut straight up the slope. The cut is susceptible to erosion in several areas. Stay on the hiking trail.

Turning left (west) in Taylor Canyon, follow the trail about .75 mile to the top of 27th Street, two blocks north of your starting point. Turn left (south) on Buchanan and follow this paved road to your car. — *Jock Glidden*

HIKE 4 *DESERET PEAK*

General description: A moderately demanding day hike or overnighter to the crest of the 11,000-foot Stansbury Mountains.
General location: Forty-two miles southwest of Salt Lake City.

Maps: Northern Utah Multipurpose Map and USGS Deseret Peak Quad.
Special attractions: Outstanding views of northwest Utah—from the Wasatch Mountains on the east to the Nevada border on the west.
Best season for hike: Late spring through fall.
For more infonmation: Salt Lake Ranger District, Wasatch-Cache National Forest, 6944 South 3000 East, Salt Lake City, UT 84121; (801) 524-5042.

The hike: While most Salt Lakers crowd into the nearby Wasatch Mountains on weekends, the Stansbury Mountains offer exceptional hiking in a less popular area but within easy driving distance of Salt Lake City.

The Stansbury Mountains are two ranges west of the Wasatch Mountains. It requires a little over an hour by car from downtown Salt Lake to reach the Deseret Peak trailhead.

From Salt Lake City follow 1-80 west about 20 miles. Take the Tooele exit, turning right after about four miles on State Highway 138 toward Grantsville. Continue another ten miles into Grantsville. In the center of town, find the Forest Service sign on the left side of the street indicating South Willow Canyon. Turn left and drive about five miles. Take the right fork here. Follow this road into South Willow Canyon about seven miles to the trailhead at the south end of the parking loop.

The Deseret Peak Trail begins its six-mile, 3,600-foot climb by ascending through a lush stand of aspen. Streams run during the spring and early summer. The trail continues through the forest for about .75 mile, where it crosses a perennial stream and jogs to the left, back along the stream bank. Within fifty feet the trail forks, with the left fork heading to Deseret Peak and the right to Willow Lakes.

The left fork to Deseret Peak continues into Mill Fork and wanders through grass-filled meadows with occasional avalanche debris, reminding you how deeply these mountains are buried in snow during winter.

From 7,800 feet at the fork, you climb to 9,600 feet in 1.5 miles. As the trail approaches the upper cirque, views of the Great Salt Lake appear to the north with Deseret Peak's 1,500-foot cliff looming to the southwest. Eventually, the trail cuts back up the glacial cirque at the head of the canyon to a ridge at 10,000 feet.

From the saddle, heavily forested, 10,305-foot Victory Mountain fills your view to the south, with the Sheeprock Mountains behind. To the north, the Great Salt Lake, Stansbury Island, and accompanying mud flats are visible.

The trail continues along the ridge, then switches back up the treeless ridgeline through patches of snow lasting into early summer. After a .5-mile hike and 1,000-foot elevation gain, you reach the top of Deseret Peak, at 11,031 feet.

On a clear day you have a commanding view of 11,928-foot Mt. Nebo to the southeast, Nevada's Pilot Peak to the northwest, the Wasatch Range on the eastern horizon, and all the desert ranges and salt flats to the west.

To complete the Deseret Peak loop, follow the trail down the mountain to the north, following the west side of the ridge overlooking South Lost Creek

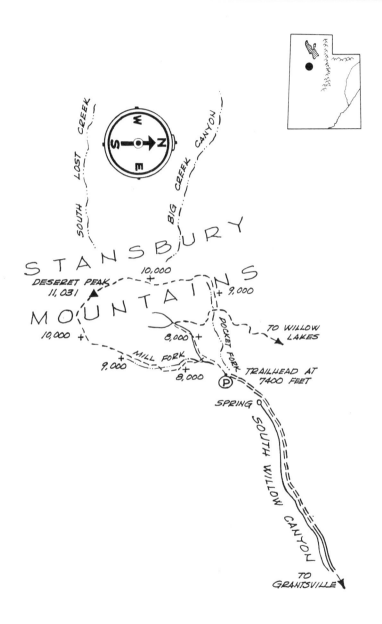

SOUTH LOST CREEK

BIG CREEK CANYON

S T A N S B U R Y

10,000 +

DESERET PEAK
11,031 ▲

+ 9,000

M O U N T A I N S

10,000 +

8,000 +

POCKET FORK

TO WILLOW
LAKES ▲

MILL FORK
9,000 +

+ 8,000

Ⓟ TRAILHEAD AT
7400 FEET

SPRING

SOUTH WILLOW CANYON

TO
GRANTSVILLE

ONE MILE
├──────────┤

and Big Creek canyons. After a 1.5-mile hike (and 1,200-foot elevation loss), the trail drops over the ridge and heads east into Pocket Fork. The trail is obvious where it crosses the ridge.

From here, the trail heads down the upper bowl and then parallels the stream bed dropping to the east. After .5 mile, the trail forks near a lone stand of aspen. To the left (north), the trail goes to the Willow lakes. A perennial stream flows through the meadow here, giving welcomed relief.

To return to your starting point, follow the trail's right fork (east) back into the trees. After about 1.5 miles, you reach the fork which you passed on the way up. It's an easy .5 mile back to the car.

The southern portion of the range, where you have been hiking, was designated wilderness in 1984. The northern portion of the range is administered by the Bureau of Land Management and is currently a wilderness study area.
— *Jim Kay*

HIKE 5 *CITY CREEK MEADOWS*

General description: A delightful day hike along the lush City Creek trail to the meadows near the crest of the Wasatch.
General location: Eight miles north of the State Capitol in Salt Lake City.
Maps: Northern Utah Multipurpose Map and USGS Fort Douglas and Mountain Dell Quads.
Special attractions: Cool, streamside hiking; diverse vegetation; and abundant wildlife.
Best season for hike: Spring through fall.
For more information: Salt Lake Ranger District, Wasatch-Cache National Forest, 6944 South 3000 East, Salt Lake City, UT 84121; (801) 524-5042. For reservations call (801) 535-7911.

The hike: If you're looking for a pleasant day hike with the trailhead only a few minutes from downtown Salt Lake, then City Creek is made to order. The area is managed as watershed by the City Department of Public Utilities, hence many strict regulations. Overnight camping, dogs and horses are prohibited. Reservations are required, but this means that you will not encounter the steady stream of hikers common elsewhere along the Wasatch. And if you can break away during the week, chances are you'll be alone.

You climb from about 6,000 feet at the trailhead to 8,100 feet at the City Creek Meadows, passing through several vegetation zones during the 4.5-mile hike. The outing is ideal for young children, because the lower section is not steep, the creek runs near the trail, and you can turn around if the kids get tired.

The trail starts at the end of the City Creek Road northeast of the Capitol. Take State Street north in Salt Lake City until you approach the Capitol Build-

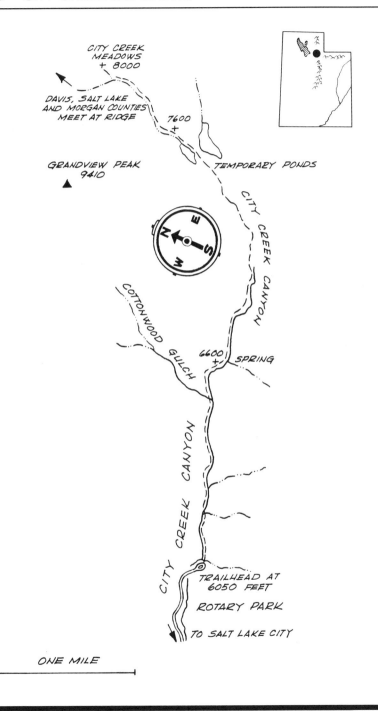

CITY CREEK
MEADOWS
+ 8000

DAVIS, SALT LAKE
AND MORGAN COUNTIES
MEET AT RIDGE

7600
+

GRANDVIEW PEAK
9410

TEMPORARY PONDS

CITY CREEK CANYON

COTTONWOOD GULCH

6600
+/

SPRING

CITY CREEK CANYON

TRAILHEAD AT
6050 FEET

ROTARY PARK

TO SALT LAKE CITY

ONE MILE

ing. Turn right and continue around the Capitol for 1.25 miles until you reach the City Creek Road. Turn left into the canyon and continue about six miles to the trailhead.

Reservations are required at least twenty-four hours in advance to get beyond the gate at the water treatment plant—about 3.5 miles up the canyon. Call 535-7911 for reservations to park near the trailhead in a campground or to get a "drive through," meaning you'll be dropped off at the trailhead. Presently, there are no "drive throughs" on weekends, and the entire road to the trailhead is closed Mondays and Wednesdays to vehicular travel.

You may be rankled by the very strict regulations, but protection of this valuable water source, along with the need to restrict automobile traffic on the narrow and tortuous City Creek Road, makes them necessary. Look on the bright side. Experiencing these regulations gives you a greater appreciation for the convenient access to most of our public lands.

Begin your hike at the gate at the end of the paved road. For .5 mile, an old jeep trail cuts through dense cover. Even on a hot summer day, the area is refreshingly cool.

Clear, spring-fed City Creek tumbles to your left. If you're quiet upon approaching one of the many pools in the creek, you may see a trout hanging lazily on the gravel bottom. The Division of Wildlife Resources stocks City Creek occasionally during the summer with rainbow trout, and a small population of native cutthroats has survived since the days of Lake Bonneville.

Cross the bridge as the jeep road becomes a foot path. Spectacular rock outcrops are above you in the canyon, and you may notice the many species of trees and shrubs in the moist river bottom: birch, box elder, dogwood, elders, bigtooth maple, cottonwood and chokecherry. Spruce and fir are on the cooler north facing slope. Beaver activity is common in this area, and you may have to skirt a few wet sections of the trail because of dam building.

A mile beyond the bridge, cross a small stream coming out of Cottonwood Gulch. A trail to the left (north) immediately after the stream leads into the Gulch (not your trail to City Creek Meadows) and offers some fine exploring around several old mines—if you have time later in the day. Be cautious around these ruins, however.

Continuing past Cottonwood Gulch for .5 mile, you enter a small meadow with the creek a few hundred feet to your right (south). There is a spring here. In late summer, there may be no water above, so you'll want to fill your water bottles.

After another mile, the trail becomes steeper as it climbs through thick aspen groves. You have been heading nearly due east but will now climb to the north and northwest, contouring around a sizable ridge. Deer sign abounds here among the thick vegetation, and it is not uncommon to surprise a blue grouse or two. After experiencing the explosive take-off of one of these high country birds from the ground or from a limb near your head, you may question who's doing the surprising.

Continue northeast toward two shallow ponds, shown as revisions on the Mountain Dell topographic map. The ponds are fed by snow melt and will probably be dry by midsummer. Skirt around the smaller pond farther to the north.

Just prior to the ponds, and beyond toward the meadows, the trail is indistinct, intermingling with many game trails. Sheep graze high in the canyon on the Wasatch-Cache National Forest, and they have contributed to the trail confusion. The appropriate topo map and a compass will help. The meadows are a mile to the north, but it is easy to head up the wrong canyon if you get a bit disoriented.

The City Creek Meadows are just below the crest of the Wasatch. The area is lush and damp in spring but can be quite dry and hot later in summer. It's an ideal spot for lunch, if you haven't stopped already along the trail.

Before heading down out of the canyon, consider making the .5-mile climb northward to the crest of the ridge where Davis, Salt Lake and Morgan counties meet. From here, among cooling breezes, you have splendid views of Grandview Peak (9,410 feet) to the west, Lookout Peak (8,954 feet) to the southeast, and much of the Wasatch to the south. — *Dave Hall*

HIKE 6 *GOBBLERS KNOB*

General description: A day hike or overnighter of intermediate difficulty.
General location: Eight miles southeast of Salt Lake City in Mill Creek Canyon.
Maps: Northern Utah Multipurpose Map and USGS Mount Aire Quad.
Special attractions: Wide variety of vegetation; abundant wildflowers in season.
Best season for hike: Spring through fall.
For more information: Salt Lake Ranger District, Wasatch-Cache National Forest, 6944 South 3000 East, Salt Lake City, UT 84121; (801) 524-5042.

The hike: This hike offers a variety of spectacular scenery. You'll ascend Porter Fork in Mill Creek Canyon and head down Alexander Basin, so there will be no backtracking. A car shuttle is required unless you don't mind a 3.5-mile walk down the Mill Creek Road at the end of the hike.

Options are available. You could backtrack from Gobblers Knob, eliminating the necessity for a shuttle or continue into Big Cottonwood Canyon via several routes to the south.

The hike up Porter Fork to Gobblers Knob and down Alexander Basin is a hefty day hike, but you could spend a night or two along the way. Camping is permitted in Mill Creek Canyon, and you may also cross the divide and camp in Big Cottonwood Canyon.

The trail gains 4,200 feet in elevation over 5.5 miles. There are only a few bothersome, steep sections. From Gobblers Knob, the trail drops another 1.75

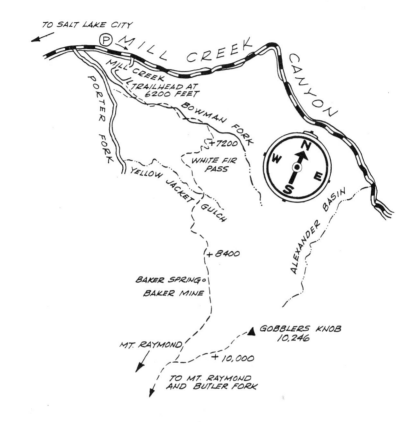

TO SALT LAKE CITY

Ⓟ MILL CREEK CANYON

MILL CREEK TRAILHEAD AT 6200 FEET

BOWMAN FORK

PORTER FORK

+7200

WHITE FIR PASS

YELLOW JACKET GULCH

ALEXANDER BASIN

+8400

BAKER SPRING○
BAKER MINE

▲ GOBBLERS KNOB 10,246

MT. RAYMOND

+10,000

TO MT. RAYMOND AND BUTLER FORK

ONE MILE

miles (3,000 feet) to the Alexander Basin trailhead.

To reach the trailhead from Salt Lake City, take I-215 south from I-80 and exit on the 39th South off ramp. Turn left under the interstate and then left again at the light on Wasatch Boulevard. Drive north for one block, turning right on the Mill Creek Canyon Road. Continue about 4.5 miles to the Terraces Picnic Area identified by a large Forest Service sign on the south side of the road.

The trail from Terraces begins at the top of the paved road inside the picnic area, but park along the Mill Creek road opposite the picnic area, since the Forest Service sometimes locks the gate.

If you plan to leave a car at Alexander Basin, drive about 4 miles farther up Mill Creek Canyon, about a mile past the Fircrest and Clover Springs picnic grounds. The trailhead is on the right side of the road as it crosses the creek.

To start your hike, go up the paved Forest Service road through the picnic area. At the top of a hill, after .5 mile, take the right fork. On your left, a steep slope leads to a picnic table. Walk southeasterly past the table onto Bowman Fork Trail, which leads into narrow Bowman Fork. The well-maintained trail is signed at the trailhead.

From 6,400 feet, the trail winds through dense canyon bottom vegetation alongside Bowman Fork for a mile, then leaves the stream to the south, enters a mature coniferous forest, and switches back up a steep hillside.

You emerge from the forest at White Fir Pass—.5 mile and more than 600 vertical feet after leaving the stream. This is a favorite camping spot and is usually littered.

From White Fir Pass, the trail contours to the south and southeast around the head of Yellow Jacket Gulch, forested mostly with aspen and mature conifers. About .75 mile from White Fir Pass, the trail crosses a ridge and enters Pole Canyon. Continue another .5 mile to Baker Spring—a small but perpetual spring. This is the last reliable source of water before the end of the hike, but may not be safe to drink without treatment.

An old miner's cabin is a few hundred yards to the southeast, still in excellent condition. A mine dump on the hillside to the southeast is visible from here. The Baker Mine itself, however, is over the ridge to the south and not visible from the trail.

From Baker Spring, the trail contours about a mile around the head of Porter Fork to the pass (about 9,400 feet) between Mt. Raymond (to the west) and Gobblers Knob (to the east). You'll pass the junction with the Desolation Trail leading to the south, to Big Cottonwood Canyon.

Wildflowers cover the slope here in the spring. The slope is also the starting point for some of the most spectacular and fatal avalanches in the Wasatch Mountains. In the winter of 1979-80, an avalanche which began on this slope continued about two miles to the northwest down Porter Fork, stopping just short of the summer homes at the bottom of the canyon.

At the saddle between Mt. Raymond and Gobblers Knob, stop to enjoy the view. This is probably the best place for lunch. Then follow the ridge line to the northeast for .75 mile to the summit of 10,246-foot Gobblers Knob. The trail appears and disappears along the ridgeline, but the ridge itself is obvious and open. The summit is just a few feet before the ridge drops off abruptly into Alexander Basin.

After enjoying the summit, scramble down the south side of the ridge to a point where you can safely enter Alexander Basin—the huge basin to the north of the knob. No trail exists here, but the basin is quite open, and you'll have no trouble finding your way. The upper part of the basin is a rockfall. Descending the rockfall, you will find that the basin becomes broad and open, and you will discover many possible routes. Pick an easy one, bearing toward the right (east) side of the canyon and head down in that direction.

As you descend farther, bear more to the right. You'll come to a hillock which distinctly divides the possible routes into left and right branches. Keep to the right of this hillock, and follow the stream bed which becomes visible at about this point. Continue on the east slope of the canyon. A distinct trail will appear entering the forest. Do not enter the stand until you have found the trail. It is on the east side of the canyon and quite clear when you get close to it.

Follow the trail north down the slope another mile to the Alexander Basin trailhead. — *Walt Haas*

HIKE 7 *ALEXANDER BASIN*

General description: A day hike or overnighter in Mill Creek Canyon.
General location: Ten miles southeast of Salt Lake City.
Maps: Northern Utah Multipurpose Map and USGS Mount Aire Quad.
Special attractions: A secluded alpine basin with many opportunities for exploration.
Best season for hike: Spring through fall.
For more information: Salt Lake Ranger District, Wasatch-Cache National Forest, 6944 South 3000 East, Salt Lake City, UT 84121; (801) 524-5042.

The hike: Alexander Basin has several features which should attract the travel-weary hiker tired of long drives to the Uintas or southern Utah. This beautiful basin, with its trailhead just a few minutes from Salt Lake City in Mill Creek Canyon, offers solitude and plenty of opportunity for exploration. Moreover, overnight camping is permitted in Mill Creek, and if you have a dog who enjoys hiking as much as you do, don't leave him behind. Dogs are permitted in the canyon as well. (Dogs are not allowed in most other nearby canyons.)

The area offers an ideal day hike or a pleasant overnighter. Alexander Basin also presents the opportunity to scale 10,246-foot Gobblers Knob or to head west into Bowman Fork for hikes past 10,241-foot Mount Raymond into Big Cottonwood Canyon.

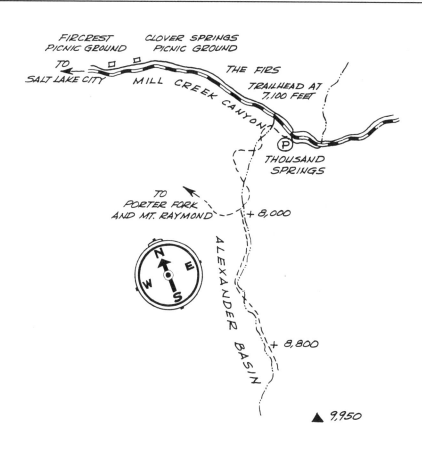

ONE MILE

The trailhead is easy to find. From Salt Lake City, take I-215 south off I-80 and exit at the 39th South off ramp. Turn left under the interstate and turn left again at the light on Wasatch Boulevard. Drive north for one block, turning right on the Mill Creek Canyon Road. Continue about 8.5 miles to the Alexander Basin trailhead on the right side of the road—about a mile beyond the Fircrest and Clover Springs campgrounds.

Don't make the mistake of heading straight up the slope from the trailhead parking area. If you do, the climbing will be extremely tough along a brush-lined trail heading to the east of Alexander Basin. The correct trail parallels the road to the northwest for a few hundred feet before heading to the southwest toward the basin. A sign with mileages to Alexander Basin (one mile), Gobblers Knob (three miles), Bowman Fork Trail (three miles), and Baker Spring (four miles) marks the spot.

This is not a difficult hike; the trail into Alexander Basin is well maintained. There are several switchbacks in the first mile, gaining elevation from 7,100 feet to about 8,400 feet. The occasionally steep trail shouldn't prove too much for anyone in reasonably good shape. Water is not present in the basin by midsummer, so plan accordingly.

The climb traverses through spruce and fir with Mill Creek occasionally visible during the steep ascent. In about a mile a trail exits right (west) to Bowman and Porter forks; continue south another .5 mile into the heart of Alexander Basin.

Once in the basin, you have views of Gobblers Knob to the south, as well as numerous high ridges and cirques.

The trail climbs over several shelves and around small islands of conifers which make good lunch spots and campsites. After climbing over the last of these steep ridges, you enter open, flat terrain at 9,000 feet. The trail mingles with game trails here, but it's impossible to become lost with the steep ridges to the east, west and south meeting at Gobblers Knob.

There is deer and coyote sign in the upper basin. If you camp in the area, watch for wildlife in the meadows in early morning. A reliable source spotted a mountain lion in this area.

Side hikes into other drainages are possible from Alexander Basin. Climbing Gobblers Knob brings you to the Mill Creek Canyon-Big Cotton-wood Canyon crest, and several hikes are possible into this canyon to the south. The trail west from Alexander Basin into Bowman and Porter forks leads to Baker Spring and to Big Cottonwood Canyon. All offer fine alpine hiking, but if you choose to stay put, spending all your time in Alexander Basin, you'll discover that this area is one of the Wasatch's special attractions.—*Dave Hall*

The pika, a relative of the rabbit and hare, is found above 8,000 feet in many of Utah's mountain ranges.—Harry Engels photo

HIKE 8 *MT. RAYMOND*

General description: A challenging day hike or overnighter to the top of the Big Cottonwood Canyon-Mill Creek Canyon divide.

General location: Ten miles southeast of Salt Lake City in Big Cottonwood Canyon.

Maps: Northern Utah Multipurpose Map and USGS Mount Aire Quad.

Special attractions: Spectacular views of Dromedary, Sunrise, and Twin Peaks to the south.

For more information: Salt Lake Ranger District, Wasatch-Cache National Forest, 6944 South 3000 East, Salt Lake City, UT 84121; (801) 524-5042.

The hike: The Mt. Raymond trail is an easy way to get a good view of the most spectacular peaks of the Wasatch Range. The hike goes up a good trail on the north side of Big Cottonwood Canyon, climbing quickly to high elevation vegetation and scenery. The hike is not difficult, and since it goes up and back by the same trail, you can turn around before the summit. There is an elevation gain of 4,000 feet from the road to the summit of Mt. Raymond.

An alternative to the Mt. Raymond hike is to head north down Porter Fork into Mill Creek Canyon. And with Big Cottonwood Canyon now open to backcountry camping, you may also opt to camp along the trail to Mt. Raymond. However, camping closer than 200 feet to a stream or spring is not permitted. Keep this in mind; water quality is at stake and the Forest Service is enforcing the regulation.

To reach the trailhead from Salt Lake City, drive south from I-80 on I-215 and exit at 6200 South. Turn left and continue 1.5 miles to the light at the mouth of Big Cottonwood Canyon. Turn left here and drive about 4.5 miles. Here you enter an "S" turn. As you finish the second turn back to your right, the signed trailhead for the Mill B North Fork Trail is on your left.

There is a turnout for limited parking. A Forest Service sign marks the route to the Desolation Trail, Mill A Basin, and the Mill Creek Road. You may want to take a quick look at Hidden Falls just a few hundred feet upstream before starting your hike.

The trail starts at 6,200 feet and climbs quickly above the canyon, switching back several times. These switchbacks have been cut off in this area, leaving erosion-prone scars heading up the slope. Stay on the trail—don't damage the area further.

After reaching the top of the first rise in about .25 mile, the trail leaves the scrub oak and drops down along Mill B North Fork. You parallel the creek for another .25 mile before entering a mature Douglas fir stand. Several campsites here show much use. There are cut trees, fire rings and litter. Toward the end of the stand, a jumble of rocks marks the spot where the trail cuts back sharply to your right and heads up the hillside.

The trail is obvious the rest of the way. You hike through a scrub oak forest, then climb through aspen and spruce-fir. The trail is continuously uphill; you'll get plenty of exercise. Wildlife use the trail regularly, avoiding the thick underbrush, and sign is abundant.

You hike among rugged outcrops and steep canyons, and the many overlooks across Big Cottonwood Canyon to the south offer ideal lunch spots. At several locations along the trail, Mt. Raymond is visible to the northeast.

At a point when you are nearly due south of Mt. Raymond, about 3.5 miles from the trailhead, turn left (northwest) on the Desolation Trail, which conntects Porter Fork in Mill Creek Canyon to Mill A Basin, Gobblers Knob, and Butler Fork. A sign marks the spot. Mt. Raymond lies ahead to the northeast.

You approach 10,241-foot Mt. Raymond on the trail which contours around the peak on the west side. Since no trail goes to the top, the best bet is to make your way from a point due west of the peak to a small ridge on the northwest side of the summit. From here, a short scramble takes you to the peak.

Like many of the Wasatch peaks, Mt. Raymond offers wonderful views in all directions. Take a few minutes to study the Great Salt Lake and Antelope Island to the northwest, the Wasatch peaks to the north, the Uintas to the east, and the peaks of the Big Cottonwood-Little Cottonwood divide to the south.

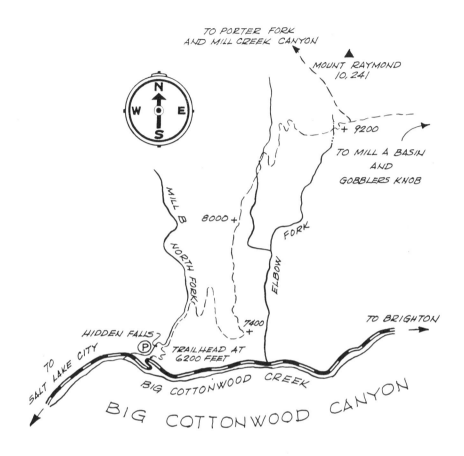

ONE MILE

There is interesting reading in the box at the top, and you may want to enter your thoughts while perched there. Among the many gems is the Ballad of Mt. Raymond. Says the author, "This was many years before us/Pre Mayor Teddy and Mormon Chorus/Pre MX and CUP/When the Ford was Model T."

You'll have to make the climb to read the rest.—*Walt Haas*

HIKE 9   *LAKE BLANCHE*

General description: A popular day hike into a rugged, glaciated canyon in the Twin Peaks Wilderness.

General location: Ten miles southeast of Salt Lake City in Big Cottonwood Canyon.

Maps: Northern Utah Multipurpose Map and USGS Mount Aire and Dromedary Peak Quads.

Special attractions: Huge glacial cirques, several lakes, and jagged peaks and waterfalls.

Best season for hike: Late spring through fall.

For more information: Salt Lake Ranger District, Wasatch-Cache National Forest, 6944 South 3000 East, Salt Lake City, UT 84121; (801) 524-5042.

The hike: This excursion into the Wasatch Mountains offers the hiker some of the best signs of glaciation and rugged alpine terrain among these 11,000-foot peaks.

To reach the trailhead from Salt Lake City, drive south from I-80 on I-215 and exit on 6200 South. Turn left under the highway overpass and continue 1.5 miles to the light at the mouth of Big Cottonwood Canyon. Turn left here and drive about 4.5 miles. Here you enter an "S" turn. A narrow, paved road exits to the right at the beginning of the first turn and winds .3 mile to the trailhead.

From here, you have to hike about 2.5 miles and gain 2,400 feet of elevation to get to Lake Blanche. The trail along Mill B South Fork is well marked and parallels the stream. It crosses a footbridge within .25 mile and cuts back to the left, remaining on the east side of the stream to Lake Blanche.

The trail passes through aspen stands along the glacially-carved canyon bottom. About 1.5 miles along, the trail begins to climb more abruptly along the east side of the canyon, away from the stream. You'll occasionally cross avalanche debris left from previous winter snows.

After .75 mile of steep climbing, the trail levels off onto an ancient, smooth rock outcropping. Notice that it was polished and etched by the most recent flow of glaciers in this region. The scratches left in the rock by debris carried along in the ice indicate the direction and force of the glacial flow.

Follow the trail through these rock outcroppings a few hundred feet to the

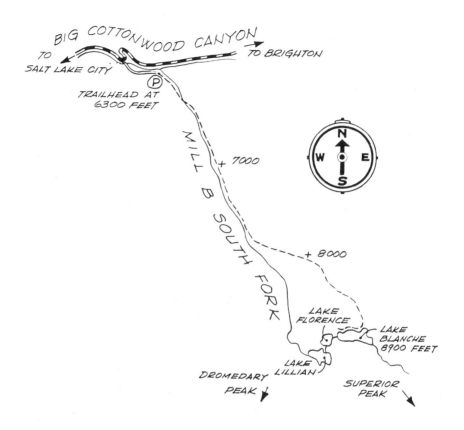

Sundial Peak and Lake Blanche.—James Kay photo

south. Lake Blanche is in a bowl with the cathedral spire of Sundial Peak beyond.

At Lake Blanche you are about 2,000 feet below the peaks of the Big and Little Cottonwood divide—Dromedary Peak (11,107 feet) to the southwest and Superior Peak (11,132 feet) to the southeast.

Lake Blanche shares the area with Lake Lillian and Lake Florence; both are just to the west and a bit below Lake Blanche. All three lakes have fair to good fishing, as long as you don't mind small rewards.

A large waterfall spills over a ledge just downstream from Lake Lillian, and during spring runoff another seventy-five-foot waterfall drops over a cliff just west of Sundial Peak.

Because of its popularity, this area receives its share of human abuse—cans, bottles, trash-filled fire pits, and other garbage which could be eliminated if hikers would carry out empty what they bring in full. Fire pits seem to be garbage magnets, attracting all sorts of tin foil and cans. A simple solution is to dismantle every fire pit you see along the way and carry a small, convenient backpacking stove. Also observe the backcountry camping regulations. While camping is permitted in Big Cottonwood Canyon, you must make your camp at least 200 feet from a lake, stream or spring. The Forest Service is enforcing this regulation.

If you're still ambitious when you arrive at Lake Blanche, continue another mile to the southeast, without benefit of a trail, into the large glacial cirque below Superior Peak. You scramble more than 1,000 feet in the process, but the trip is worth it.

To reach this canyon, follow the stream that enters Lake Blanche on the east, staying to the northeast side of the Sundial Peak ridge. Several small lakes dot the area, and you certainly will see more marmots and pikas than people. The high alpine scenery is superb, with huge walls and jagged peaks all around you. A reputable source has even made note of an occasional lurking moose in the general vicinity. — *Jim Kay*

HIKE 10 *LONE PEAK VIA DRAPER RIDGE*

General description: A relatively long and steep ascent to the principal summit of the Lone Peak Wilderness.

General location: Twenty miles southeast of Salt Lake City.

Maps: Trails Illustrated Uinta National Forest Map and USGS Draper Quad.

Special attractions: Spectacular alpine summit with beautiful views in every direction.

Best season for hike: Late spring through early summer. Summer and autumn are also suitable, but the outing may be hot and water sources unpredictable.

For more information: Pleasant Grove Ranger District, Uinta National Forest, Box 228, Pleasant Grove, UT 84062; (801) 785-3563. Also, Salt Lake Ranger District, Wasatch-Cache National Forest, 6944 South 3000 East, Salt Lake City, UT 84121; (801) 524-5042.

The hike: Should a monument be erected at the base of Lone Peak, its bronze plaque might read: "Lone Peak stands as a memorial to the dedication and perseverance of many conscientious Utahns who, over a period of nearly fifteen years and against almost insurmountable political and bureaucratic odds, succeeded in securing for the enjoyment of present and future generations a nearly pristine piece of Utah's rapidly vanishing wilderness."

In addition to its unique position as part of Utah's first congressionally designated wilderness, Lone Peak, the piece de resistance of the Lone Peak Wilderness, is among the most delightful mountain experiences in the Wasatch range.

Because much of the Draper Ridge route is located on public and private lands of diverse ownership and because no public agency has assumed responsibility for its maintenance, the Draper Ridge "trail" consists of linearly connected—and sometimes interconnected—segments of firebreaks, jeep trails, horse, game, cattle, and foot trails.

Backcountry camping is permitted on the Little Cottonwood side of Draper Ridge. Keep in mind, however, that camping closer than 200 feet to any water source is not permitted. And remember that dogs are still prohibited in the canyon.

To reach the trailhead, take I-15 to the Draper exit south of Salt Lake City and follow State Highway 71 into Draper. From the corner of Highway 71 and 700 East, drive one block south, then turn east toward the mountains, following the paved road about two miles to a fork. Turn right on the well-graded dirt road.

Follow this road 1.5 miles until a switchbacked jeep trail appears on a hillside a few hundred yards east of the road. Several well-worn jeep tracks leave the road to a flat area where you will find space to park.

From the parking site at an elevation of 5,110 feet, the Draper Ridge route follows the jeep trail .4 mile directly south, then turns abruptly east to follow a firebreak up the ridge for a mile. The firebreak segment gains 2,130 feet and ends in a rock outcropping. From the outcropping, descend southeasterly along a brush-covered gully .25 mile and intercept a horse/foot trail easily visible low on the opposite slope. Another .25 mile traverse northeast along the foot trail brings you to a small meadow at an elevation of 7,400 feet.

For the next .75 mile, the trail follows the drainage above the meadow while it ascends 900 feet to the east toward the base of a rock-covered, windswept ridge. Occasionally ill-defined due to the hardness of the rocky soil, the trail follows the ridge .75 mile until it reaches a 9,322-foot rocky prominence from where Lone Peak's summit becomes easily visible for the first time. The trail skirts to the left of the prominence, crosses the ridge, and begins a very gentle traverse along the eastern slope to a meadow with trees.

From the meadow, the trail follows the drainage .5 mile, drifting northeast toward a flat spot along an impressive granitic ridge about 600 feet above the meadow. As you cross this ridge, the trail becomes indistinct. But beyond, the route toward Lone Peak and its cirque is obvious. It traverses beneath the base of the granitic ridge along its southwestern side. Hiking along the large outcroppings of granite is especially delightful, as well as immensely picturesque.

The traverse continues for a mile (with a 1,000-foot elevation gain) and you

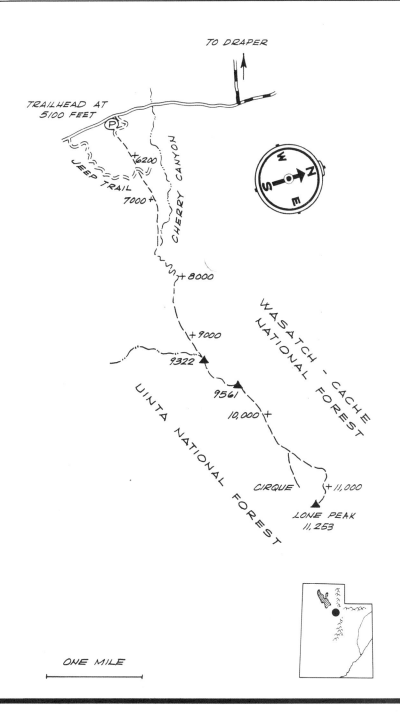

TO DRAPER

TRAILHEAD AT
5100 FEET

JEEP TRAIL

X 6200

7000 X

CHERRY CANYON

+ 8000

+ 9000

9322

9561

10,000 X

WASATCH - CACHE
NATIONAL FOREST

UINTA NATIONAL FOREST

CIRQUE

+ 11,000

LONE PEAK
11,253

ONE MILE

arrive on the northwest shoulder of Lone Peak. A gentler, lower traverse among the outcroppings brings you into the cirque.

From the shoulder, the summit is reached via a .25 mile, 450-foot scramble along an often exposed, though well protected, rocky ridge. Late in spring and occasionally into summer, the ridge crest may be covered with deep, hard snow. An ice ax, rope, and snow climbing experience are recommended.

Once on top, the sights are spectacular. But the panorama can elicit a range

Lone Peak in Utah's first congressionally designated wilderness area—the Lone Peak Wilderness.—Alexis Kelner photo

of emotions—depending on your philosophical alignment.

The newcomer to Utah or one of the state's many visitors will be awestruck by the views west to the Great Basin, north and south along the Wasatch, and east to the Uintas. However, the Utahn, more familiar with local population and development trends may view the sights with a more critical eye. Looking over Salt Lake Valley, air quality will most likely come to mind, as will the loss of farmland and wildlife winter range to residential tracts.

There is indeed irony in the proximity of the Lone Peak Wilderness to Utah's capital city, but the area's convenience is unparalleled, and to those optimistic wilderness advocates, Lone Peak is a reminder that hard-fought battles can mean environmental victories.

From the summit, you can choose to retrace your ascent route or continue .5 mile southeast along the summit ridge to a low pass above Bells Canyon. From here, you can descend into Bells Canyon and intercept the Bells Canyon trail. Of course, a car shuttle is necessary for this option. — *Alexis Kelner*

HIKE 11 *LONE PEAK AREA VIA LAKE HARDY*

General description: An overnighter through the heart of Utah's first congressionally-designated wilderness.
General location: Sixteen miles southeast of Salt Lake City.
Maps: Trails Illustrated Uinta National Forest Map and USGS Lehi, Draper, Dromedary Peak, and Timpanogos Cave Quads.
Special attractions: Spectacular geologic formations; alpine ridges and valleys; panoramic views of northern Utah.
Best season for hike: Early summer through fall.
For more information: Pleasant Grove Ranger District, Uinta National Forest, Box 228, Pleasant Grove, UT 84062; (801) 785-3563. Also, for information on the Little Cottonwood Canyon side, contact Salt Lake Ranger District, Wasatch-Cache National Forest, 6944 South 3000 East, Salt Lake City, UT 84121; (801) 542-5042.

The hike: The rocky cirques, wooded canyons, alpine meadows and ridges of the Wasatch are no more common than in the Lone Peak Wilderness east of Salt Lake City. A demanding but spectacular ascent to this area is from the town of Alpine in Utah County, climbing past Lake Hardy and descending through Bells Canyon on the Little Cottonwood Canyon side.

Bells Canyon, a major drainage under 11,253-foot Lone Peak, has long been a favorite, if somewhat secret, three-season hiking area. Day trips into Bells Canyon are popular, but you must hike nearly seven miles and 5,000 feet in elevation to the top. Until December, 1981, Salt Lake City water regulations prevented backcountry camping in Little Cottonwood Canyon. So few hikers chose to make a one-day hike up Bells Canyon. This ban on camping has been lifted, and new hiking options are now available. After crossing the ridge from Lake Hardy, you may choose to spend a night on the Little Cottonwood side.

Keep in mind that wilderness regulations require that you make camp *at least 200 feet from the nearest water source.* Forest Service personnel do enforce this regulation.

A car shuttle is necessary if you choose this hike over the ridge. Of course, you could ascend from Dry Creek, spend a night or two, explore the area, and return to your car along the same route.

To leave a car at Bells Canyon, turn south off the Little Cottonwood Canyon Road (9555 South; State Highway 209) at 3100 East. Pass the Granite Elementary School on your right after .25 mile, then cross 9800 South. In another .25 mile, the road makes a ninety-degree turn to the right and, almost immediately after, Dimple Dell Road (3050 East) turns to the left. Turn here, drive a few hundred yards down the hill, and turn left onto Bells Canyon Road (10025 South). In .25 mile, turn left on Wasatch Boulevard and park a car at the dead end. This is the bottom of Bells Canyon.

To reach the trailhead, return to the Little Cottonwood Canyon Road and drive west to State Street. Enter I-15 at 90th South.

Drive south around the Point of the Mountain and take the Alpine exit off I-15 to Alpine. Continue past the market on Main Street about .75 mile and turn right on Pioneer Road (600 North). When it intersects diagonally with Grove Drive in .25 mile, turn left and follow Grove another mile to a ninety-degree turn to the right. A few hundred yards after this turn, you'll notice a high chain link fence on the right, protected by large boulders. Across the road a jeep trail heads north through sagebrush flats. Park here.

This jeep road crosses about a mile of private property (respect it) before reaching the Uinta National Forest boundary.

As you look north from the trailhead at 5,250 feet, Lone Peak forms the sharp summit on the extreme left of the skyline. The peak's east ridge slopes gradually to the right—the horizon broken by a rocky outcropping—before climbing to the more rounded summit of 10,877-foot Big Horn. Lake Hardy, your destination for the first night, is behind and to the right of the Big Horn summit.

There are a couple of routes to Lake Hardy, either up the main drainage below the lake or along the slopes nearby. However, the most popular route follows the jeep road about a mile from the trailhead and then switches back up 1,300 vertical feet over the next 1.5 miles to the First Hamongog at the wilderness boundary. (Hamongog is a biblical term for meadow.)

Two signed trails leave the First Hamongog. One heads to the west to the Second Hamongog; the other takes a steeper and more direct route (east, then north) to Lake Hardy.

Take the trail to the Second Hamongog, situated beneath Big Horn. Notice the prominent ridge which drops south from this peak, with tree and brush cover ending about two-thirds of the way up the ridge at granite cliffs. From the Second Hamongog, the trail climbs northeast along the west side of this

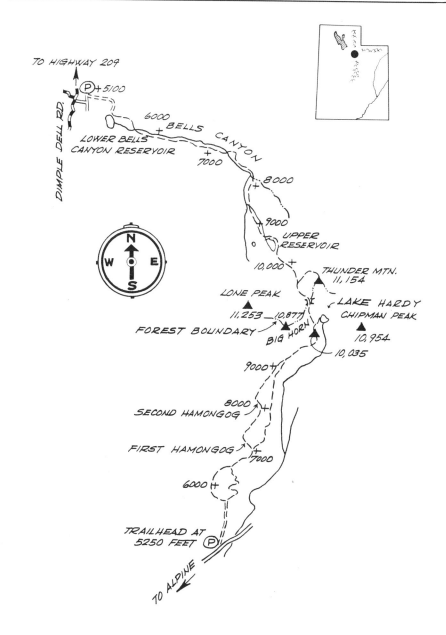

TO HIGHWAY 209

P +5100

DIMPLE DELL RD.

6000

BELLS CANYON

LOWER BELLS
CANYON RESERVOIR

7000

8000

9000

UPPER
RESERVOIR

10,000

THUNDER MTN.
11,154

LONE PEAK

LAKE HARDY
CHIPMAN PEAK

11,253 — 10,877

FOREST BOUNDARY

BIG HORN

10,954

10,035

9000

8000

SECOND HAMONGOG

FIRST HAMONGOG

7000

6000

TRAILHEAD AT
5250 FEET P

TO ALPINE

ONE MILE

Mountain goats, transplanted from Washington by the Division of Wildlife Resources, are doing well in the Lone Peak area.—Harry Engels photo

ridge (about a mile) before crossing to the east side. The trail then traverses northeast into the bowl at just under 10,000 feet framed by Big Horn, Thunder Mountain (11,154 feet), and Chipman Peak (10,954 feet).

Picturesque islands of conifers and wildflowers dot the granite slopes above timberline. The slopes allow fairly unrestricted cross-country travel.

Lake Hardy sits in a bowl north of the imaginary line between Big Horn and Chipman Peak. As you hike toward the lake, notice the bowl is divided by a north-south ridge, indicated by a 10,035-foot location on the topo map.

The route climbs the west side of this ridge, through beautiful secluded pockets, finally topping the crest of the ridge and dropping northeast to the lake.

As you approach Lake Hardy, stay midway up the granite slopes to the west of the lake. A cairned route winds through draws and granite boulders, among wildflowers, grasses and stunted shrubs. Lightning-struck and weathered conifers attest to the harsh conditions and provide endless photographic and sketchbook compositions.

While there are springs at lower elevations, Lake Hardy offers the only reliable water near the crest. Purifying your water before drinking is recommended.

The Lake Hardy area has good campsites, rewarding beauty and opportunities for after-dinner exploration. The lake doesn't get the "pounding" that some areas get across the ridge in Little Cottonwood Canyon, but that is no reason not to observe common sanitation and backcountry rules. A backpacker stove is recommended here, and remember to carry out *all* trash. Check with the Forest Service for current fire regulations.

The easiest and most scenic route to Bells Canyon is to return to the ridge, .25 mile west of Lake Hardy. Another .25 mile to the northwest, a grassy meadow just south of the saddle makes a good high campsite. Along this route, as well as elsewhere on the trail, you may see grouse, woodpeckers and many passerine species. Also look for red-tailed hawks and golden eagles soaring above the ridges.

You might also climb a mile due east from Lake Hardy to the saddle north of Chipman Peak. Here, you get a magnificent view of upper Hogum Fork before traversing northwest under and to the west of the ridgeline toward Bells Canyon.

From the saddle at the head of Bells, the view is spectacular in every direction. Rugged peaks and ridgelines flank the saddle to the east and west, while the panorama of Box Elder Peak, Mt. Timpanogos and Utah Lake spreads to the south.

Dominated by an upper cirque, Bells Canyon descends to the north from a 10,400-foot saddle northwest of Lake Hardy. A nice side-trip from here is to traverse northeast, climbing a few hundred feet under Thunder Mountain (11, 154 feet). About .5 mile from the saddle above Bells, climb to the 11,000-foot saddle just north of Thunder. From here or from the cliff-top perch on Thunder Mountain, the three cirques of Hogum Fork spread out to the east, while all of upper Little Cottonwood Canyon can be seen in the distance.

Pick your route carefully down to Upper Bells Canyon Reservoir. Use ridges and avoid the boulder accumulation in drainages when possible. Stay on the right (east) side of the canyon to find the upper reservoir, about 1.5 miles from the ridge.

As you descend Bells Canyon, observe the distinct vegetative changes. Keep an eye out for mountain goats, introduced from Washington by the Division of Wildlife Resources. And note the cirques, basins, moraines and polished tracks left by glaciers.

Just below Upper Bells Canyon Reservoir, a cairned route starts on the left (west) side of the creek. (Note that older editions of the Dromedary Peak topo incorrectly show the trail on the other side.) Within .5 mile, the stream cascades down a steep granite gorge, and the trail veers farther left (west), continuing on the west side of a rocky ridge which divides the canyon. The trail passes through dense spruce-fir forests, a secluded willow and wildflower meadow, and, after another .5 mile, onto the center of a ridge dividing the upper forks of Bells Canyon Creek. From the ridge to this spot, you've descended about 2,000 feet.

Incredible avalanche debris obscures the trail. Stay out of the gullies and thread your way through the deadfall and sumac until you are above the ravine where the upper forks combine.

A small park is .5 mile down the canyon where the drainage from Thunder Mountain enters from the southeast. Reach it by hiking along the east side of the stream or climb higher to the east and descend the ridge. (Trail improvements and realignment may eventually address this confusing section.)

The trail is on the right (northeast) side of the stream here. Again, the USGS topo may be in error. It continues down the canyon in good shape to Lower Bells Canyon Reservoir—2.5 miles below. Along the way, many waterfalls are heard, and spur trails lead to scenic views.

Some of the lower sections of the trail are a bit tricky, since they are straight down the fall line and quite eroded—not pleasant hiking after a strenuous climb over the ridge.

When the canyon widens a mile before Lower Bells Canyon Reservoir, work your way through the confusion of trails to the right (north) side of the canyon, around the reservoir, and down the road to your car.

Remember that the final .75-mile stretch of the trail is on private property. Past complaints from landowners have resulted from hikers straying off the trail here and from using the lower reservoir.

The Forest Service plans continuous improvement of the Bells Canyon trail as finances permit, and access at the mouth of Bells is being negotiated.

The route from Dry Creek Canyon across the ridge and down Bells Canyon traverses a variety of land—private, watershed, Forest Service multiple use, and pristine wilderness. Treat each with equally high respect.—*Jim and Valerie Pissot*

HIKE 12 GREAT WESTERN TRAIL— UINTA NATIONAL FOREST

General description: Multiple use trail threading through sixty-five miles of the Uinta National Forest.

General location: Twenty miles southeast of Salt Lake City in Little Cottonwood Canyon south to Spanish Fork Canyon, twenty miles southeast of Spanish Fork.

Maps: Trails Illustrated Uinta National Forest Map; Uinta National Forest

Travel Plan Map; and USGS Brighton, Charleston, Bridal Veil Falls, Wallsburg Ridge, Twin Peaks, Two Tom Hill, Strawberry Reservoir NW and SW Quads.
Special attractions: Spectacular scenery, cultural and geological features, wildlife and diverse vegetation.
Best season for hike: June to October.
For more information: Uinta National Forest, 88 West 100 North, Provo, UT 84603; (801) 377-5780.

The hike: The Great Western Trail, planned as a continuous route from Mexico to Canada, traverses some of the most spectacular scenery in the west. The portion through the Uinta National Forest stretches for sixty-five miles and skirts Lone Peak and Timpanogos wilderness areas, then travels the spine of the Uinta National Forest — Strawberry Ridge — to Spanish Fork Canyon.

Representing the pioneer spirit, the trail is marked with the symbol of a covered wagon inside the silhouette of Utah, and is open to hikers, horses, and mountain bikers. All terrain vehicles are allowed in designated locations.

Hiking possibilities incorporating the Great Western Trail in the Uinta National Forest are endless. Study a map and choose a portion that piques your interest. The trail enters the Uinta National Forest at its northern edge, near Lone Peak Wilderness.

Take State Highway 209 and 210 east of Sandy past the Snowbird and Alta ski resorts. Half a mile past Alta, the road continues as Forest Road #028. Just before Albion Campground, you'll find the trailhead to Lake Mary on the left side of the road. Hike east about a mile to the junction with Dry Fork Trail #032.

After descending into the Dry Fork drainage, you climb up the ridge to the east, where Ridge Trail #157 begins. For about fifteen miles, the trail follows the ridge, ending at the summit of the Alpine Scenic Loop Road. Views along the way include Sunset Peak at 10,648 feet, the historic Mineral Basin mining area, Forest Lake, and Mt. Timpanogos at 11,750 feet. Numerous trails and roads intersect the route, providing various access opportunities.

The route then follows State Highway 80 past Sundance Ski Area to Provo Canyon, southwest on U.S. Highway 189 to Vivian Park, then east up the South Fork. The trail is picked up again near Trefoil Ranch and heads south through Shingle Mill Canyon, then turns east past Lightning Peak at 10,056 feet to Windy Pass at 8,932 feet. You'll agree the pass is aptly named if you spend a night here, as the wind blowing over the ridge sounds like ocean waves breaking over your tent.

The Great Western Trail continues on an easterly course, following various trails and roads to Strawberry Peak at 9,714 feet, where it bends south along Strawberry Ridge. Hiking along the ridge, you are treated to views of some of the most rugged country in the forest. Mountain peaks line the route to the west; Strawberry Reservoir lies to the east and can be accessed by side trails and roads.

The route descends south on trail and road to Indian Creek Road, then drops into Tie Fork on a trail which passes through oak on the southern slopes

Uinta
National Forest

and conifer on the northern slopes. Meadows and a stream filled with beaver dams hug the trail. Another primitive road finishes the Uinta portion of the Great Western Trail at the Big Sky Cafe on U.S. Highway 50/6 in Spanish Fork Canyon.—*Heber Ranger District*

HIKE 13 *RED PINE LAKES*

General description: A popular day hike or overnighter into the Lone Peak Wilderness.

General location: Sixteen miles southeast of Salt Lake City in Little Cottonwood Canyon.

Maps: Trails Illustrated Uinta National Forest Map and USGS Dromedary Peak Quad.

Special attractions: Beautiful views of Little Cottonwood Canyon, Salt Lake Valley, and the Red Pine cirque; and fishing for cutthroat trout.

Best season for hike: Late spring through fall.

For more information: Salt Lake Ranger District, Wasatch-Cache National Forest, 6944 South 3000 East, Salt Lake City, UT 84121; (801) 524-5042.

The hike: This hike into Utah's first wilderness area is a popular one for Salt Lake Valley residents. The trailhead is forty minutes from downtown, and the trail ascends through some of the Wasatch's finest alpine terrain.

Backcountry camping is permitted in Little Cottonwood Canyon. However, you are not permitted to camp within 200 feet of any water source. Respect this regulation; Forest Service rangers will be seeing that you do. The restriction on dogs has not changed, and fines up to $299 are handed out regularly, so take note.

To reach the trailhead, take I-215 south from I-80 just east of Salt Lake City. Exit I-215 at 6200 South and turn left under the highway overpass. Continue four miles to the mouth of Little Cottonwood Canyon, passing the light at the mouth of Big Cottonwood Canyon along the way. Drive an additional six miles up the canyon to the trailhead. Park at the White Pine parking area a mile beyond the Tanner Flat Campground. The parking lot is on the right (south) side of the road. A trail to both White Pine Lake and the Red Pine lakes begins here.

A well-constructed bridge crosses Little Cottonwood Creek 100 yards south of the parking lot amid a thick stand of aspen and spruce. The trail contours for a mile to the west and southwest amid several slide areas before reaching the White Pine Fork. The White Pine Trail cuts back sharply to the left (east) here. A slide during the winter of 1979-80 obliterated the crossing to the Red Pine lakes, but the new, well-marked bridge is now a few hundred feet upstream.

After crossing the White Pine Fork, the trail contours for .5 mile north, west and then south around a ridge into Red Pine Canyon. At this point, you enter the Lone Peak Wilderness. Immediately after entering the wilderness, notice the Little Cottonwood Canyon road snaking its way west down the canyon toward the Salt Lake Valley. The view is beautiful, and it's not uncommon to come across a hiker snapping a few pictures here.

Many wildflower species show their colors along the trail in early summer, Uinta ground squirrels are common, and the remarkable forces of avalanches are evident on some of the steeper aspen and spruce-fir slopes.

Notice long rope-like strands of dirt in several areas along the trail. Pocket gophers have left these. They burrow through the snow during winter and push soft dirt into the tunnels. When the snow melts, the dirt settles to the ground in the many designs you see.

About a mile after entering the wilderness, a trail crosses the Red Pine Fork to the right (west) and continues into Maybird Gulch. Do not take this route, but continue for .75 mile to Red Pine Lake.

The final stretch to the lake may have large patches of snow into mid-summer, making the going sloppy and the trail difficult to locate in spots. If you run into this trouble, hike south into the basin above and you can't miss the lake.

Red Pine Lake, a popular day hike near Salt Lake City.—Dave Hall photo

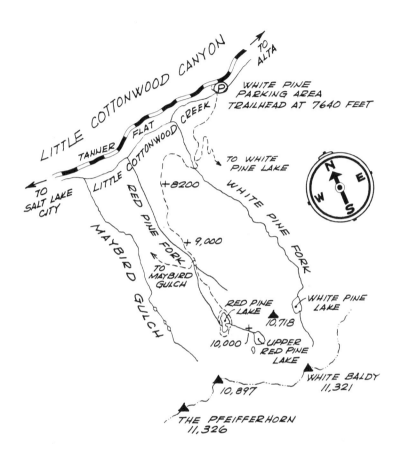

ONE MILE

Red Pine—deep, clear and with conifers around much of the perimeter—is one of the prettier of the Wasatch lakes. The granitic slopes of the Little Cottonwood/American Fork ridgeline loom to the south, and the knife-edge to the west above Maybird Gulch is spectacular. At the southeast end of the lake a large boulder makes a perfect lunch spot. It is located where the stream from Upper Red Pine Lake enters. Sitting on the rock, look north down the lake and across Little Cottonwood Canyon to Twin, Dromedary and Superior peaks (all over 11,000 feet). Golden eagles often circle lazily on midday thermals above the ridgeline to the west.

Unfortunately, this area has some of the repugnant signs of Homo sapiens. Several old fire rings dot the area, and there is evidence of ax cuttings in standing trees. In a few locations trash has been burned carelessly and left for a more responsible person to pack out.

For hikers interested in a lake with even more alpine qualities, Upper Red Pine lies .5 mile to the southeast over a steep knoll. There is no trail, and you must scramble over large rocks near the lake. Talus slopes rise to the east and south, where you may hear the peculiar squeak of a pika. If you're observant, you might spot one of these small relatives of the rabbit and hare among the rocks above the lake. A yellow-belly marmot may also waddle across your path.

There are some nice cutthroat trout in the lake, but the fishing is usually slow until the water has warmed in mid-summer. The lake can be icebound into late June.

And if you're up for a final challenge before heading back down to Red Pine Lake and out to the trailhead, Thunder Mountain to the northeast (10,718 feet) presents breathtaking views north across the canyon, east to White Pine Canyon and White Pine Lake, west to the Salt Lake Valley and the Pfeifferhorn (11,326 feet) and south along the Red Pine divide. Don't forget your camera.—*Dave Hall*

HIKE 14 *THE PFEIFFERHORN*

General description: A very challenging day hike or overnighter to the crest of the Wasatch Mountains.

General location: Sixteen miles southeast of Salt Lake City in Little Cottonwood Canyon.

Maps: Trails Illustrated Uinta National Forest Map and USGS Dromedary Peak.

Special attractions: Spectacular views in rugged alpine country.

Best season for hike: Summer through fall.

For more information: Salt Lake Ranger District, Wasatch-Cache National Forest, 6944 South 3000 East, Salt Lake City, UT 84121; (801) 524-5042.

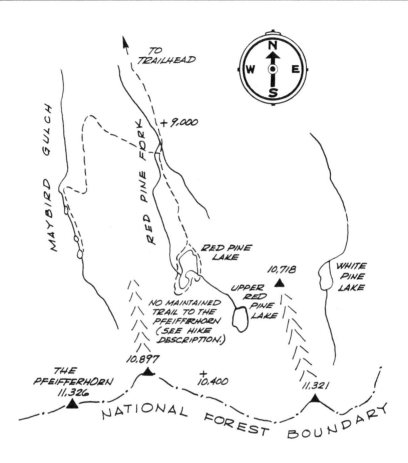

TO TRAILHEAD

N
W E
S

+ 9,000

MAYBIRD GULCH

RED PINE FORK

RED PINE LAKE

10,718

WHITE PINE LAKE

UPPER RED PINE LAKE

NO MAINTAINED TRAIL TO THE PFEIFFERHORN (SEE HIKE DESCRIPTION.)

10,897

+ 10,400

11,321

THE PFEIFFERHORN 11,326

NATIONAL FOREST BOUNDARY

ONE MILE

The hike: Red Pine Lake offers access to many points along the rugged, winding ridge that divides Little Cottonwood Canyon from American Fork Canyon. Here, the granite core of the range is exposed in a series of dramatic alpine peaks which provide spectacular views and immensely satisfying climbs. No technical equipment is required to ascend the Pfeifferhorn, at 11,326 feet the third highest summit on the ridge (after the Twin Peaks at 11,489 and 11,443 feet, respectively).

For trailhead information, consult the hike to the Red Pine lakes on page 57. The Pfeifferhorn hike continues past Upper Red Pine Lake to the ridge.

Climbing the Pfeifferhorn from the trailhead on the Little Cottonwood Canyon Road is an all-day affair, involving about ten miles for the round trip and 3,700 vertical feet. You should be in good condition and allow at least eight hours for the trip. Sunglasses and sun screen are recommended, particularly early in the season.

With the backcountry camping regulations now in effect in Little Cottonwood Canyon, you may choose to camp at Red Pine Lake or at another suitable spot along the way. Remember that regulations specify that you make camp at least 200 feet from the nearest water source.

From Red Pine Lake at 9,600 feet, follow a well-beaten path from the stream that enters from Upper Red Pine Lake. The trail climbs steeply through conifers and soon bends away from the stream. As the ground becomes rockier, the trail gets harder to follow, though a few cairns have been left by previous parties. Watch and listen for pikas in this rocky country. Climb across several small talus fields to a line of trees on the horizon marking the rim of the Upper Red Pine Lake basin—.5 mile from Red Pine Lake.

You emerge on a low ridge about .25 mile southwest of the upper lake. Climb along it southwest to the main ridge another .25 mile away. It's steep here, but the crest is not far off. If you come in late July, you'll find the lovely magenta blossoms of Parry primrose nodding in shaded crevices and fragrant pennyroyal with its delicate lavender pompons.

The crest of the ridge, about 1,000 feet above Red Pine Lake, is a good place to stop for breath. Enjoy the exhilarating views of American Fork Canyon and Mt. Timpanogos to the south, smoky blue in the midday light and marbled with snow fields. In midsummer, large fields of lupine bloom in the meadows along this ridge, beautifully set off against the gray granite and pale green grass.

Contour westward, passing below peak 10,897 on your right, and rejoin the crest .25 mile later as it narrows to a knife-edged file of gigantic blocks. The easiest route keeps slightly below and to the left of the crest here, requiring both hands for safety and balance. The knife edge is about 150 yards long.

You can see the pyramidal summit of the Pfeifferhorn straight ahead. The best route climbs alongside a steep, smooth granite chute. Keep to the left, where protruding rocks and grassy ledges make for easier going. Once again, it looks steep from a distance, but turns out to be no worse than a staircase. Four hundred vertical feet bring you panting to the top.

The views from the Pfeifferhorn are among the most dramatic in the

The Pfeifferhorn from Maybird Gulch.—James Kay photo

Wasatch. You can look northwest into the deep cirques of Hogum Fork and Bells Canyon as the ridge twists westward to Lone Peak. Beyond lie the Oquirrhs and the Stansbury Mountains; to the south, American Fork Canyon empties into Utah Lake; and far below, a matchstick city spreads toward the Great Salt Lake, a turquoise smear on the far horizon. Across the canyon to the north, the red summits of Twin, Dromedary, and Superior Peaks contrast handsomely with the younger, lighter granite exposed by the deep avalanche scars which corrugate their flanks. To the northeast, the main ridge pitches and zigzags toward Snowbird and Alta, with the dark, slab-like Uinta Mountains just visible on the eastern horizon.

In early summer, deep snow makes possible a variation in the descent. At the base of the summit cone, you can glissade down a snow-filled gully into Maybird Gulch, where within a mile a marked trail rounds the dividing spur to meet Red Pine Fork less than a mile below Red Pine Lake. (In late summer, this route is impractical, due to the extensive talus fields exposed on the floor of the gulch.) If you elect to descend by retracing your steps, simply cross the knife-edge (keeping below and to the right), contour to the right of peak 10,897, and meet the spur from Upper Red Pine Lake near a clump of wind-stunted evergreens.—*John Tallmadge*

HIKE 15 *MT. TIMPANOGOS*

General description: A spectacular—and popular—ascent to the summit of the second highest mountain in the Wasatch Range. Suitable as a day hike or overnighter.

General location: Timpanogos forms the eastern wall of Utah Valley — thirty miles southeast of Salt Lake City.

Maps: Trails Illustrated Uinta National Forest Map and USGS Aspen Grove and Timpanogos Cave Quads.

Special attractions: Spectacular panoramas, one of the most beautiful glacial tarns in Utah, and delightful approaches along sheltered cirques and exposed ridges.

Best season for hike: Late autumn, as the aspen turn brilliant gold. The terrain, however, is suitable for hiking from early summer to early winter.

For more information: Pleasant Grove Ranger District, Uinta National Forest, Box 228, Pleasant Grove, UT 84062; (801) 785-3563.

The hike: Mt. Timpanogos, at 11,750 feet, is the most prominent mountain along the 200-mile length of the Wasatch Range. Its seven-mile crest, often said to resemble the profile of a reposing woman, rises abruptly 7,000 feet from the Utah Valley floor and provides a spectacular, and in the wintertime almost Himalayan, backdrop to the communities of American Fork, Lehi, Pleasant Grove, and Orem. A wilderness area since 1984, the Mount Timpanogos Wilderness encompasses 10,750 acres of National Forest system land.

Timpanogos is composed mostly of intermingled and horizontally bedded layers of limestone and quartzite and exhibits considerable evidence of glaciation along its eastern and northern flanks. Vegetation ranges from grasslands and mountain brush at lower elevations to lichens in the alpine regions. Mountain goats were introduced on Timpanogos in 1981 and are flourishing.

In the language of the Ute Indian tribe, *Timpanogos* originally stood for "rocky stream" and referred specifically to the creek flowing down American Fork Canyon north of the mountain. During settlement of the area, the pioneers transferred the name to the river south of the mountain. Still later, the newly labeled Timpanogos River was renamed the Provot River after an army officer who explored the canyon. *Timpanogos* was then transferred again, to the only other nearby geological feature of any prominence, the mountain itself.

According to legend (actually based on a story written in this century), the crest of Mt. Timpanogos is a remnant of an Indian Princess who slowly petrified as she languished for her warrior-husband-to-be while he was away on an "extended deer hunt."

To reach the trailhead, take the Alpine Loop Road (State Highway 92) which travels around Timpanogos from the Alpine exit on I-15 to U.S. 189 in Provo Canyon. Take the Loop Road to the recreational home community of Aspen Grove—about 19 miles from I-15 and five miles from U.S. 189.

Look for an open field west of the homes. A few hundred yards farther west, turn south. The trailhead is at a paved parking lot just off the Loop Road.

The Timpanogos trail begins at an elevation of 6,900 feet and proceeds almost directly westward through a grove of aspen into the lower portion of Primrose Cirque. After .8 mile and a gentle 600-foot climb, the trail steepens as it begins to switchback the headwall of the cirque. The switchbacks continue for about two miles while the trail ascends to an elevation of 10,000 feet and enters a hanging valley often covered with magnificent displays of mountain flowers. Another .5 mile of very gentle hiking brings you to the "traditional" lunch knoll overlooking Emerald Lake and a nearby rock shelter. From here, the summit is visible another .5 mile to the southwest—1,300 feet straight up!

During lunch, area etiquette commands one to ponder the age-old question: Is it a glacier above Emerald Lake or a snowfield? For those who care to deliberate, it should be noted that at the time of the earliest known "first winter ascent" of Timpanogos on February 19, 1916, a climber described a "large ice crevice" and a "number of deep beautiful crevices" along the upper area of what he called a "glacier".

Dancing on Mt. Timpanogos' 11,750-foot summit? A routine weekend activity in the 1920s for these Wasatch Mountain Club members.—Wasatch Mountain Club photo

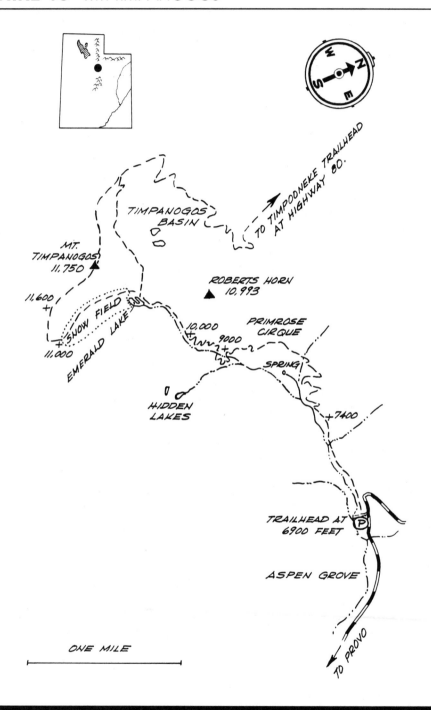

TIMPANOGOS BASIN

TO TIMPOONEKE TRAILHEAD AT HIGHWAY 80.

MT. TIMPANOGOS 11,750

ROBERTS HORN 10,993

11,600

SNOW FIELD

PRIMROSE CIRQUE

10,000

9000

EMERALD LAKE

11,000

SPRING

HIDDEN LAKES

7400

TRAILHEAD AT 6900 FEET

ASPEN GROVE

TO PROVO

ONE MILE

The shelter near Emerald Lake was constructed in 1959 as an "aid station/rest stop" for use during annual community climbs of Mt. Timpanogos that would include thousands of participants attempting the summit on the same day. More than 8,000 hikers made the day hike one year. These one-day assaults were discontinued in 1970 due to resource damage. The Pleasant Grove Ranger District reports that the Aspen Grove side of the mountain may never recover from this overuse.

The route continues .75 mile up the gentle snow field/glacier above the lake. Ascent is generally straightforward, though severe winter conditions can leave behind a very steep, sometimes overhanging cornice at the top of the pass.

From the pass at 11,500 feet, the trail to the summit traverses in a northwesterly direction along the western slope of the ridge crest. The summit is .8 mile beyond and 450 feet above the pass. A small, open, metal, hut-like structure, built as a triangulation station for the county, dominates the summit block where dedicated hikers of the early 1920s danced at sunrise.

From the summit, two options are available for descent to Aspen Grove. The first option traces the ascent route. The second follows a descending trail .5 mile northwest along the ridge to a pass, then swings back abruptly for a mile to Emerald Lake. From the lake, descent to Aspen Grove follows the ascent trail.

Many hikers prefer a third option, a route that does not return to Emerald Lake or to Aspen Grove. This route follows the ridge to the pass northwest of the summit, but instead of swinging back to Emerald Lake, continues about a mile into Timpanogos Basin and eventually terminates five miles farther on at the Timpooneke trailhead and ranger station six miles northwest of Aspen Grove. If two vehicles are available, a return shuttle can be organized in advance of the hike. If not, the hiker can take his chance on hitching a ride with passing motorists.

Incidentally, the Timpooneke Trail is also an excellent ascent route to Mt. Timpanogos. It is a bit longer than the Aspen Grove route, but is a more gradual climb and is shaded during much of the morning.—*Alexis Kelner*

HIKE 16 *SANTAQUIN PEAK*

General description: A day hike or possible overnight trip to the top of 10,685-foot Santaquin Peak.

General location: Eighteen miles south of Provo in the Uinta National Forest.

Maps: Trails Illustrated Uinta National Forest Map, and USGS Payson Lakes and Birdseye Quad.

Special attractions: Views of Utah Lake and Mt. Nebo.

Best season for hike: Late spring; late summer through fall.

For more information: Spanish Fork Ranger District, Uinta National Forest, 44 West 400 North, Spanish Fork, UT 84660; (801) 798-3571.

The hike: Santaquin Peak and Loafer Mountain provide a good change of pace from the more popular areas overlooking the Salt Lake Valley. A pleasing combination of alpine and pastoral scenery unfolds as the trail winds its way along several drainages.

The hike begins from the Mt. Nebo Scenic Loop Road. Take I-15 to the Payson exit, fifteen miles south of Provo. In Payson take 600 East heading south; this road leads into Payson Canyon. You reach Maple Dell on the right

HIKE 16 *SANTAQUIN PEAK*

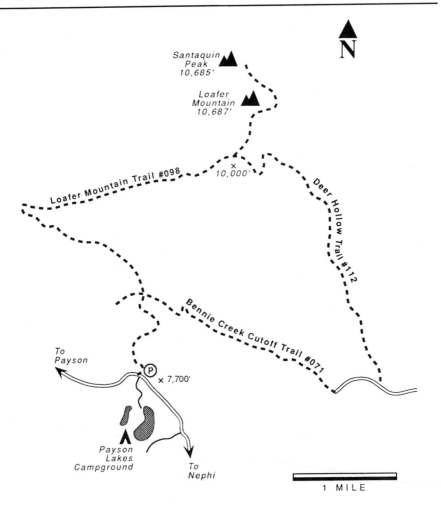

after about 5.5 miles. There is a large metal bar gate here, used to close the road under winter and other adverse conditions. Continue about seven miles up the narrow, winding road to the Loafer Mountain trailhead just north of Payson Lakes (about .75 mile before Payson Lakes Campground).

From the trailhead at 7,700 feet, the trail climbs about 3,000 feet over 5.5 miles. It's a good day outing but certainly not overwhelming for hikers in good condition.

The route follows the well-marked Loafer Mountain Trail #7098 about four miles to a saddle overlooking a cirque, descending to the east. Leave the main trail here and proceed northwesterly up the ridge, veering to the northeast within .25 mile toward the summit ridge. From Loafer Mountain (10,687 feet), Santaquin Peak is visible to the west, separated by a deep chasm.

Although the terrain is very steep in places, Santaquin Peak can be reached from the northern end of the Loafer Mountain ridge by descending through fir-covered slopes to the saddle connecting the two. From the low point, ascend the ridge to the summit of Santaquin Peak—about a mile and 450 vertical feet away.

Much of the area is open, providing a number of variations to adventure-some hikers armed with a topo map. Not all the contiguous land is national forest, hence, be prepared to make local inquiries on the availability of private land for hiking. This is particularly true for the territory to the north overlooking Spanish Fork Canyon. Several hundred acres are involved, with access limited, if not forbidden.

For a good overnight loop trip, backtrack to the saddle where you first left the main trail. The Loafer Mountain Trail connects with Deer Hollow Trail #7112 at the saddle. Deer Hollow winds its way three miles southeast to its end at Forest Road #123. Follow the road west about .5 mile to the Bennie Creek Cutoff trailhead at the end of the road. Bennie Creek intersects the Loafer Mountain Trail about 1 mile north of the trailhead and your vehicle. — *Karin and Dennis Caldwell*

HIKE 17 *MT. NEBO*

General description: A strenuous 5,000-foot climb to the top of Mt. Nebo's south summit in the Mount Nebo Wilderness.
General location: Eight miles northeast of Nephi; 30 miles south of Provo.
Maps: Northcentral Utah Multipurpose Map and USGS Mona and Nebo Basin Quads.
Special attractions: Spectacular views of northern and central Utah.
Best season for hike: Late spring through fall.
For more inforrnation: Spanish Fork Ranger District, Uinta National Forest, 44 West 400 North, Spanish Fork, UT 84660; (801) 798-3571.

The hike: Mt. Nebo is a demanding trip—not recommended for hikers looking for an easy day hike. The hike can be done in a day, but you may find a two-day backpack more enjoyable. You climb 5,000 feet in about five miles.

To get to the trailhead, take Interstate 15 to Nephi and turn east on State Highway 132 (at the light on 100 North). Continue east about six miles and turn left on the Nebo/Salt Creek Road. Bear left in 3.3 miles (do not take the Nebo Loop Road) and drive about 1.5 miles to the trailhead on the left, .25 mile beyond the Andrews Canyon sign.

The trail begins at 6,450 feet and climbs west for about .5 mile before meeting the established trail out of Andrews Canyon at about 7,200 feet. Several switchbacks through the next .5 mile ascend through sage and maple/oak thickets. It can be hot along this stretch, so bring plenty of water. Look back along the Andrews Creek drainage for a nice view.

After this first mile and a 1,400-foot elevation gain, the trail enters a relatively flat sagebrush and grass meadow. The views east to the Golden Ridge area, southeast to the Manti-LaSal National Forest, and north into the Salt Creek drainage are superb.

Follow the trail west .5 mile up another set of steep switchbacks to Andrews Ridge. Aspens and conifers become more common here. You will discover that the trail splits into two major routes and several side trails. (During the summer of 1981, there was seismic equipment in the area. Its presence may explain the numerous trails.) From the junction, the left trail follows the south slope of Andrews Ridge and the right trail (recommended) continues near the ridge. The trails rejoin after about .5 mile.

At this junction, an old trail heads southeast into Quaking Asp Canyon. Turn right (north). The summit trail crosses two very small drainages and enters a third, larger one in the next .75 mile, climbing about 500 feet in the process. Even late into the summer, the snow fields that remain in the basins above the trail may provide some water in the gulches. However, it would be wise to check with the Spanish Fork Ranger District on the current water quality conditions before making the hike.

The trail forks after entering the third basin. The Nebo Basin Trail continues north. Turn left (west) and make the steep ascent (600 feet in .5 mile) to a saddle on the ridge. The views west into Juab Valley and beyond are spectacular.

Turn right (north) on the ridge and continue 1.5 miles through stands of limber pine and then above tree line to the 11,877-foot summit.

The final stretch is spectacular. At the southern end of the summit, there is a beautiful alpine meadow. A small snow bank to the east and below the ridge may last all year when the snowfall has been heavy.

An old flag-shaped sign sits on top, placed there by the Wasatch Mountain Club. Incidentally, it is now known that the highest point on the ridge is actually two peaks north (11,928 feet), but the trail ends at the south summit.

You can reach this higher peak by scrambling along the knife-edge to the north .5 mile to the middle peak (11,824 feet) and then another .5 mile to the actual summit. However, use caution along this precipitous ridge. If you have doubts about the climb, don't make it.

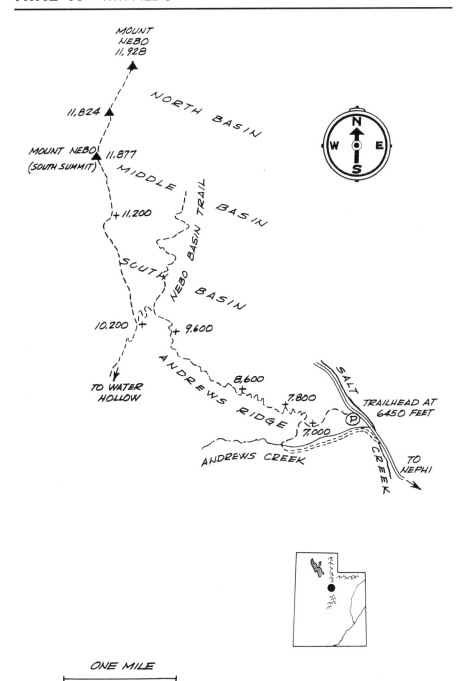

MOUNT
NEBO
11,928

NORTH BASIN

11,824

MOUNT NEBO
(SOUTH SUMMIT) 11,877

MIDDLE BASIN

11,200

NEBO BASIN TRAIL

SOUTH BASIN

10,200   9,600

TO WATER
HOLLOW

ANDREWS RIDGE

8,600

7,800

7,000

SALT CREEK

TRAILHEAD AT
6450 FEET

ANDREWS CREEK

TO
NEPHI

N
W   E
S

ONE MILE

71

Rocky Mountain bighorn sheep have been reintroduced to the Mount Nebo area by the Division of Wildlife Resources.— John George photo.

The views from the top of the South Summit are fantastic. To the north are the other peaks of the Nebo ridge; to the northeast are the many peaks of the Wasatch that ring Utah Valley. Views to the east and south are of the Uinta and Manti-LaSal National Forests. To the west you can see the basins and ranges of the Great Basin.

Mt. Nebo has many plant species. The alpine zone has daisies, buckwheat, lichens, and hardy grasses. The subalpine zone hosts limber pine, lupine, several species of beardstongue, gentians, columbine, bluebells, Indian paintbrush, and many others. Lower down are aspen, Douglas fir, sagebrush, maple, oak, and numerous plants of the composite family.

This area is critical wildlife habitat. You may see rodents, grouse, and a variety of other birds. Hikers with keen eyes will see agile sharp-shinned hawks darting between trees and riding thermals above the ridges. The Nebo area is also home to one of Utah's most important elk herds. Deer are also common. Recently, Rocky Mountain bighorn sheep were reintroduced to the area. — *Gary McFarland*

HIKE 18 *DANIELS CANYON NATURE TRAILS*

General description: Two interpretive trails in Daniels Canyon in the Uinta National Forest, Heber Ranger District.

General location: Eight or sixteen miles southeast of Heber City along U.S. Highway 40.

Maps: Northeastern Utah Multipurpose Map; Uinta National Forest Travel Plan Map; USGS Center Creek and Twin Peaks Quads.

Special attractions: Spectacular scenery and views, and diverse vegetation.

Best season for hike: June through October.

For more information: Heber Ranger District, Uinta National Forest, Box 190, Heber City, UT 84032; (801) 654-0470.

The hike: The Whiskey Springs Nature Trail and the Foreman Hollow Trail are two short loop trails easily accessed from Heber City along U.S. Highway 40.

To reach the Whiskey Springs trailhead, drive eight miles southeast of Heber City on U.S. Highway 40 to the Uinta National Forest. The Whiskey Springs Picnic Area is located just inside the national forest boundary. The 500-foot nature loop is an easy, paved and gravel trail with interpretive plant signs along the way.

Foreman Hollow Trail #071 is near the summit of Daniels Canyon, sixteen miles from Heber City on U.S. Highway 40. The trail is accessed from a trailhead in Lodgepole Campground. Foreman Hollow is a three-mile loop of moderate difficulty. There are spectacular views of Strawberry Reservoir to the southeast, and Strawberry Peak (9,714 feet) and Twin Peaks (9,712 and 9,653 feet) to the southwest. Educational signs along the well-maintained trail note interesting facts about the native vegetation and wildlife. Campsites, water and restrooms are available at Lodgepole Campground. —*Heber Ranger District*

HIKE 19 *DRY CANYON/CLEGG CANYON*

General description: A number of day hike possibilities in Daniels Canyon in the Uinta National Forest, Heber Ranger District.

General location: Ten miles southeast of Heber City on U.S. Highway 40.

Maps: Uinta National Forest Travel Plan Map; USGS Center Creek Quad.

Special attractions: Panoramic views, wildlife, diverse vegetation.

Best season for hike: June through October

For more information: Heber Ranger District, Uinta National Forest, Box 190, Heber City, UT 84032; (801) 654-0470.

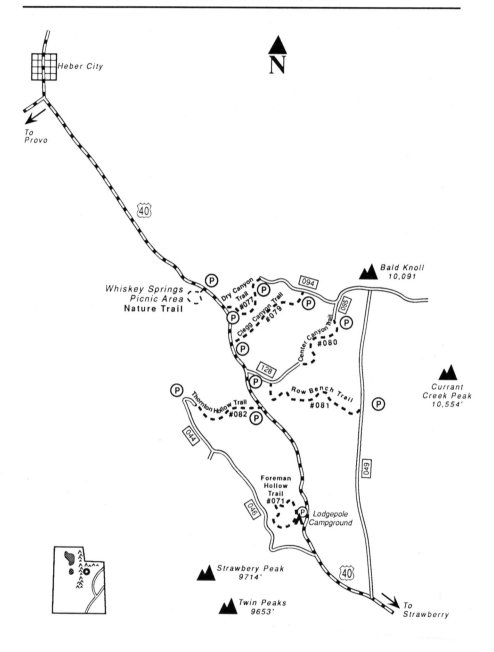

Beautiful views await hikers on Dry Canyon Trail.

The hike: These two point-to-point trails in Daniels Canyon are easily accessed on U.S. Highway 40 and connect via Forest Service road, providing vehicle shuttle or loop hike opportunities. Hiking information, maps and supplies for your trip can be obtained at nearby Heber City.

To reach Dry Canyon Trail #077, drive nine miles southeast of Heber City on U.S. Highway 40. The trailhead is on the left side of the highway, 1.5 miles past the Uinta National Forest boundary.

Water is not available along either of the trails, so be sure to carry a sufficient supply, especially in the warm summer months. Be prepared, as well, for summer afternoon thunderstorms.

The 3.25 mile trail is a moderately difficult route which is quite steep as it passes through a narrow canyon. At the top, hikers are treated to a breathtaking view of the surrounding mountains, including Bald Knoll (10,091 feet) to the east.

You'll find Clegg Canyon Trail #079 also on the left another mile up the highway. This trail is nearly six miles long and passes through canyon country, meadows, and evergreen and aspen stands. The trail is relatively flat at each end and steep in the middle, making it an easy to moderately difficult hike. Clegg Canyon is closed to all motorized traffic.

Clegg Canyon and Dry Canyon trails meet Forest Road #094 within one mile of each other, making a 10.5 to 11.5 mile loophike (depending on whether a second vehicle was left at either trailhead on the highway). — *Heber Ranger District*

HIKE 20 *CENTER CANYON*

General description: A short day hike in Daniels Canyon in the Uinta National Forest, Heber Ranger District.
General location: Thirteen miles southeast of Heber City.
Maps: Uinta National Forest Travel Plan Map; USGS Center Creek and Twin Peaks Quads.
Special attractions: Panoramic views, wildlife, diverse vegetation.
Best season for hike: June through October.
For more information: Heber Ranger District, Uinta National Forest, Box 190, Heber City, UT 84032; (801) 654-0470.

The hike: The Center Canyon Trail is open only to foot, horse, or mountain bike travel. Water is not available along the trail, so be sure to carry a sufficient supply, especially in the warm summer months. Be prepared for afternoon thunderstorms during the summer, too. Hiking information, maps and supplies for your trip can be obtained at nearby Heber City.

To reach Center Canyon Trail #080, drive about eleven miles from Heber City, then turn left (east) on Forest Road #128 for about 2.5 miles to the trailhead. The trail, four miles long, is relatively steep as it climbs through Center Canyon to a ridge, following a small stream for most of its length. There are great views of the surrounding mountains, including Currant Creek Peak to the southeast at 10,554 feet.

Center Canyon connects with Forest Road #095 which intersects Forest Road #094 about .5 mile to the north. You could have a vehicle waiting here or hike the road west and pick up the Clegg Canyon or Dry Canyon trails (see Hike 19). — *Heber Ranger District*

HIKE 21 *ROW BENCH*

General description: A moderate day hike in Daniels Canyon in the Uinta National Forest, Heber Ranger District.
General location: Twelve miles southeast of Heber City.

Row Bench Trail.

Maps: Uinta National Forest Travel Plan Map; USGS Co-op Creek and Twin Peaks Quads.
Special Attractions: Panoramic ridgeline views, wildlife, diverse vegetation.
Best season for hike: June through October.
For more information: Heber Ranger District, Uinta National Forest, Box 190, Heber City, UT 84032; (801) 654-0470.

The hike: To reach Row Bench Trail #081, drive about eleven miles from Heber City, then turn left (east) on Forest Road #128 for about one mile to the trailhead on the right (south) side of the road.

The trail is nearly six miles long, runs along a ridge above Row Hollow and provides beautiful views of the surrounding area. You pass through evergreen forest, thick stands of aspen, gambel oak and other shrubby growth interspersed with brief patches of grassy meadow. The well-maintained trail climbs upward continuously and is rated moderately difficult. It intersects Forest Road #049 at its eastern end.

Water is not available along the trail, so be sure to carry a sufficient supply, especially in the warm summer months. Be prepared for summer afternoon thunderstorms. Hiking information, maps and supplies for your trip can be obtained at nearby Heber City. — *Heber Ranger District*

HIKE 22 *THORNTON HOLLOW*

General description: A short day hike in Daniels Canyon in the Uinta National Forest, Heber Ranger District.

General location: Twelve miles southeast of Heber City on U.S. Highway 40.

Maps: Uinta National Forest Travel Plan Map; USGS Twin Peaks Quad.

Special attractions: Panoramic ridgeline views, wildlife, diverse vegetation.

Best season for hike: June through October.

For more information: Heber Ranger District, Uinta National Forest, Box 190, Heber City, UT 84032; (801) 654-0470.

The hike: The Thornton Hollow Trail is open only to foot, horse, or mountain bike travel. Water is not available along the trail, so be sure to carry a sufficient supply, especially in the warm summer months. Be prepared for summer afternoon thunderstorms. Hiking information, maps and supplies for your trip can be obtained at nearby Heber City.

Thornton Hollow Trail #082 begins twelve miles from Heber City on the right (west) side of U.S. Highway 40. Thornton Hollow is an easy to follow, scenic trail running over three miles to a ridgetop. It features rocky stream crossings, shady pine needle-carpeted trail, aspen groves and grassy meadows. The trail is well-maintained and of moderate difficulty. It connects with Forest Road #044 at the western national forest boundary. — *Heber Ranger District*

HIKE 23 *LOG HOLLOW/NOBLETTS CREEK*

General description: An enjoyable day trip on two trails sharing the same trailhead in the Uinta National Forest near the western boundary of the High Uintas Wilderness.

General location: Seventeen miles northeast of Heber City on State Highway 35.

Maps: Northeastern Utah Multipurpose Map, Uinta National Forest Travel PlanMap, USGS Soapstone Basin Quad.

Special attractions: Interesting geologic features, spectacular views, wildlife and diverse vegetation.

Best season for hike: June through October.

For more information: Heber Ranger District, Uinta National Forest, Box 190, Heber City, UT 84032; (801) 654-0470.

The hike: Drive eight miles north from Heber City on U.S. Highway 40, turn right (east) and drive seven miles to Francis. Take State Highway 35 southeast

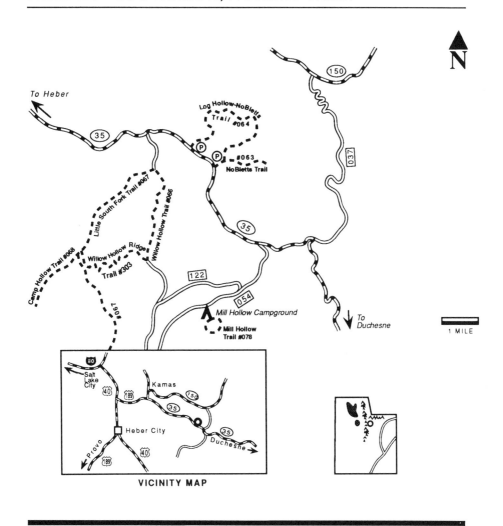

VICINITY MAP

along the South Fork Provo River about ten miles. The trailhead is located about two miles from the Uinta National Forest boundary on the left side of the highway. Both the Nobletts Creek Trail and the Log Hollow-Nobletts loop begin at this trailhead.

If you have plenty of time, you might begin the day by hiking the short, generally easy Nobletts Creek Trail #063. This 1.5-mile, well-maintained trail passes through some interesting geologic formations. The key feature is Nobletts Creek, an underground stream that surfaces as a large spring near the end of the trail.

After exploring the Nobletts Creek area, hike back to the junction near the trailhead and take the left fork up Log Hollow-Nobletts Trail #064. The trail is initially rather steep as it follows the left fork of Nobletts Creek. At the top of the canyon, the trail crosses a grassy meadow and meanders along the ridge. You can enjoy spectacular views of the surrounding valleys and peaks, including Iron Mine Mountain to the east and Soapstone Mountain to the southeast. As the ridge ends, the trail turns south down Log Hollow Canyon to Nobletts Canyon and Highway 35.

The trail, nearly seven miles long, is lined with conifer and aspen stands and scrub oak. It's about a mile back to the trailhead and your car, making this an easy loop to complete with or without a vehicle shuttle. —*Heber Ranger District*

HIKE 24 *ROUND, SAND AND FISH LAKES*

General description: A rigorous overnighter to grayling and trout lakes in the upper Weber River drainage.

General location: Nineteen miles east of Oakley and 50 miles east of Salt Lake City in the western Uinta Mountains.

Maps: Northeastern Utah Multipurpose Map and USGS Whitney Reservoir Quad.

Special attractions: Good fly fishing for grayling and brook trout.

Best season for hike: Late June through September.

For more information: Kamas Ranger District, Wasatch-Cache National Forest, Box 68, Kamas, UT 84036; (801) 783-4338.

The hike: These lakes are for well-conditioned trekkers seeking good high country fishing, particularly for the beautiful Arctic grayling. The trailhead is less than two hours from Salt Lake City, with several miles over improved dirt road suitable for passenger cars.

The trail begins at 8,000 feet and climbs through a rocky fir forest, ending below timberline in a broad, U-shaped basin boasting many small ponds and lakes. Round Lake sits just below 10,000 feet; Sand and Fish Lakes are about 200 feet higher. The area is about 3.5 miles from the trailhead.

This trail attracts heavy horse traffic, so expect to see a few ruts and mud holes on the steeper sections of the route.

To reach the trailhead, take the Wanship exit off I-80 and drive about ten miles to Oakley on U.S. Alternate 189. Turn left on Canyon Road (.25 mile north of the Oakley General Store—your last stop for trail munchies). The intersection is clearly marked with a sign indicating "Weber Canyon, Smith and Morehouse."

The trailhead is nineteen miles from this intersection. You begin traveling on an improved dirt road after twelve miles. The road to Smith and Morehouse Reservoir turns right at this point. Do not turn here. Pass the Thousand Peaks Ranch sign, and after four miles on the dirt road, bear right at a minor intersection. Before long you cross the Weber River. About .25 mile beyond,

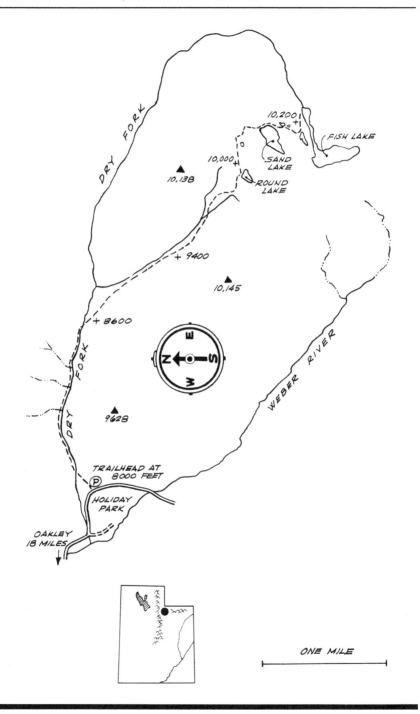

pass the entrance to Holiday Park. Do not enter the park; rather, bear left and continue .5 mile to the trailhead. It is on the left just after crossing Dry Fork Creek. There is a small dirt parking area. The trailhead is on private land, so respect the right to use it.

From the trailhead, the route heads northeast through an aspen grove for .25 mile to the first crossing on Dry Fork Creek. Watch this crossing very carefully, especially with small children in tow. Normally low and easily waded, Dry Fork Creek can quickly rise to hazardous levels in midsummer due to upstream releases for irrigation. With care, older children and adults can cross safely at any time. Incidentally, you follow the stream for 1.5 miles, so don't overload your water bottles yet. There's plenty ahead, although treatment for Giardia is recommended (see page 16).

After the stream crossing, the trail proceeds northeast along Dry Fork's left (north) side through lodgepole pines and firs. The trail becomes rocky, climbing slowly. While you still have your wind and energy, relax and enjoy the abundant wildflowers. You should see yarrow, cinquefoil, assorted sunflowers and daisies, Indian paintbrush, geraniums, and monkshood.

After climbing about 600 feet in 1.5 miles, cross Dry Fork Creek again in a large clearing near the downstream end of an old, washed-out beaver pond. Watch carefully for this spot, with the trail heading south for about 100 feet after the crossing. (Note that the crossing is mistakenly shown as being past the upstream end of the clearing on the USGS map; other than this error, the map trail description is accurate.) While at the clearing, look upward to the southeast at a knobby peak (10,138 feet). You ascend the slope to the right and pass the peak on the south side. Check your water now. While there are creeks in the next stretch of trail, none are reliable and may be dry when you hike.

From Dry Fork Creek, head south on a smooth, gentle trail for about 100 feet, then bear left (east). In about .25 mile at 8,600 feet, begin climbing a rocky trail, still tracking southeast. The trail again levels out, but you'll soon hit a steep stretch looking much like a stream bed. Keep your eyes and wildflower guide open, because there are white columbine, parrotsbeak, monkshood, false hellebore, cow parsnip, purple penstemon, red and yellow monkeyflowers, bluebells, wild strawberry, and others. This damp area is ideal habitat for many of the showier wildflowers.

From here on, continue to the southeast until you reach Round Lake about two miles from the crossing. It seems like five miles, especially just before Round Lake where the trail is steepest. Cross the outlet stream from Round Lake, which actually is the trail for about fifty feet. Be careful—the algae-coated rocks are slippery.

Round Lake is small and sits at 9,940 feet elevation. The one good campsite is on the northwest corner where the trail meets the lake and will accomodate three small tents. Don't pitch tents close to the water's edge, because the area is fragile, and the water typically creeps up overnight with irrigation releases upstream. Do other hikers a favor and pack out some of the extra garbage in the area.

Round Lake has been stocked with Arctic grayling and brook and cutthroat trout. All readily take small flies, especially dries. The north and northeast shores are best for fly casting, but the largest fish may be on the other side, where many trees have fallen into the water. While fishing, note all of the elephanthead plants in the wet meadows around the lake.

Sand Lake is just southeast of Round Lake, .5 mile on the trail. At about the halfway mark, you skirt a large meadow on the north side. Look to your right (south) and notice a beautiful waterfall against the heavily timbered hillside. The fall is the stream outlet from Sand Lake.

Sand Lake has only a few poor-to-fair campsites on the north and northwest corners, plus one just below the dam (not shown on the USGS map). The largest site could accomodate one party with up to three small tents. The inlet meadow on the southwest corner of the lake is wet and muddy.

Sand Lake contains small grayling and has poor fly fishing due to the steep, timbered, debris-ridden shoreline. Round Lake certainly is more productive and attractive for fishing.

Fish Lake is due south of Sand Lake, another .5 mile on an easy trail. The trail meets Fish Lake on a long, narrow arm extending northeast from the main lake body. Although not shown on the USGS map, Fish Lake has a rock dam at the extreme northeast end of the arm.

The plant community around Fish Lake is similar to that around Round and Sand lakes, and you are still below timberline. The lake has many good shoreline campsites, particularly on the long arm, so you should have no trouble bringing a larger party in. The lake contains mostly brook trout and grayling and often has good fly fishing. The outlet stream looks as if it could hold some nice trout as well.

The Round-Sand-Fish lakes area has received no official Forest Service wilderness designation. However, the area is part of the Lakes Roadless Area—recommended for wilderness by Utah conservationists.

Future hikers can enhance its qualities by packing out some of the accumulated trash, which the Forest Service says has become a particular problem here in recent years. — *Bill Geer*

HIKE 25 *THREE DIVIDE LAKES*

General description: A day hike or overnighter to beautiful alpine terrain in the Uinta Mountains.
General location: Fifty miles east of Salt Lake City.
Maps: Northeastern Utah Multipurpose Map and USGS Mirror Lake Quad.
Special attractions: Alpine scenery at the head of the Provo and Weber River drainages; good flshing.
Best season for hike: Late spring through fall.
For more information: Kamas Ranger District, Wasatch-Cache National Forest, Box 68, Kamas, UT 84036; (801) 783-4338.

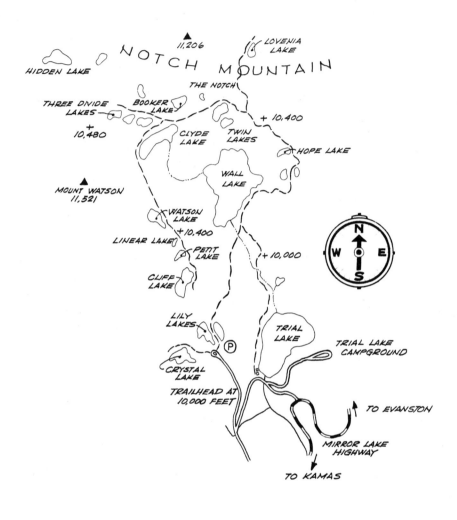

ONE MILE

84

The hike: The western Uinta Mountains, from Kamas east to Bald Mountain, offer spectacular high lake country and a family of peaks over 10,000 feet. This is the Lakes Roadless Area, headwater country of the Provo and Weber Rivers.

To reach the trailhead, drive about twenty-six miles east of Kamas on State Highway 150 (the Mirror Lake Highway). Turn left toward Trial Lake at a long, 180-degree turn to the right. Drive on pavement for a few hundred yards, continuing on a gravel road for .75 mile. Turn right toward Crystal Lake (signs

Blue grouse—or fool hens, as they're sometimes called—are common at higher elevations in Utah.—Harry Engels photo

mark the spot). The trailhead is .5 mile ahead at the end of the road, just north of a horse ramp at the west end of the parking area. This trailhead leads to many areas of the upper Provo and Weber drainages, so don't be discouraged by several cars in the trailhead parking area.

The Three Divide Lakes are about three miles from the trailhead and only about 400 feet higher in elevation, so the hike is relatively easy. These beautiful alpine lakes sit among a cluster of lakes at just over 10,400 feet. The area is bordered by the Notch Mountain peaks to the north (11,263 feet is the tallest) and by boulder-strewn Mount Watson (11,521 feet) to the southwest.

Beginning at about 10,000 feet, the trail passes Lily Lakes in a few hundred yards, then contours north for a mile before reaching the Notch Mountain Trail just south of Wall Lake. This section of trail, incidentally, is not shown on the 1972 Mirror Lake topographic map.

At Wall Lake, the trail angles to the east through a lovely series of ponds and small meadows and then ascends several switchbacks .75 mile to the broad meadows near Twin Lakes.

The Notch, a 10,000-foot pass leading to Lovenia and Ibantik Lakes and the upper Weber drainage, is .25 mile to the north. Leave the trail here, proceeding due west an eighth mile to Twin Lakes. A trail runs .5 mile along the north shore of the larger, upper lake, up a series of boulders, and on to large Clyde Lake at the base of Mount Watson. From Clyde Lake, the Three Divide Lakes are all within .5 mile to the north.

Fishing is good here, particularly for small brook trout. There are also cutthroats in some of the nearby lakes. Campsites are plentiful in the many stands of spruce and fir, with spring water available throughout the year. Check local Giardia conditions with the Forest Service before drinking unboiled water.

From a base camp near any of the Three Divide Lakes, you can take side trips through the Notch to Lake Lovenia. You can make the 1,100-foot climb up Mount Watson or explore the Hidden Lake area to the northwest on the shoulder of the Middle Fork Weber River. This is a lovely area in the shadow of Mount Watson.

Because of this area's proximity to the Mirror Lake Highway, it gets heavy use, especially during the midsummer months. But it's wide open country, and you should be able to find a quiet niche for your campsite.

Mule deer, some moose and elk inhabit the area. Small mammals, including weasels, voles and muskrats, provide interesting diversions from your hiking in the high lakes country. Extensive pine marten research was done on the northern reaches of the Middle Fork Weber River.

An alternative route back to your car—one which supplements your wilderness experience in the Lakes region—offers an intriguing cross-country hike.

Hike around the west end of Clyde Lake and find the trail heading south. Follow a series of terraces and lakes (Watson, Linear and Petit) .75 mile down to Cliff Lake. Foot traffic has created a trail from the south end of Cliff Lake along the west edge of Lily Lake, connecting to Lakes Country Trail #066. Turn left here for less than .25 mile back to the trailhead.

There are numerous options in this splendid alpine wilderness, but we'll leave it to you to discover them. — *Margaret Pettis*

HIKE 26 *HIDDEN LAKE*

General description: An enjoyable overnighter to a secluded lake in the Uinta Mountains.

General location: Forty-four miles east of Salt Lake City.

Maps: Northeastern Utah Multipurpose Map and USGS Mirror Lake and Erickson Basin Quads.

Special attractions: Alpine scenery; fine fishing for cutthroat and brook trout.

Best season for hike: Early summer through fall.

For more information: Kamas Ranger District, Wasatch-Cache National Forest, Box 68, Kamas, UT 84036; (801) 783-4338.

The hike: This Hidden Lake truly is hidden—some experienced backcountry hikers have gotten lost along the way. So follow your topo maps carefully and keep your compass handy.

Take State Highway 150 (the Mirror Lake Highway) about twenty-six miles east of Kamas. Turn left toward Trial Lake at a long, 180-degree turn to the right. Drive on pavement for a few hundred yards, continuing on the gravel road for .75 mile. Turn right toward Crystal Lake (signs mark the spot). The trailhead is .5 mile ahead at the end of the road. This trailhead leads to many areas in the upper Provo and Weber drainages, so don't be discouraged by several cars at the trailhead parking area.

The hike is not difficult—4.5 miles to the lake with a net loss in elevation of about 300 feet. Whatever difficulty you may encounter will be in orienteering on the second half of the trip in. The intermittent, unsigned trail has few distinct landmarks, and the tendency is to stay too low along the North Fork of the Provo River, bypassing Hidden Lake.

The hike begins at 10,000 feet just east of Crystal Lake. The trail is an old road for a few hundred yards, becoming a well-trodden pack trail as it swings around Crystal Lake.

The trail jogs south, crosses a bridge, and then climbs about 250 feet to a saddle in .5 mile. Mount Watson (11,521 feet) is immediately north, and Haystack Mountain, with its long ridge close to 11,000 feet, stretches to the south.

From the saddle, there's a gentle descent to the west, and Long Lake appears in a mile through intermittent stands of conifers. There are a few excellent campsites around the lake.

Trail #066 crosses the dam at Long Lake and continues west about a mile to Island Lake, then northwest along Smith and Morehouse Creek.

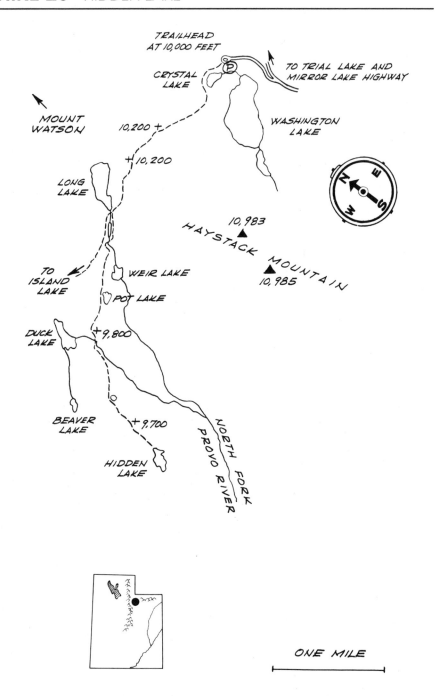

TRAILHEAD
AT 10,000 FEET

CRYSTAL
LAKE

TO TRIAL LAKE AND
MIRROR LAKE HIGHWAY

MOUNT
WATSON

10,200 +

+ 10,200

WASHINGTON
LAKE

LONG
LAKE

10,983

HAYSTACK

TO
ISLAND
LAKE

WEIR LAKE

MOUNTAIN

POT LAKE

10,985

DUCK
LAKE

+ 9,800

BEAVER
LAKE

+ 9,700

NORTH FORK
PROVO RIVER

HIDDEN
LAKE

ONE MILE

Angler at pretty Hidden Lake in the upper Provo drainage.—Dave Hall photo

About .5 mile past Long Lake, a well-established trail on your left heads southwest past Weir and Pot lakes.

About .25 mile southwest of Pot Lake, the trail descends a few hundred feet to a large meadow. The upper portion of the North Fork of the Provo River snakes through this open stretch. The stream's source is just .25 mile to the northwest at Duck Lake.

Continue south along the right (west) side of the stream. Within .25 mile the trail leaves the stream and continues to a small unnamed pond north of Hidden Lake. There's a spring on the west side of this pond, and some feisty brook trout can be found in its shallow waters. This is also good blue grouse country. You may spot a few of these "fool hens" along the trail.

Use your compass from here. The trail is once again intermittent, but Hidden Lake is nearly due south on the bench, about .75 mile away. Avoid the temptation to lose elevation to the east toward the Provo.

Hidden Lake has a few good campsites, mostly on its southeast side. There are steep slopes and broken terrain on the west.

Since firewood is becoming scarce around the lake, a backpacker stove is recommended for cooking. If you must build a fire, build it so that ashes blow away later, leaving no sign of your presence.

There are a few deep holes in the lake, offering a good opportunity for a midday dip. This deep water also enables trout to survive the winter. Some large cutthroat and brook trout lurk in the depths and occasionally dimple the surface in the shallows. They're not easy to catch, but when you do hook into one, it will give you a fine fight—not to mention a mouth-watering meal. — *Dave Hall*

HIKE 27 *FOUR LAKES BASIN*

General description: A popular backpack to alpine lakes in the western Uinta Mountains.
General location: Fifty-five miles east of Salt Lake City.
Maps: Northeastern Utah Multipurpose Map, High Uintas Wilderness Map, and USGS Hayden Peak Quad.
Special attractions: Beautiful views of the western Uintas, including the upper Duchesne River and Rock Creek country.
Best season for hike: Summer through early fall.
For more information: Duchesne Ranger District, Ashley National Forest, Box 1, Duchesne, UT 84021; (801) 738-2482. Also, Kamas Ranger District, Wasatch-Cache National Forest, Box 68, Kamas, UT 84036; (801) 783-4338.

The hike: Although not as remote and quiet as some other Uinta Mountain hikes, this trip is considered a basic west-side approach to the interior High Uinta Wilderness. You get there quickly, too—just off the Utah Highway 150 trailhead two miles north of Mirror Lake. Once on the trail, you're soon in roadless country.

This route is also the most popular access to the Highline Trail which courses across the great backbone of the east-west Uinta Mountains. At first, you will see many hikers, some out for a stroll to Scudder Lake. Then, there are the more serious hiker/anglers who find solitude and fast fishing off the main trail at Wilder, Wyman and Packard lakes—about 3.5 miles in. Most of the traffic, however, is to the many lakes in Naturalist Basin, located to the north in the shadow of Mount Agassiz (12,428 feet) and Spread Eagle Peak (12,540 feet). When you reach the invitingly cold water of Pigeon Milk Spring farther east, Rocky Sea Pass and access to the upper Rock Creek drainage are to the north, but you will head south past grayling-filled Carolyn Lake to Four Lakes Basin.

The trailhead is easy to find. Take State Highway 150 (the Mirror Lake Highway) east from Kamas into the Uintas. About 2.5 miles past Mirror Lake and just after passing from Duchesne into Summit County, the Highline Trail parking lot turn is to the right. Expect to find the large parking lot filled, especially at the height of the hiking season.

From the trailhead just east of Hayden Pass (10,347 feet), the trail descends two miles to a point just east of Scudder Lake, a popular destination for day hikers. A mile beyond, a trail heads right (south) to Wilder, Wyman and

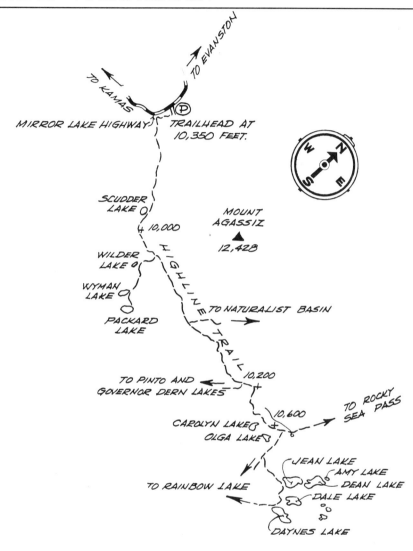

TO EVANSTON

TO KAMAS

MIRROR LAKE HIGHWAY

TRAILHEAD AT
10,350 FEET.

SCUDDER
LAKE

10,000

WILDER
LAKE

WYMAN
LAKE

PACKARD
LAKE

MOUNT
AGASSIZ

12,428

HIGHLINE TRAIL

TO NATURALIST BASIN

TO PINTO AND
GOVERNOR DERN LAKES

10,200

CAROLYN LAKE
OLGA LAKE

10,600

TO ROCKY
SEA PASS

JEAN LAKE
AMY LAKE
DEAN LAKE
DALE LAKE

TO RAINBOW LAKE

DAYNES LAKE

ONE MILE

Packard lakes. Continue straight (east) here, mostly contouring on the gently undulating trail below Mount Agassiz.

The steep trail to Naturalist Basin heads left (north) as you pass around the rocky spur south of Agassiz. The basin and its lakes make a nice side excursion, but be prepared to see many other hikers.

In 1.5 miles, the trail heading south to Pinto and Governor Dern lakes and Grandaddy Basin exits to the right (south). The Highline Trail continues eastward, beginning to climb after this junction. The trail ascends about 600 feet in just over a mile—the only real climb you have into Four Lakes Basin.

About .25 mile before the rocky ridge to the east, the trail south to Four Lakes Basin exits to the right. However, you should hike an additional few hundred yards east toward Rocky Sea Pass to Pigeon Milk Spring. The water is cold and delicious here, and many hikers go a bit out of their way to fill their water bottles. Pigeon Milk was named for the sometimes slightly discolored glacial "milk" flowing here. However, the water quality is not affected.

Heading south and then east for about a mile, skirt around the rock slides protecting Four Lakes Basin. Your first glimpse of the basin is of Jean and Dean lakes, visible from the 10,900-foot ridge to the west. Dale and Daynes lakes are a bit lower to the southeast.

Swampy meadows, almost the type you would expect to see dinosaurs rise from, grace the scenery throughout this region. These meadows are found so consistently that they seem almost deliberately spaced for variety. Some of the lakes, including those back toward the trailhead, are often eerily forged with cold morning mist.

Nearly all the lakes offer fine fly fishing due to open meadow shorelines and cooperative, while not large, trout. The west end of Dean Lake along the open cliffs is an especially productive site for catching hungry cutthroat trout.

You may want to make this hike before branching out into the remainder of the Uintas. It is the doorstep to almost all the trails on the west side of these unique and scenic mountains. — *Hartt Wixom*

THE HIGH UINTAS *AN OVERVIEW*

Northeastern Utah's High Uinta Mountains are a range of superlatives. They embrace the state's highest peak—13,528-foot Kings Peak—and the headwaters of major rivers which produce ninety percent of Utah's in-state water. They are important habitat for large big game herds as well as for more secretive and rarer species. Three-fourths of the state's bird species are found in the Uintas. There are hundreds of alpine lakes sprinkled through its many drainages.

The Uintas are an isolated and biologically intact alpine sanctuary. From the high, rugged peaks along its 11,000-foot, seventy-mile backbone to its willow-covered and richly forested river basins, the High Uintas are more like the Northern Rockies than are other Intermountain ranges.

The Uinta high country.

On the north slope, long meadows are flanked by virgin lodgepole pine and spruce forests, harboring rare species like the pine marten, goshawk, black bear and cougar. Research is being conducted to verify the possible presence of the Canada lynx, wolverine and timber wolf. Utah's largest elk and moose herds are found here, and mule deer are common. In addition, there are bald and golden eagles, osprey, owls, hawks, weasels, mink, and the ever-present beaver.

The Uinta's largest rivers begin on the south slope, high in the alpine basins, fifteen-twenty miles from trailheads. The lower Yellowstone River tumbles through steep, heavily-timbered country, and the Uinta River slices an 80-foot vertical gorge through the range's largest glacial canyon.

Historically, the Uintas are a lively chapter in the discovery of the American West. First recorded by Father Escalante in 1776 and by John Wesley Powell in 1869, the Uintas have been hunted by the Utes, trapped by the pioneer Rocky Mountain Fur Company (notably Jim Bridger, William Ashley and Andrew Henry), surveyed by great American explorers/geologists Hayden, Agassiz, Gilbert, Cleveland and others, tie-hacked for construction of the Union Pacific Railroad across Wyoming, and grazed by Uintah Basin and southern Wyoming sheepmen.

Today the Uintas offer spectacular opportunities for family camping, rugged hiking and climbing, riding, fishing and hunting by nearly 100,000 visitors yearly.

Established in 1931 as a Forest Service primitive area, 247,000 acres of the Uintas were granted protection from commercial timber harvesting, road construction, summer housing expansion, off-road vehicles, and mining (after 1983). In 1984, the High Uintas Wilderness was established, encompassing 456,704 acres of the Uinta Mountains.

While considerable North Slope acreage was added to the High Uintas Wilderness, some of the most pristine middle elevation North Slope lands were ignored along with the alpine eastern Bollies. Conservationists continue to push for wilderness designation of this primeval landscape. Critical issues surrounding oil and gas leasing on the East Fork of the Blacks Fork and Stillwater drainages, and timber harvesting proposals by the Ashley National Forest on the South Slope and eastern reaches of the range still threaten the integrity of the area.

Since the High Uintas Wilderness was designated, two herds of native bighorn sheep have been reintroduced in the area. For a decade, the Utah Wilderness Association (UWA) has pushed for reintroduction of this extirpated species back into its native habitat. When considerable acreage on the eastern North Slope was closed to sheep grazing, the dream became reality. This has renewed interest in seeking ways to further reduce the domestic sheep grazing in key areas in the Uintas to allow the existence of the native bighorn.

And finally, in 1991, a High Uintas Wilderness Limits of Acceptable Change (LAC) Task Force was created to properly manage the wilderness to assure the wild values do not get trampled by growing numbers of wilderness users, horse packing, sheep grazing and a host of other management concerns. — *Margaret Pettis and Dick Carter*

For more information on the Uintas, contact the Utah Wilderness Association, 455 E. 400 South, Salt Lake City, UT 84111 or call (801) 359-1337.

HIKE 28 *STILLWATER DRAINAGE*

General description: Several short two-day hikes or a longer five-day trip.
General location: Sixty miles east of Salt Lake City in the Uinta Mountains.
Maps: Northeastern Utah Multipurpose Map, USGS Hayden Peak and Christmas Meadows Quads, and High Uintas Wilderness Map.
Special attractions: Cirques and massive peaks at the upper basins; good fishing.
Best season for hike: Late spring through fall (late snows may restrict upper basin travel).
For more information: Evanston Ranger District, Wasatch-Cache National Forest, Box 1880, Evanston, WY 82931; (307) 789-3194 or (801) 642-6662 (June - October).

The hike: The Stillwater drainage of the Bear River offers three destinations: West Basin, with Kermsuh Lake; Middle Basin, with McPheters and Ryder lakes; and Amethyst Basin, containing Amethyst and Ostler lakes. Each has incredibly beautiful alpine scenery of high rock walls, pockets of spruce, scattered ponds, and wet meadows. Good fishing exists throughout the three basins, and water is abundant.

You could easily spend a week in this beautiful drainage—visiting each of the three basins. For a weekend outing, choose one of the three.

From Kamas on the west end of the Uinta Mountains, take State Highway 150 (the Mirror Lake Highway) over Bald Mountain Pass, past Mirror Lake and the Highline trailhead (which serves the western end of the High Uintas Wilderness) toward Evanston, Wyoming. About fifteen miles north of Mirror Lake and just after crossing the Bear River, turn right on the dirt road to Christmas Meadows Campground. Follow this road 4.5 miles to the end where you will find the trailhead. (From Evanston this road is about thirty-three miles south on Highway 150).

The trail to the three basins begins at 8,800 feet at the south end of the Christmas Meadows Campground. If you choose to follow Stillwater Fork for the first 1.5 miles, rather than the trail, trout fishing is good in its deep, clear pools. Staying on the east flank of the drainage, the trail passes beaver ponds, springs, and aspen and talus slopes.

After 2.5 miles, the Amethyst Basin trail heads to the left (east). It climbs a steep, rocky slope for 1,000 feet before leveling out on the north shoulder of Ostler Fork, north of Salamander Lake. Hidden in the lodgepole pine across Ostler Fork, the route to this little lake is a real test of orienteering.

Hiking south through several meadows, spruce parklands, and finally a spectacular broad meadow from which the first unobstructed view of magnificent LaMotte and Ostler peaks can be enjoyed, the trail to Amethyst Basin splits at the base of the large meadow. From here, it heads .5 mile southwest to Ostler Lake, or a mile beyond, to Amethyst Lake, nestled in the farthest crook of the basin.

This large, picturesque lake sits at the base of centuries of talus from the Ostler-LaMotte ridge. Wind-scoured spruce dot its rocky shore and fingerling meadows. If you camp here, Ostler, Toomset, and two small unnamed lakes are within an hour to the northwest.

If you choose to stay on the main Stillwater Fork trail, continue two miles past the Amethyst Basin Trail and find the trail on the right (west) to West Basin and Kermsuh Lake. Crossing Stillwater Fork and immediately climbing a series of switchbacks and several steep pitches, the trail sits high above the West Basin creek, making water along this stretch unreachable. Older editions of the topographic map are in error at this point. The trail does not cross the creek flowing out of West Basin but remains high on the north side of the deep creek bed and enters a sizable open meadow, where it then crosses the creek and offers a stunning view of the walled head basins.

The trail winds about two miles through a diverse forest to kidney-shaped Kermsuh Lake. The large meadow mentioned above and several others along

Amethyst Meadows and Ostler Peak, Uinta Mountains.—John George photo

the northern shore of Kermsuh offer excellent campsites and abundant water. There are hidden ledges and potholes with much evidence of wildlife, exquisite ancient pockets of spruce, and a lovely lake which drains into Kermsuh from the south. Rugged, vertical Hayden Peak (12,473 feet) looms above this small lake to the southwest, and Kletting Peak (12,055 feet) on the northwest provides a wall of stone above the tiny basin.

To reach Ryder, McPheters and the other lakes of the Middle Basin, follow the main Stillwater trail past the West Basin turnoff. After two miles, the trail crosses the Stillwater Fork and climbs 500 feet up a steep shoulder on the south

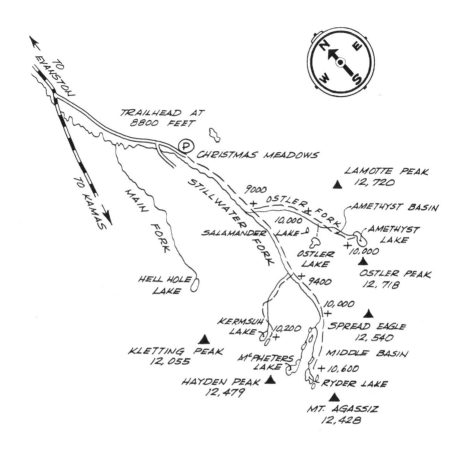

TRAILHEAD AT
8800 FEET

CHRISTMAS MEADOWS

TO EVANSTON

TO KAMAS

MAIN FORK

STILLWATER FORK

9000

OSTLER FORK

SALAMANDER FORK

10,000

HELL HOLE LAKE

OSTLER LAKE

9400

LAMOTTE PEAK
12,720

AMETHYST BASIN

AMETHYST LAKE
10,000

OSTLER PEAK
12,718

10,000

KERMSUH LAKE

10,200

SPREAD EAGLE
12,540

KLETTING PEAK
12,055

McPHETERS LAKE

MIDDLE BASIN

10,600

HAYDEN PEAK
12,479

RYDER LAKE

MT. AGASSIZ
12,428

ONE MILE

bank of Middle Basin Creek. The trail leads westerly another mile to Ryder Lake, which, with McPheters and over two dozen tiny lakes and potholes, offers an incredible view of the bowl, nestled close to 11,000 feet. Surrounding the bowl are Mount Agassiz (12,428 feet) on the south, Hayden Peak on the northwest, and across the Stillwater Fork, magnificent Spread Eagle Peak (12,540 feet) and Ostler Peak (12,718 feet). These splendid peaks form a narrow ring encircling the lakes of the Middle Basin.

Just over the Agassiz-Spread Eagle ridge sit the lakes of Naturalist Basin; beyond the Spread Eagle-Ostler ridge lies Rock Creek. This is high alpine country at its finest—spectacular scenery and outstanding opportunities for exploration.—*Margaret Pettis*

HIKE 29 *WEST FORK BLACKS CREEK*

General description: An overnighter to the headwaters of the Blacks Fork River.

General location: Thirty-four miles northeast of Kamas on the North Slope of the Uinta Mountains.

Maps: Northeastern Utah Multipurpose Map and USGS Lyman Lake, Elizabeth Mountain, Explorer Peak and Red Knob Quads, and High Uintas Wilderness Map.

Special attractions: Lush alpine meadows; good fishing; excellent opportunities to view wildlife.

Best season for hike: Late spring through fall (be prepared for snow in early spring).

For more information: Evanston Ranger District, Wasatch-Cache National Forest, Box 1880, Evanston, WY 82931; (307) 789-3194 or (801) 642-6662   (June - Oct.).

The hike: The West Fork Blacks Fork River is a superb journey into the northwestern portion of the High Uintas Wilderness. This drainage is replete with moose, mule deer, elk, small mammals, and raptors. The hike offers level traversing of lush meadowlands, a survey of rich wildlife habitat, and an ascent into the alpine lakes and ponds for which the Uintas are famous. This is the High Uintas at its finest.

Take State Highway 150 (the Mirror Lake Highway) east from Kamas. Pass the Bear River Ranger Station on the right after about forty-five miles. Two miles beyond, turn right on the North Slope Road. This graded, well-traveled route across the Uinta North Slope provides access to many of the drainages.

Climb about thirteen miles to Elizabeth Pass (10,235 feet). This pass divides the Bear River drainage of the Great Basin from the Blacks Fork drainage of the Green River.

Cross Elizabeth Pass and descend past Fish Lake another five miles to the Lyman Lake junction. Turn right here (south, then west) back along the river.

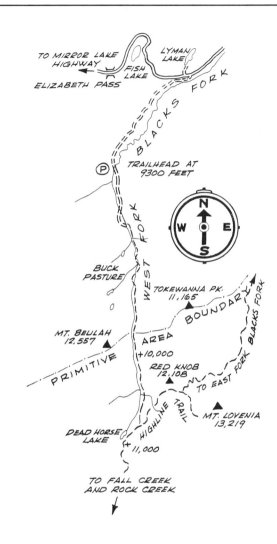

ONE MILE

Follow this rocky road (eroded in spots but usually passable for two-wheel vehicles) about 4.5 miles to a major river crossing. Park here to begin the hike.

The hike is gentle, about 11 miles (and about 1,600 feet elevation gain) from the trailhead to Dead Horse Lake—a popular destination below the Uinta backbone. Plan to spend two to four days in the upper drainage in order to explore it fully. The upper meadows, alpine potholes on the high western ledge and below Dead Horse Lake, and the lake itself offer the finest Uintas scenery. Golden eagles are a common sight.

The hike begins at about 9,300 feet and climbs slowly along a jeep trail for 4.5 miles to Buck Pasture at 9,700 feet. The trail begins on the left (east) side of the river and then makes several crossings before passing the wilderness boundary and reaching the long meadow.

Note that the topo map shows several pothole lakes to the west in this area.

There is some ORV damage in some of the lower meadows, resulting from off-road use during wet spring conditions. This activity poses a real management problem for the Forest Service.

The trail follows the river course through a series of rich meadows and offers superb scenery of the high ridgelines paralleling the river. The ridgeline exceeds 11,000 feet to the east and west, with 12,557-foot Mount Beulah to the southwest of Buck Pasture and 12,108-foot Red Knob and 13,165-foot Tokewanna peaks to the southeast. Forests of lodgepole pine, subalpine fir, and eventually spruce, harbor deer, elk, pine marten, goshawks, and other interesting wildlife species. Moose are common and can be seen leaving the willows for the forest each evening.

Once in Buck Pasture, Dead Horse Lake is another 6.5 miles. Here, the rugged Uinta spine looms to the south more than 1,000 feet above.

From Dead Horse Pass at just under 11,600 feet, high above its namesake lake, you can drop to the south into the head of Fall Creek (by way of Ledge and Phinney lakes) and Rock Creek (by way of Lightning, Helen, Triangle, and Reconnaissance lakes), thus exploring the very head of that south slope drainage. To see this spectacular alpine country, allow several more days.

Another side trip is the route along the Highline Trail, out of the east side of the head basin, over to the East Fork Blacks Fork. This spectacular route passes between Red Knob and 13,219-foot Mt. Lovenia. Allow an additional day for this trip.

Water abounds in the West Fork drainage, and campsites are readily available. Use of a stove not only makes your presence less noticeable to future hikers, but increases your chances of seeing moose near the river.
— *Margaret Pettis*

HIKE 30 *KINGS PEAK*

General description: A forty-mile backpack to Utah's highest peak—13,528-foot Kings Peak.

General location: In the eastern half of the High Uintas Wilderness.

Maps: Northeastern Utah Multipurpose Map; USGS Gilbert Peak NE, Bridger Lake, Mount Powell, and Kings Peak Quads; and High Uintas Wilderness Map.

Special attractions: Emerald-green Henrys Fork Basin and a dozen lakes below 13,000-foot peaks.

Best season for hike: Mid-July to mid-August.

For more information: Mountain View Ranger District, Wasatch-Cache National Forest, Lone Tree Road, Highway 44, Mountain View, WY 82939; (307) 782-6555.

The hike: Many hikers just *have* to scale the highest peak around. In Utah, that means 13,528-foot Kings Peak—a rocky spire in the eastern half of the High Uintas Wilderness. What makes Kings Peak such a fine backpack is not only the exciting scramble to the peak, but also the beautiful alpine terrain and trout fishing along the way.

Choose the time of your hike carefully. Snow remains in the high country into summer, and the mountains are crowded on the July 4 and July 24 weekends.

There are several approaches to Kings Peak—either from the north or south. However, many hikers consider the route along the Henrys Fork the best because the distance from the trailhead to Kings Peak, about sixteen miles, is shorter than two alternate routes along the Yellowstone and Uinta rivers on the Uintas' south slope.

From the Henrys Fork Campground trailhead at about 9,400 feet, the trail climbs more than 4,100 feet to the top.

To reach the trailhead, take I-80 east of Evanston, Wyoming and turn right on the I-80 business route to Fort Bridger. Drive about three miles and turn right on Wyoming State Highway 414 toward Mountain View. In Mountain View, pick up Wyoming State Highway 410 toward Robertson. About seven miles south of Mountain View, Highway 410 makes a ninety-degree turn to the west. Continue south here into the Uintas.

Continue toward the Bridger Lake Guard Station. After about thirteen miles, turn left towards the Henrys Fork. In another eleven miles, just before the road crosses the river, turn right toward the Henrys Fork Campground—about .75 mile along the west side of the river.

At the trailhead, a wooden Forest Service map points out the many lakes and peaks located in the area you'll be hiking.

The trail follows the Henrys Fork for 5.5 miles, gaining about 700 feet of elevation before reaching a junction in a meadow northeast of Bear and Sawmill lakes. The quickest route to Kings Peak is to continue straight (south) rather than turning right (west) here. The quicker route heads past Dollar Lake to the east of Henrys Fork. Most hikers, however, choose to take a few extra days on the "scenic" route—past Bear and Sawmill lakes and on to Henrys Fork Lake, about four miles from the junction. This loop rejoins the trail past Dollar Lake about a mile southeast of Henrys Fork Lake and before reaching

Gunsight Pass.

Camping and fishing along this route are excellent. Above Henrys (follow the creek), you will find good fishing at Lake Blanchard, the small lake to Blanchard's east; and at Castle and Cliff lakes. These lakes offer fast fly-fishing for cutthroat trout, especially at inlets and outlets; and the stream just below Blanchard has plenty of pan-sizers. No one will go hungry.

Most of the lakes here are above timberline, leaving the area near Henrys Fork Lake—at about 10,800 feet—with the best campsites. The Forest Service suggests that you choose your campsite carefully. Areas around lakes and streams get heavy use.

Water is abundant in the basin, but treatment is recommended to avoid the possibility of contracting giardiasis (see page 16).

Watch for wildlife in this region and also notice Kings Peak to the south. On a clear day, it appears as an inverted V-notch just above the large rock slide.

Where the trails join at 11,000 feet, east of Henrys Fork and south of Dollar Lake, it is about two miles to 11,888-foot Gunsight Pass. The entrance to the pass is, indeed, shaped like a rifle's sight, and you can't miss it. The trail does not continue through the low notch as easily as it may appear from below. There are thickets and boulders here, and the trail switches back up the west slope to the pass.

Brook and cutthroat trout from a Uinta lake.—Dave Hall photo

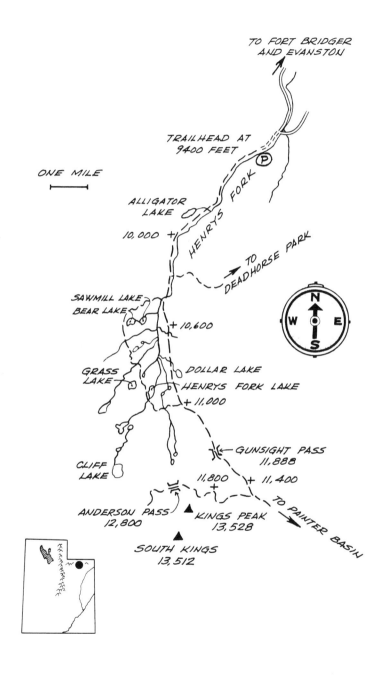

TO FORT BRIDGER
AND EVANSTON

TRAILHEAD AT
9400 FEET

ONE MILE

ALLIGATOR
LAKE

10,000

HENRYS FORK

TO
DEADHORSE PARK

SAWMILL LAKE
BEAR LAKE

+ 10,600

N
W   E
S

GRASS
LAKE

DOLLAR LAKE
HENRYS FORK LAKE

+ 11,000

GUNSIGHT PASS
11,888

CLIFF
LAKE

11,800
+

+ 11,400

ANDERSON PASS
12,800

▲ KINGS PEAK
13,528

TO PAINTER BASIN

▲
SOUTH KINGS
13,512

If you're lucky enough to find clear weather at the pass, you'll have beautiful views down into Painter Basin on the Uintas' south slope, as well as back down the Henrys Fork.

Since the trail to Kings Peak drops toward Painter Basin and then climbs westward to Anderson Pass, there is a strong temptation to avoid loss of altitude by crossing onto the steep, rubble-strewn rock slides to the south. This is a mistake, as anyone who has tried it quickly discovered. The rocks are loose and dangerous, and you eventually have to drop down to the meadow below.

So, follow the trail down from Gunsight Pass. The trail descends about 400 feet quickly, then heads through the flats 1.5 miles to the Anderson Pass cutoff. Turn right (west) here and begin climbing toward the pass.

The trail climbs 1,400 feet over the next three miles, including an 800-foot climb in just over a mile. The east slope of Kings Peak looms to the west, then south, as you climb, and the views down along the upper Uinta River are spectacular.

At Anderson Pass, you get your first glimpses of the spacious Yellowstone drainage to the southwest. In fact, the trail contours to the west and then drops down into the basin. But you head southwest here, up the ridge to the top of Kings Peak.

It's only about .5 mile to the top, but you've got more than 900 vertical feet, and there is no trail. You have to hop the boulders. Near the top, watch your step carefully, because there is considerable exposure to the west. You know you're at the top—even in a blowing mist—by the plaque commemorating mountain explorer and scientist Clarence King. A mailbox offers a diary in which you can record your experience.

With any luck in the weather, you can enjoy a remarkable view from the top of Kings. The Yellowstone drainage to the southwest looks like moonscape photos—tundra without timber. In the Uinta River basin to the east, you see forested slopes near Lake Atwood bordered by rocky ridges. Several small lakes lie below you in cliff country. And one of the most beautiful views is right down the Henrys Fork basin to the north, where you can admire many lakes and emerald meadows. — *Hartt Wixom*

HIKE 31 *BURNT FORK*

General description: An overnight backpack to high country lakes in the Uinta Mountains.

General location: Northeast end of the Uinta Mountains, about twenty miles south of Burntfork, Wyoming.

Maps: Trails Illustrated Ashley National Forest Map; USGS Whiterock Lakes, Chepeta Lake, and Fox Lake Quads; and High Uintas Wilderness Map.

Special attractions: Timberline and alpine scenery typical of the Uintas; excellent fishing; good opportunities to view wildlife.

Best season for hike: Mid-summer through early fall.

For more information: Mountain View Ranger District, Wasatch-Cache National Forest, Lone Tree Road, Highway 44, Mountain View, WY 82939; (307) 782-6555.

The hike: Hiking opportunities in the eastern Uinta Mountains are often ignored, probably because most hikers pour into the western end of the range near Salt Lake City. However, hikers who haven't spent time in this part of the state are missing something. The area has spectacular terrain, abundant wildlife, fast fishing, and relatively light hiking pressure. You will scarcely feel the weight of a heavy pack due to the spectacular lake and forest scenery.

Beginning at the Spirit Lake Campground at 10,200 feet, this hike traverses the upper reaches of the middle and north forks of Sheep Creek and then enters the Burnt Fork drainage. The Burnt Fork lakes sit around 10,700 feet; so elevation gains from the trailhead amount to less than 600 feet.

The eleven -mile hike to Island Lake passes other beautiful alpine lakes, offering excellent campsites. And the upper Burnt Fork region along the way boasts several small but fish-filled lakes requiring off-trail exploring.

To reach the trailhead, take I-80 east of Evanston, Wyoming and turn right on the I-80 Business Route to Fort Bridger. Drive about three miles and turn right on Wyoming State Highway 414. Follow Highway 414 through Mountain View, Lonetree and Burntfork. Turn right about 2.5 miles past Burntfork and drive on the graded road about 13.5 miles. Turn right toward Spirit Lake and continue another six miles on rough road to the trailhead. You find the trailhead .25 mile past the Spirit Lake Campground on the left. There is no parking at the trailhead but the Spirit Lake Lodge will watch your car for a fee.

From the trailhead, the trail climbs slowly for 1.5 miles before reaching Tamarack Lake. Jessen, Lily Pad, Lost, and Hidden lakes are all nearby—draining to the Middle Fork.

At the west end of Tamarack Lake, the trail climbs about 400 feet into a huge meadow as you cross into the Burnt Fork drainage. Just .5 mile into the meadow (just before you enter the High Uinta Wilderness), a trail down the North Fork Sheep Creek to Hickerson Park leaves to the right (north). In McCoy Park, two miles farther, you meet the trail from Beaver Mountain Reservoir to Fish Lake and beyond. Turn left (south) here.

A mile to the south, in the shadow of the ridge, you find cigar-shaped Fish Lake, well named. There is good camping and fishing near the outlet stream which runs a mile northwest into Burnt Fork. About halfway down the south side of Fish Lake, you may find fast fly fishing for brook trout a pound or more in weight. These trout can be selective, but if you hit a "good day," there'll be plenty of food for your party for dinner. These brookies are especially beautiful during the fall, when their spawning colors are richest.

The unmaintained and unmarked trail from Fish Lake heads west about 1.5 miles, descending about 500 feet to Burnt Fork. The Burnt Fork Trail turns right (north) here, and the trail from Fish Lake continues another 4.5 miles to Island Lake, crossing several meadows which can be difficult to follow in wet grass.

However, you may want to make a cross-county trip to Island Lake because

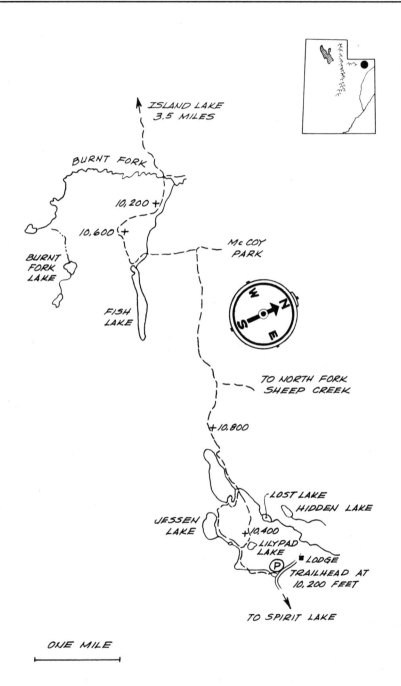

of the scenic lakes and good fishing up against the ridge. However, if you do choose this option, don't expect easy travel and have someone along with map-reading experience.

From Fish Lake, contour west and south around the ridge about a mile to Burnt Fork Lake. In this lake and in the one half a mile above it are some of the West's most brilliantly-colored cutthroat trout. Trout also can be found in the stream and the many waterfall holes below Burnt Fork Lake. These trout hit almost any fly.

You may see big game such as moose and deer about anywhere in the region. Elk can be found here at times, although they are constantly on the move. You may also see golden eagles, several hawk species, and other birds of prey. This country abounds in food-rich meadows and lake borders—hence the abundant wildlife. And you're likely to see far fewer people than in other areas of the Uintas. But beware: mosquitoes, deer flies and horse flies can be a problem at times.

Water and good campsites are abundant in the area. However, you may want to check the water quality conditions with the Mountain View Ranger District. Presently, the Forest Service recommends boiling all water. Giardiasis (see page 16) has become widespread in Utah and, unfortunately, even some "pristine" streams have been affected. You can do your part by observing backcountry sanitation rules.

West of Burnt Fork Lake there is no trail, but you can easily make your way over meadows to several lakes, including one under a talus slide with nothing but the designation "130" on Division of Wildlife Resources maps. This lake, Round Lake (.5 mile farther to the west), and Island Lake offer excellent brook and cutthroat possibilities.

There are several small lakes west of Island in the shadow of North Burro Peak (12,686 feet) and South Burro Peak (12,726 feet).

Before heading back to the trailhead, you may also choose to take a trail at the west end of Island Lake south across the divide (11,280 feet), past Divide Lake, and down among the many lakes at the head of the Uinta River drainage.
— *Hartt Wixom*

HIKE 32 *ROCK CREEK*

General description: A three- to five-day backpack in the Rock Creek drainage on the south slope of the Uinta Mountains.

General location: Forty miles northwest of Duchesne in the High Uintas Wilderness.

Maps: Northeastern Utah Multipurpose Map, High Uintas Wilderness Map, and USGS Tworoose Pass and Explorer Peak Quads.

Special attractions: A vast wilderness drainage with many lakes, abundant wildflowers and wildlife, good fishing, solitude, and views; easy access to other areas of the High Uintas.

Best season for hike: Summer and early fall.

For more information: Duchesne Ranger District, Ashley National Forest, Box 1, Duchesne, UT 84021; (801) 738-2482.

The hike: Rock Creek drains a large region on the south slope of the Uinta Mountains. Its deep, forested canyon offers leisurely woodland walking and good trout fishing, while its upper basins provide alpine camping and climbing, with easy access to other parts of the range via major passes and trails. Many routes can be planned from the trailhead near the Upper Stillwater Reservoir, and loop trips of three-seven days are particularly convenient.

The extended backpack follows Rock Creek for about 10 miles, then angles northeast another four miles to Phinney and Anderson lakes—in the heart of the High Uintas Wilderness. The trail out parallels a long ridge extending south from Explorer Peak, drops into beautiful Squaw Basin, then follows the East Fork to Rock Creek and the trailhead.

The fourteen-mile trip up Rock and Fall creeks gains 2,400 feet through some of the Uintas' finest country. However, if you don't have the time for this loop, make a shorter trip by hiking up the East Fork on the way in and spending a day or two in Squaw Basin.

To reach the trailhead at the Upper Stillwater Reservoir, take State Highway 87 (the Moon Lake Highway) north from Duchesne about sixteen miles and turn left on Forest Route 134. Drive about three miles into Mountain Home, turning left again.

Follow the signs to Rock Creek. You cross Mountain Sheep Pass about nine miles west of Mountain Home, then enter the spectacular Rock Creek canyon, which rapidly deepens as you head upstream (northwest) into the mountains. The road is paved to the trailhead, which is about twenty-five miles from Mountain Home at a parking lot with restrooms and a horse ramp.

Because of the reservoir, older editions of the Twooroose Pass topographic map do not correctly show the first few miles of the trail. Rather than climbing along the east side of Rock Creek, the trail now heads north along the left (west) side of the reservoir. You can see the spectacular peaks at the head of Rock Creek from here; but the trail soon enters the forest, and the peaks disappear from view until you get to the meadows below Phinney Lake.

About 2.5 miles from the trailhead, Cabin Creek enters from the right (east), and the West Fork comes in from the left (west) a few hundred yards farther on. The West Fork Trail heads to Grandaddy Basin, Naturalist Basin, and Four Lakes Basin. The Rock Creek Trail drops down to cross the creek here, continuing north along the east side as shown on the Twooroose topo map.

About 1.25 miles past the West Fork junction, you cross the East Fork and meet the trail to Squaw Basin. If you choose to make the shorter trip and climb to Squaw Basin from here, you'll gain 1,300 feet in 1.5 miles, with no water and very little shade. In 1974 a great forest fire burned 2,900 acres in Rock Creek Canyon, and this steep, exposed trail still provides evidence of its effects. However, the area is healing well and is now thick with ten-foot tall lodgepole

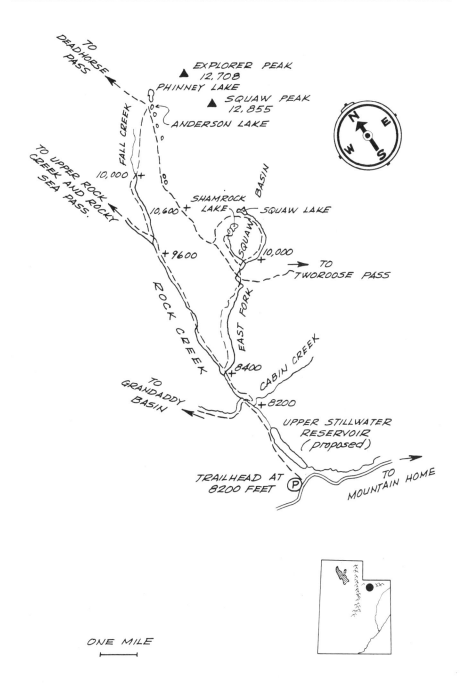

TO DEAD HORSE PASS

EXPLORER PEAK
12,708
PHINNEY LAKE

SQUAW PEAK
12,855

ANDERSON LAKE

FALL CREEK

TO UPPER ROCK CREEK AND ROCKY SEA PASS.

10,000

SQUAW BASIN

SHAMROCK LAKE

SQUAW LAKE

10,600

SQUAW

9600

10,000

TO TWOROOSE PASS

ROCK CREEK

EAST FORK

CABIN CREEK

8400

TO GRANDADDY BASIN

8200

UPPER STILLWATER RESERVOIR
(proposed)

TRAILHEAD AT
8200 FEET

TO MOUNTAIN HOME

ONE MILE

pine. In early summer, you're also likely to find lupine, fireweed, and other pioneer flowers in bloom.

Still, the main trail offers a more pleasant, if lengthier approach to Squaw Basin, particularly in the heat of summer. Continue up Rock Creek Canyon, through the burned-over forest where, curiously, occasional clusters of pines appear to have escaped the fire. There are numerous camping spots along the rocky floor of the canyon, if you are inclined to spend the first night in the forest.

Water from the creek should be boiled to prevent giardiasis, but if you come in June or July, you should find good water trickling in small rivulets from melting snow far above. However, avoid any spots where beaver have been active, as they are known to carry *Giardia* (see page 16).

About 1.75 miles above the East Fork junction, the trail bends away from the creek and continues along the base of the steep mountain slope that bounds the Rock Creek flood plain. You can hear the stream along here although it is hidden in the trees.

Four-and-one-half miles above the junction, the trail crosses Fall Creek and forks, the left branch ascending Rock Creek to Lightning Lake and the Highline Trail, while the right fork climbs along Fall Creek four miles to Phinney Lake.

Take the right (more northerly) fork. Immediately past the junction, the Fall Creek Trail begins to climb steeply, but after about a mile it levels off in a meadow at about 9,600 feet. In another mile, the trail crosses the creek, and .75 mile beyond, you come to one of the world's greatest swimming holes.

As Fall Creek crosses the 10,000-foot contour, it cuts into a thin formation of red and blue shale. This very soft rock weathers easily; in fact, you could crumble it in your hand. The creek slices through it in a narrow chute, with several plunge pools deep enough for diving and swimming.

Just above the falls, two streams meet to form the main creek, and the shale between them is so neatly beveled it looks engineered, like the prow of a ship or a concrete bridge pylon. Below these cliffs you can find perfect skipping rocks, flat flakes of shale whose edges have been scoured and rounded by the stream. This is a wonderful spot for lunch, photography, or a late swim after a hot day of hiking.

Beyond the falls, the trail ascends a ridge dividing the two tributaries, and the forest opens into broad alpine meadows in about .75 mile. Suddenly, you are surrounded by the huge peaks of the High Uintas, gigantic crumbling piles of buff, gray, and rust-colored metamorphic rocks. Explorer Peak (12,706 feet) and Squaw Peak (12,855) rise on your right, with Yard Peak (12,706) and Dead Horse Pass on your left. Phinney Lake lies .5 mile farther on, just past the junction with the Ledge Trail. There are eight lakes in this basin, with plenty of camping and fishing. Phinney and Continent lakes are particularly good for brook trout and cutthroats.

At the junction with the Ledge Trail, .25 mile before Phinney Lake, you can turn left (northwest) to meet the Highline Trail in a mile and ascend Dead Horse Pass at 11,600 feet to the West Fork Blacks Fork on the

Uintas' North Slope.

To complete the trip to Squaw Basin, turn right (south) on the Ledge Trail and contour along the base of the huge, talus slopes below Explorer Peak. Here, the red quartzite which forms the bulk of the High Uintas has been quarried by frost into great rectangular blocks, forming labyrinths for small mammals. The rocks look bare from a distance, but up close they reveal gaudy mats of lichen—slate gray, black, clay blue, and bright chartreuse.

The trail winds to the south, among numerous small unnamed lakes fed by snow melt. This is forested country broken by numerous meadows and immense fields of wildflowers. Often you will see trails of flowers snaking up toward the talus along hidden drainages. At times, the trail climbs up rocky spurs, offering splendid views of the gray peaks across the headwaters of Rock Creek. If you take the Ledge Trail late in the day, you are likely to see moose and deer, not to mention a spectacular sunset over the far peaks.

Four miles from the junction at Phinney Lake, the trail turns left (east) and climbs 450 vertical feet in .75 mile. From the ridge, you can see the densely forested floor of Squaw Basin. Squaw Peak (12,855 feet) and Cleveland Peak (12,584 feet) border the basin to the north, with Cleveland Pass and the immense, mesa-like Brown Duck Mountain to the east.

Descend a steep .5 mile to the junction with the East Fork Trail on the floor of the basin. Take Trail #066 1.5 miles to Big Meadow. You can also bushwhack 0.5 mile east to Shamrock Lake.

At Big Meadow, the trail to Tworoose Pass and Brown Duck Basin enters from the east. Fly fishermen enjoy casting for small, feisty brook and cutthroat trout in the East Fork's deep meanders.

The trail climbs out of the meadow gradually, entering the burned-over area and reaching 9,744 feet in 1.5 miles before descending toward Rock Creek.

It's a steep, hot, dusty descent, but you'll be glad you're not climbing it. Take a moment on top to view the immense area of the burn and to appreciate the vigor with which new plants are returning to colonize the ashy soil.

In 1.25 miles, you arrive at Rock Creek, and from there, it's about four gentle miles back to the trailhead. — *John Tallmadge*

HIKE 33 *YELLOWSTONE DRAINAGE*

General description: An extended trip to the many lakes and high basins of the Upper Yellowstone drainage.

General location: Thirty-five miles north of Duchesne in the High Uinta Wilderness.

Maps: Northeastern Utah Multipurpose Map; USGS Burnt Mill Spring, Lake Fork Mountain, Garfield Basin, and Mount Powell Quads; and High Uintas Wilderness Map.

Special attractions: One of the Uinta's longest, most primitive and scenic basins.

Best season for hike: Mid-July to late August.

For more information: Roosevelt Ranger District, Ashley National Forest, Box 333-6, Roosevelt, UT 84066; (801) 722-5018.

The hike: The more than 20-mile length of the Yellowstone drainage has just about everything typical of the entire 100-mile-long Uinta Mountains. From the 10,200-foot trailhead near the end of the Hells Canyon Road (or alternate but longer trail at road's end on Yellowstone Creek), you climb through vast forests of Engelmann spruce and lodgepole pine, then into the treeless tundra in the Garfield Basin. No drainage in the Uinta Mountains has more trout-filled lakes and streams than this one, and in a variety of meadow, cliff edge, and arctic-like waters.

To reach the trailhead, drive about twenty miles north on State Highway 87 from U.S. 40 in Duchesne through Mountain Home until you enter the Uinta and Ouray Indian Reservation. Continue another four miles, then turn right at the Yellowstone Creek turnoff. Cross the Lake Fork River, turn left within .25 mile and head north again. About .25 mile after entering the Ashley National Forest, the Hells Canyon Road forks to the left. This is a rough road and may not be suitable for some two-wheel-drive vehicles, especially in inclement weather. Forest Service side roads exist along the way, so follow your topo maps carefully for about ten miles to the trailhead at Center Park. Look for the trailhead sign to Swasey Hole. (If you encounter trouble on this road, an alternate trailhead is at the end of the maintained road to the east, paralleling the Yellowstone River.)

On the way in from the Center Park trailhead above Hells Canyon, you will find plenty of water.

After 4.5 miles, the trail skirts to the east of Swasey Hole. Several peaks over 11,300 feet protect this pothole-filled area on the west and north. You might see deer and elk anywhere from Swasey Hole on. Moose are less numerous in the southern Uintas than they are to the north, but seeing one of these beautiful animals is possible, as the big mammals have moved over the summit in some regions. Bird life of all kinds is especially abundant before you get beyond timberline. You may see blue grouse, hawks, eagles, and Clark's nutcrackers. Various sparrows and finches are also common.

Four miles beyond Swasey Hole, you reach Bluebell and Spider lakes. Five Point and Superior lakes are another one and two miles, respectively.

Around the sprawling Spider Lake, meadows stretch everywhere, with excellent fly fishing in clear, cold feeder ponds. Wherever trees form a windbreak, there are luxuriant campsites. And you are never without scenic mountain backdrops, including the highest point in the Uintas, 13,528-foot Kings Peak (and slightly lower South Kings) in the northeast corner of Garfield Basin.

Around all these 11,000-foot lakes, you find lush meadows and plenty of cooking wood. But a backpacker stove with ample fuel is recommended,

Swasey Lake in the Yellowstone drainage, Uinta Mountains.
—John George photo

especially in the treeless terrain north of Superior Lake.

There is a fair amount of hiking traffic in midsummer near the trail-side lakes like Five Point. But there are, nevertheless, some oversized fish in all of these lakes. Five Point, Superior and Little Superior have produced trout to six pounds. However, the best part is you never know when a little pond nearby may yield a surprise catch.

One thing you are certain to see is the result of glacial action, including cirques at most of the stream canyon heads, smoothed-over ridges, and gouged-out lake basins.

The ridge tops, incidentally, provide some scenic routes if you prefer to travel that way rather than on the forested trails. But be sure to pick out a prominent landmark (like the Wilson Peak ridge, north of Five Point Lake on the north side of Garfield Basin) to keep track of your location. You can find most of the lakes in this basin, too, by merely following streams into the high meadows below the baldies.

Two lakes in the uppermost Yellowstone drainage, North Star and Tungsten—about three miles beyond Superior Lake—have a reputation for growing giant cutthroat trout. In this alpine country, it means two- to four-pounders, with an occasional shorter, but possibly heavier, brook trout.

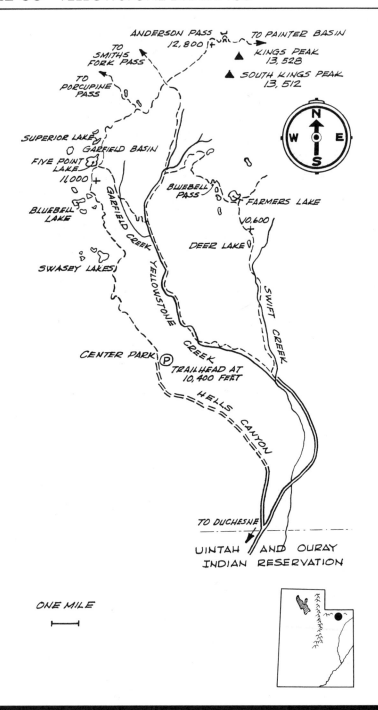

ANDERSON PASS
12,800

TO PAINTER BASIN

TO SMITHS FORK PASS

▲ KINGS PEAK
13,528

▲ SOUTH KINGS PEAK
13,512

TO PORCUPINE PASS

N
W E
S

SUPERIOR LAKE

○ GARFIELD BASIN

FIVE POINT LAKE
16,000

BLUEBELL PASS

FARMERS LAKE

10,600

BLUEBELL LAKE

DEER LAKE

SWASEY LAKES

GARFIELD CREEK

YELLOWSTONE CREEK

SWIFT CREEK

CENTER PARK ℗

TRAILHEAD AT 10,400 FEET

HELLS CANYON

TO DUCHESNE

UINTAH AND OURAY INDIAN RESERVATION

ONE MILE

Moose are imposing figures along many Uinta trails.—John George photo

And no matter how far you look in this basin, you won't see air or water pollution, telephone lines, pavement, nor likely anything artificial. It is also as harsh as it is wildly scenic; a snowstorm in July is not uncommon at this elevation of around 11,500 feet.

In such country, particularly considering the long distances back to civilization, make certain you have sufficient supplies of food, matches, warm clothing, and are wearing top-notch hiking boots. If you don't like one lake or meadow, you can find another nearby. Truly, the Yellowstone has everything, including 12,700-foot Anderson Pass into Painter Basin just north of Kings Peak.

It is not likely you will find other campers or hikers north of Superior Lake in this upper terrain. The Yellowstone backcountry offers plenty of room for exploration, and you can't always be certain what you'll find next.
—*Hartt Wixon*

HIKE 34 *EASTERN UINTA HIGHLINE TRAIL*

General description: A twenty-one-mile hike along the summit of the Uinta Mountains to the eastern edge of the High Uintas Wilderness.

General location: Twenty-five miles northwest of Vernal.

Maps: Trails Illustrated Flaming Gorge/East Uintas Map; Ashley National Forest Map; and USGS Leidy Peak, Whiterocks Lake, and Chepeta Lake Quads.

Special attractions: High altitude views of the eastern Uinta Mountain Range; good fishing and camping.

Best season for hike: July 15 through September 15.

For more information: Vernal Ranger District, Ashley National Forest, 353 N. Vernal Ave., Vernal, UT 84078; (801) 789-1181.

The hike: Those who enjoy leaving the bustle of everyday life behind, and who wish to avoid the crowds in some backcountry areas, will enjoy the remoteness of this trail. The Highline Trail is so named because it follows the high summits of the entire Uinta Mountain Range. This section of trail follows the boundary between the Vernal and Flaming Gorge ranger districts to the eastern edge of the High Uintas Wilderness. The trail continues through the wilderness area to its end at the Mirror Lake Highway.

There are two main vehicle access routes to the Highline Trail. To begin the hike on the eastern end, drive twenty miles north from Vernal on U.S. Highway 191 to the Red Cloud Loop Junction (FR #018). Turn left on this paved road for about 2.5 miles, then another left onto a gravel road for about eleven miles to the Leidy Peak/Hacking Lake Junction (FR #043). Follow this road about ten miles to its end to find the trailhead.

The other route is accessed by traveling west from Vernal on State Highway 121 through Lapoint, then north to Whiterocks. Pick up Forest Road #117 by Elkhorn Guard Station, just north of Whiterocks, and drive about twelve miles to the junction of Forest Road #110 to Chepeta Lake, about nine miles further.

Although the Highline Trail is marked and maintained by the Forest Service, some portions of trail above timberline do not have an established trail path, but are clearly marked with rock cairns. Areas below timberline are marked with blazes on trees. Count on two days to hike from the beginning of the trail on the eastern end to Chepeta Lake, and another day to hike to the wilderness boundary and back.

The trail is used by both backpackers and horsepackers. All drinking water obtained along the trail should be boiled before use to insure its purity.

Hikers should be in good physical condition for this trip. You are hiking primarily above timberline where the terrain is mostly open and rocky. The altitude climbs from 10,625 feet at Hacking Lake to an elevation of 11,500 feet near Leidy Peak, descending to 10,560 feet at Chepeta Lake and climbing again to a high point of 12,200 feet at the wilderness area boundary.

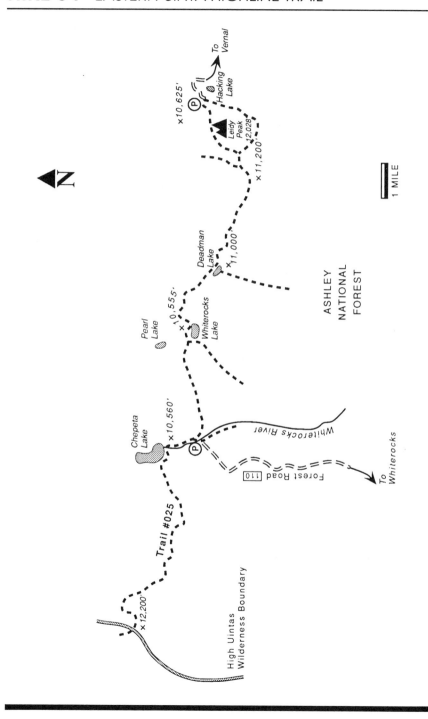

Numerous backcountry lakes with trout fishing opportunities dot the Eastern Uinta Highline Trail.—Chris Cauble photo

There are several trails that tie in with the Highline Trail. Numerous backcountry lakes with trout fishing opportunities dot these side trails as well as the main trail. Hiking, fishing and exploring possibilities are endless. —*Michael Bergfeld*

HIKE 35 *JONES HOLE CREEK*

General description: An easy day hike or overnighter in Dinosaur National Monument.

General location: Twenty-eight miles northeast of Vernal.

Maps: Trails Illustrated Dinosaur National Monument Map and USGS Jones Hole Quad.

Special attractions: A deep, scenic canyon with a permanent stream; trout fishing; prehistoric Indian rock art.

Best season for hike: Spring through fall.

For more information: Dinosaur National Monument, Quarry Visitor Center,

Box 127, Jensen, UT 84035; (801) 789-8807.

The hike: You won't see any dinosaur bones in Jones Hole, but you will see country typical of the rest of Dinosaur National Monument—deep, sheer-walled canyons etched into the high plateaus at the eastern end of the Uinta Mountains. Jones Hole Creek, rushing from limestone springs to join the Green River, has carved a gorge over .5 mile deep. An easy trail follows the creek for four miles, descending about 600 feet to its confluence with the Green River in Whirlpool Canyon.

The trailhead at Jones Hole Fish Hatchery is reached by paved road from Vernal or by graded and paved roads from the Dinosaur Quarry Visitor Center. From U.S. 40 (Main Street) in Vernal, take U.S. 191 north for five blocks, turn right on 500 North, and after about two miles, bear left past the county dump. The hatchery is thirty-five miles farther on a well-signed road.

The route from the Quarry is more difficult, but a free map and directions are available at the Visitor Center information desk. To reach the Quarry, drive thirteen miles southeast of Vernal on U.S. 40. Turn left in Jensen on State Highway 149 and continue another seven miles to Dinosaur National Monument and the Quarry Visitor Center.

When you get to the fish hatchery, park in the gravel area at the downstream (left) end of the tanks. The trail begins on the left bank and follows the creek closely for most of its length.

Surrounded by semi-arid sagebrush and pinyon-juniper uplands, Jones Hole is an oasis. The stream issues from several springs in the limestone canyon walls just above the hatchery and tumbles through a boulder-strewn channel lined with boxelder, watercress, horsetails, and, in early summer, an explosion of yellow monkey-flowers. Drawn by the water and the lush growth, wildlife concentrates in the canyon. You might see a mule deer ducking through the underbrush or hear a yellowbelly marmot whistling from its hideout on a talus slope. Canyon wrens and other songbirds also add their tunes to the constant background music of the creek.

About 1.5 miles down the trail, a plank bridge crosses the creek. Short side trails just beyond this bridge lead to a group of 1,000-year-old pictographs from the Fremont Culture and to a small waterfall on Ely Creek, a tributary stream entering from the right (west). If you visit the pictographs, please don't touch them—the iron-oxide paint used by the Fremonts has withstood centuries of weather, but the pressure of many fingers, as well as the acids and oils in your skin, can quickly wear away this prehistoric art.

Buff-colored Weber sandstone dominates the upper part of Jones Hole and forms monolithic walls reminiscent of Zion Canyon. When you cross Ely Creek however, you also cross the Island Park Fault and step back about 200 million years in time. Older rocks have been uplifted into view on the downstream side of the fault, forming stepped walls as hard limestone and sandstone layers alternate with softer shale beds. A close look at trail-side boulders and ledges may reveal fossils of corals, crinoids, and brachiopods that lived in the ancient seas which left these strata.

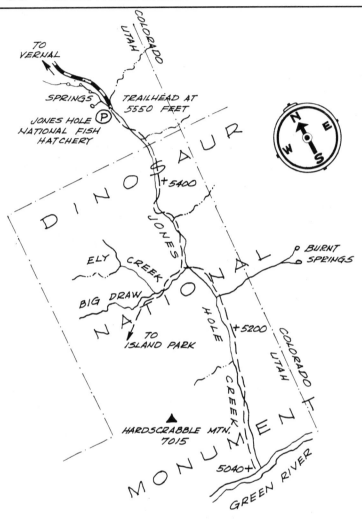

ONE MILE

About two miles beyond Ely Creek, the trail ends at the Jones Hole river camp, a popular stop for raft parties floating the Green River. Overnight use of the campsites is reserved for river groups only, but hikers may picnic.

If you plan an overnight hike in the Jones Hole area, you must obtain a free backcountry permit and low impact camping handout at the Quarry Visitor Center. There is an established campsite at the mouth of Ely Creek; camping elsewhere along Jones Hole Creek is not permitted. Water from both Jones Hole and Ely creeks must be boiled or chemically purified before drinking. Bring your backpacker stove; campfires are prohibited, since wood is not plentiful and fires, however small, create ash and debris which mar the site and are difficult to erase.

There is some good fishing in Jones Hole Creek. Remember, a Utah license is required even though you are in a National Monument.

Pets are not allowed on the trail. And, as in other backcountry areas, carry out all that you carry in. Be particularly careful with garbage—scavenging skunks have become a problem at the river camp. As in any national park or monument, do not disturb any natural, historic or archaeological resource. Let those who come after you enjoy all that you have enjoyed. — *Linda West*

HIKE 36 *DINOSAUR NATIONAL MONUMENT*

General description: Hiking routes in deep canyons and along benches for hikers with route-finding and desert hiking skills.
General location: Twelve miles east of Vernal.
Maps: Trails Illustrated Dinosaur National Monument Map (see quad index on this map for your area of interest).
Special attractions: Solitude, overwhelming silence, steep canyons and dramatic vistas.
Best season for hike: April, May and September, October.
For more information: Dinosaur National Monument, Quarry Visitor Center, Box 127, Jensen, UT 84035; (801) 789-8807. For information on the Colorado portion of the park, contact Dinosaur National Monument, Box 210, Dinosaur, CO 81610; (303) 374-2216.

Dinosaur National Monument is a land that has changed little over the past hundred years. Few visitors travel away from the river corridors or "developed" areas. While the park has few trails developed and marked in the traditional sense, there is unequalled opportunity to travel undeveloped "routes" through narrow slickrock canyons or along benches with vast, sweeping views.

You can stop at any ranger station to discuss the hiking potential of a particular area. Rangers can provide you with recommendations and alternatives, and will point out the fragile nature of this cold desert.

A free backcountry permit is required for overnight travel. Camping is closed in some areas such as the Cub Creek area and Jones Hole Creek (escept the established site at Ely Creek) and restricted during the summer in the inner river canyons.

Spring and fall are optimum times to hike, although hikers familiar with summer desert hiking can select a variety of routes to challenge their skills. Access is limited by snow during the winter.

You should carry at least one gallon of water per person per day in the summer. Water is scarce in some areas of the park. All available water should be treated before drinking.

Dinosaur National Monument can provide the backcountry traveler with an isolated wilderness experience in rugged terrain amidst dramatic scenery, almost total silence (actually measured at less than twelve decibels of ambient sound!) and surprises only the desert can provide. — *Herm Hoops*

Because the above describes a general area instead of a specific hike, there is no map. — *Editor*

HIKE 37 *TULE VALLEY*

General description: A little-known day hike or overnighter in a greasewood desert and wetlands ecosystem.

General location: West of the House Range, fifty miles west of Delta.

Maps: Northcentral Utah Multipurpose Map and USGS Chalk Knolls, Coyote Knolls and Swasey Peak NW Quads.

Special attractions: Solitude in an undeveloped valley; wetlands and warm water springs.

Best season for hike: Fall, winter and spring.

For more inforrnation: House Range Resource Area, Bureau of Land Management, Box 778, Fillmore, UT 84631; (801) 743-6811.

The hike: Most wilderness hikes in Utah are in the high country or the canyons. Tule Valley is a change of pace. Located in the Great Basin, west of the House Range, Tule is an undeveloped desert valley sprinkled with wetlands. The hike is on an old road with no elevation change. From Delta, take U.S. 6/50 west about twelve miles through Hinckley to the Antelope Spring dirt road. Turn

Notch Peak from Tule Valley.—Peter Hovingh photo

123

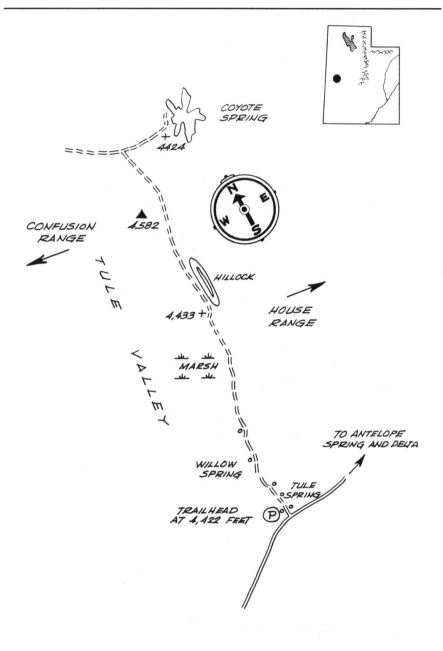

COYOTE SPRING

+ 4424

CONFUSION RANGE

4,582

T U L E

HILLOCK

4,433 +

HOUSE RANGE

MARSH

V A L L E Y

TO ANTELOPE SPRING AND DELTA

WILLOW SPRING

TULE SPRING

TRAILHEAD AT 4,422 FEET

P

ONE MILE

right and continue about twenty-four miles. Turn right again toward Antelope Spring. Proceed another twenty-two miles through the House Range via Dome Canyon Pass to Tule Spring. A dirt road turns to the right and continues a few hundred yards to a corral at Tule Spring.

At Tule Spring (4,422 feet) where the hike begins, a rough road heads north 6.5 miles to Coyote Spring. Interestingly, although you gain and lose some elevation along the way, Coyote Spring is at 4,424 feet—a net gain of two feet over more than six miles.

The water at Tule Spring and Coyote Spring, as well as other springs nearby, is of questionable quality. The Bureau of Land Management recommends that you bring your own water.

There is a sizable wetland 2.5 miles north of the trailhead on the left (west). Another .5 mile beyond, a rise of a few hundred feet offers a break in the scenery. If you plan an overnighter, this is an interesting camping area. From the top of the hillock, you can look south and see your car at the trailhead.

Views from Tule Valley include the steep side of the House Range to the east, the Deep Creek Mountains to the northwest, and the low-lying Confusion Range to the west. Nevada's Mt. Moriah and Wheeler Peak are also on the western horizon. Twisters and storms are often seen kicking up salt in the adjacent salt flats. Hiking in stormy weather is an experience, watching clouds swirl around the peaks of the House Range and the Deep Creek Mountains.

Tule Valley was once an extension of Lake Bonneville. If you look carefully, you'll see ancient shorelines on the mountains around the valley.

Tule Valley has approximately twenty springs, most of which originate below the surface (1,500-3,000 feet), causing warm water temperatures. Cattle, sheep, and occasionally oil rigs use the water.

Of course, the water and marshes provide habitat for waterfowl, marsh hawks, blackbirds, rails, and marsh wrens, as well as for relic populations of the western spotted frog, a leech, and a giant water bug.

You may find obsidian chips around and between the springs, left by prehistoric Native Americans. Most certainly, the springs were stop-off points during travel and provided an important source of food.

After hiking north about six miles from Tule Spring, you intersect an east-west road. Turn right (east) and continue .5 mile to Coyote Spring. You may spot ducks and even a goose or two on the open water here. Most waterfowl in the general vicinity are found thirty miles to the north at the Fish Springs National Wildlife Refuge, but Coyote Spring attracts birds as well.

From Coyote Spring, you can backtrack to your car or take an overland route southwest to the trailhead. — *Peter Hovingh*

HIKE 38 SWASEY PEAK

General description: A day hike or overnighter in the Great Basin.

General location: Forty miles west of Delta in the House Range.

Maps: Northcentral Utah Multipurpose Map and USGS Swasey Peak and Marjum Pass Quads.

Special attractions: Spectacular views of the Great Basin in Utah and Nevada; small population of bristlecone pine.

Best season for hike: Late spring through fall.

For more information: House Range Resource Area, Bureau of Land Management, Box 778, Fillmore, UT 84631; (801) 743-6811.

The hike: At 9,678 feet, Swasey Peak is the highest point in the House Range. From the top, after an off-trail, 1,700-foot climb, you'll have a panoramic view northwest to the Deep Creeks, northeast to Whirlwind Valley and Mt. Nebo, southeast to the Tushar Mountains and 12,173-foot Delano Peak, south to the Sevier Dry Lake, and west across Tule Valley to the Confusion Range. In addition, Wheeler and Pilot peaks and Mt. Moriah are visible in Nevada.

To reach the trailhead for this 4.5-mile hike, take U.S. 6/50 west from Delta and through Hinckley for about twelve miles before turning right on the Antelope Spring Road. After another twenty-four miles, turn right toward Antelope Spring. Travel an additional nine miles into the House Range. As the road swings west and then south toward Dome Canyon Pass, the Sinbad Spring Road exits to the right. Fill your water bottles at Antelope Spring—just off the road. Incidentally, there are extensive trilobite beds here. You may want to stop briefly to hunt for some of these fossils.

Beyond the junction, continue 3.2 miles to a large open area. Park here. You begin by bushwhacking up the slope on the right (northeast) side of the road. There is no water on the mountain, so plan on toting a supply with you.

The first section of the hike may not appear difficult when you consult the appropriate topo maps. You climb about 600 feet in less than a mile and overlook a steep dropoff to the west. But the thick mountain mahogany can be a nuisance until you reach the area.

A small population of bristlecone pine exists along the ridge. Continue northeast .5 mile to the first of two lower summits. The top is another .5 mile along the ridge.

To return to your car, hike down the ridge to the northwest. After .75 mile, swing to the west and then south, staying above the steep terrain to the west. You meet the Sinbad Spring Road in a flat, southwest of Swasey Peak. Follow the road to the left (southeast) about a mile to your car.—*Peter Hovingh*

9,059 ▲

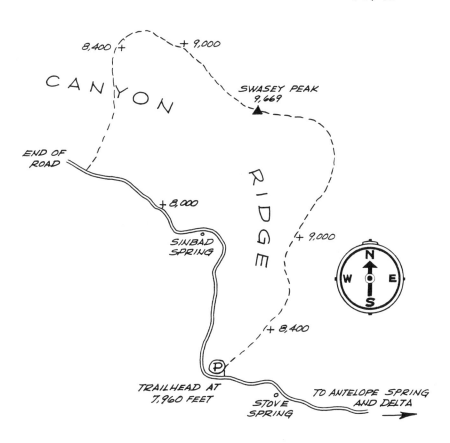

8,400 +   + 9,000

C A N Y O N

SWASEY PEAK
9,669
▲

END OF
ROAD

R I D G E

+ 8,000

SINBAD
SPRING

+ 9,000

+ 8,400

TRAILHEAD AT
7,960 FEET

STOVE
SPRING

TO ANTELOPE SPRING
AND DELTA
→

ONE MILE

HIKE 39 *NOTCH PEAK*

General description: A day hike to the top of 9,655-foot Notch Peak in the House Range.

General location: Forty-four miles southwest of Delta.

Maps: Northcentral Utah Multipurpose Map, and USGS Notch Peak and Miller Cove Quads.

Special attractions: Solitude; bristlecone pines; spectacular views of the Great Basin in Utah and Nevada.

Best season for hike: Spring and fall.

For more information: Warm Springs Resource Area, Bureau of Land Management, Box 778, Fillmore, UT 84631; (801) 743-6811.

The hike: The nine-mile round trip to the top of Notch Peak (9,655 feet) — part of an 80,000-acre Bureau of Land Management (BLM) wllderness study area — offers an opportunity to get away from throngs of hikers in more popular backcountry areas.

The hike is not difficult, in spite of a 3,000-foot climb. Most of the trip is along a dry wash. Only the final .25 mile to the top is relatively steep.

No water exists along the route, so be certain to fill water bottles in Delta before driving to the trailhead. Flash flooding can be a problem in late summer and early fall.

After getting final provisions in Delta, drive west on U.S. 6/50 about thirty-eight miles. Turn right on a dirt road. This road is not signed, and you may miss it unless you watch carefully. After 4.7 miles, turn left; then continue another 1.3 miles and turn right onto the Miller Canyon Road. A sign marks the spot.

In 5.5 miles bear left into Miller Cove. About three miles farther along, stop at an old stone cabin on the right. A miner working active mines in the area uses this cabin. Please respect this property.

Hike along the road to the west about a mile and pass through a deeply-cut canyon. The walls on the left (south) side rise several hundred feet. The hiking is easy here — along the rough gravel road on relatively flat terrain.

After .75 mile, the canyon opens and the drainage splits. Hike to the left (southwest) of a large, rounded knob which you will see straight ahead. There is no conspicuous trail here, but the open wash makes the going easy.

Occasionally, the walls of the meandering wash narrow, and the hiking is similar to canyon hiking in southeastern Utah. Normally, however, dry slopes rise from the wash. Pinyon and juniper dot the sage-covered hillsides at the lower elevations. Fir and mountain mahogany become more common as you climb.

About 3.5 miles from the trailhead, the wash becomes steeper, and you climb over a few tricky ledges. A good lunch spot is just above a massive tree which has fallen across the canyon. Slightly above the trunk is a bristlecone pine — one of the first you'll see along the trail.

128

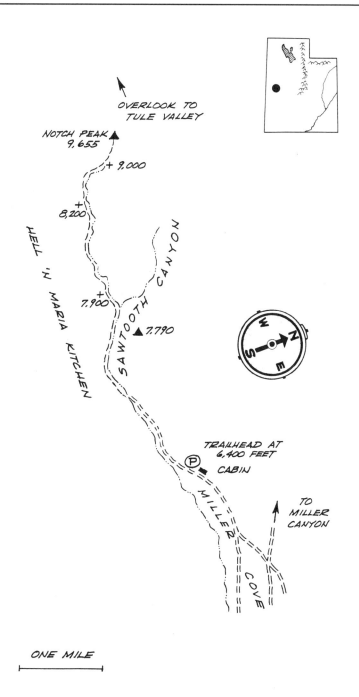

OVERLOOK TO
TULE VALLEY

NOTCH PEAK
9,655

+ 9,000

+
8,200

HELL 'N MARIA KITCHEN

SAWTOOTH CANYON

+
7,900

▲ 7,790

TRAILHEAD AT
6,400 FEET

CABIN

TO
MILLER
CANYON

MILLER COVE

ONE MILE

In another .5 mile, the wash becomes indistinct. Begin climbing on the sage and mountain mahogany hillsides, heading northwest .5 mile to an obvious saddle east of Notch Peak.

At the saddle, look at the spectacular chasm on the mountain's west side, dropping 4,500 feet to Tule Valley.

Notch Peak is a steep .25 mile to the west. The views from the top are rewarding. The Deep Creek Mountains are to the northwest, the Confusion Range to the west, the Wah Wahs to the south, and Sevier Lake and the mountains of the Fishlake National Forest to the east.

The Wasatch Mountain Club has left a small mailbox in a rock cairn at the top. Among those who have signed the log are a few hang glider pilots who packed their gear to the peak for an aerial descent to Tule Valley. The log indicated that they were scared, but there was pride and a $500 bet on the line.

On the trip down, you may want to take a brief side trip to a small bristlecone pine grove. It is on the southeast side of the knob east of Notch Peak. A .25 mile hike from the saddle and around the knob brings you there. — *Dave Hall*

HIKE 40 *WAH WAH MOUNTAINS*

General description: An interesting day hike into a Great Basin range.
General location: Thirty miles southwest of Milford.
Maps: Southwestern Utah Multipurpose Map, and USGS Lamerdorf Peak and Sewing Machine Pass Quads.
Special attractions: Remote cross-country hiking; few people; bristlecone pines.
Best season for hike: Late spring through fall.
For more information: Beaver River Resource Area, Bureau of Land Management, 444 South Main, Cedar City, UT 84720; (801) 586-2458.

The hike: This excursion into the Wah Wah Mountains makes an easy day hike. Most hikers eat lunch at one of the summits a few miles in and make the round-trip in four to five hours. Overnight hikes heading farther into the range are possible but not popular due to the scarcity of water.

Part of the attraction of the Wah Wahs, like other Great Basin ranges, is their remote nature and the stark contrast they present with the desert below. Just getting to the mountains is an interesting trip. You won't see many people on the way to the trailhead, and the chances of seeing someone along the trail are even slimmer.

Take State Highway 21 west from Milford. Drive about twenty-four miles, passing through the San Francisco Mountains, and turn left on a gravel road near mile post 54. Bear right in about 2.5 miles and continue southwest another thirteen miles to the backbone of the Wah Wahs. Park at the high point (about

Pronghorn antelope are more common now in many parts of the Great Basin.—
John George photo

8,100 feet). If you continue on to the west side of the Wah Wahs, you descend into Pine Grove where several small mines are being reactivated.

There is no formal trailhead by the road, and travel in the backcountry is mostly cross-country. A few game trails exist, but consider the ridgeline your guide. Springs just a few miles to the west in Pine Grove provide the only water.

Beginning at the high point in the road, climb northeast through the forest for .5 mile to a knoll. A fence here runs north-south. Follow it north another .5 mile to the next high point, at around 8,600 feet.

About .75 mile from the trailhead, look for signs of revegetation following a burn approximately fifty years ago. Mule deer and even antelope have been spotted here, as well as a long list of birds.

Continue the gentle ridge walk through conifers to an unnamed peak (9,393 feet) a mile to the northwest, passing over one high point (8,946 feet) along the way. Heading north for .25 mile, you leave the forest and enter more open country which falls off to the west. There are splendid views to the west of Pine Valley — more than 4,000 feet below — and the Great Basin.

Wah Peak (9,383 feet) is .25 mile to the north. Bristlecone pines (some are several thousand years old) can be found on the ridge to the east of Wah.

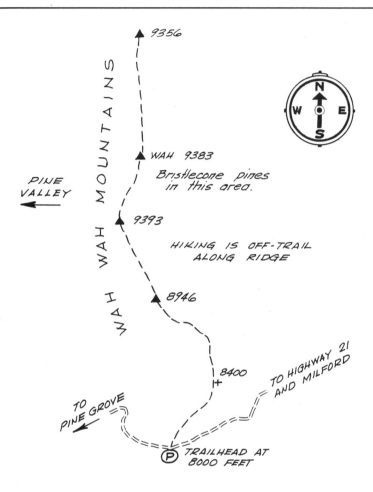

9356

WAH WAH MOUNTAINS

WAH 9383

Bristlecone pines
in this area.

PINE
VALLEY

9393

HIKING IS OFF-TRAIL
ALONG RIDGE

8946

8400

TO HIGHWAY 21
AND MILFORD

TO
PINE GROVE

P TRAILHEAD AT
8000 FEET

ONE MILE

You may want to hike another mile along the ridge before making the return to your car. An option is to take an extended trip to the north. However, little water is available, so most hikers do the short day hike.

When you make the Wah Wah trip, plan to spend some time exploring the Great Basin in your car at the end of the hike. Some fascinating abandoned towns and old mining operations are in the area, and you can almost be assured that each gravel road you take will offer new attractions.

The old mining town of Frisco — now a ghost town — is particularly interesting. It is in the San Francisco Mountains just off Highway 21 and makes an easy side trip after leaving the Wah Wahs. Following the discovery of silver here in the late 1800s, there were 4,000 residents. Today, although a few of the claims have been reactivated, there is little more than the many old buildings.
— *Bill Viavant*

HIKE 41 *DELANO PEAK*

General description: A day hike to 12,173-foot Delano Peak in the Tushar Mountains.

General location: Seventeen miles east of Beaver.

Maps: Trails Illustrated Fishlake National Forest Map, USGS Delano Peak and Shelly Baldy Peak Quads, and Fishlake National Forest Travel Map.

Special attractions: Spectacular views of southern Utah.

Best season for hike: Late spring through fall.

For more information: Beaver Ranger District, Fishlake National Forest, Box E, Beaver, UT 84713; (801) 438-2436.

The hike: The Tushar Mountains, east of Beaver, don't have the reputation of the spectacular Wasatch Range near Salt Lake. Therefore, few hikers realize there are higher peaks in the Tushars—most notably, 12,173-foot Delano Peak.

This part of the Fishlake National Forest offers high alpine scenery and excellent opportunites for day hikes or overnight backpacking trips. The Tushar Mountains were at one time home for one the state's largest deer herds.

Two approaches are recommended to Delano Peak and 11,985-foot Mount Holly — one near Elk Meadows Ski Resort, the other from the Big John Flat Road. Both trails can be done individually or as part of a longer loop hike, necessitating a car shuttle. Portions of both routes are along existing trails. Once you're above timberline, you will be traversing your own trail much of the way.

Take State Highway 153 about eighteen miles east of Beaver to Elk Meadows Ski and Summer Resort. Continue another mile on 153 past Elk Meadows to the beginning of Trail #175, which leaves the highway on your left (northeast). The trailhead is not signed, but you should be able to spot the blazes on trees.

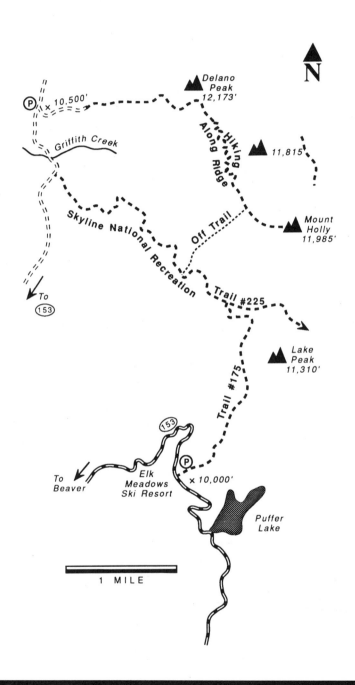

The route proceeds north about 2.3 miles, where it intersects with the Skyline National Recreation Trail #225. Turn left (northwest) for about .5 mile. At this point you will see a ridgeline running northeast to southwest. Mount Holly is about 1.5 miles along the ridge.

From there, you can hike back to the northwest about two miles to arrive at Delano Peak. The recommended route is along the ridge and is steep and rough in places. The saddle between the two peaks is just over 11,500 feet. Delano Peak cannot be seen during the ascent, but once on the relatively flat top, you get the most impressive views of the Tushar Mountains.

Much of the hike is above timberline and the views are spectacular. Puffer Lake is to the south, the Great Basin ranges are to the west, Belknap and Mt. Baldy peaks rise to the north and Piute Reservoir is visible to the east.

The second, more primitive approach to Delano Peak begins from the Big John Flat Road. Drive about sixteen miles east of Beaver on Highway 153 and turn left onto Forest Road 123. Follow this dirt and gravel road (not recommended for low clearance vehicles) 3.6 miles north to the flat. Keep to the right and proceed another 1.8 miles to the trailhead. (You should be about .5 mile past Griffith Creek.) The trail begins on an old jeep road that has been closed and posted with a "no motorized vehicle" sign.

From the trailhead at about 10,500 feet, the route proceeds east for about .5 mile, gaining about 800 feet. The jeep road narrows to a hiking trail, and Delano Peak and the route to the top are clear.

The trail continues east, climbing another mile to the saddle north of Delano Peak, just over 11,800 feet. The trail to the saddle may become obscure in places, but your destination is clearly visible. Once at the saddle, it's an easy .5 mile, 350-foot climb to Delano Peak. — *Tim Randle*

HIKE 42 *SKYLINE NATIONAL RECREATION TRAIL*

General description: A day hike along the "skyline" of the Tushar Mountain Range.

General location: Fifteen miles east of Beaver.

Maps: Trails Illlustrated Fishlake National Forest Map, USGS Delano Peak and Shelly Baldy Peak Quads, and Fishlake National Forest Travel Map.

Special attractions: Spectacular views of several mountain ranges and the east and west side of the Tushar Mountain Range.

Best season for hike: July through October.

For more information: Beaver Ranger District, Fishlake National Forest, Box E, Beaver, UT 84713; (801) 438-2436.

The hike: The Skyline Trail was placed on the National Recreation Trail System in 1979. Craggy peaks around the trail give the experience of being on

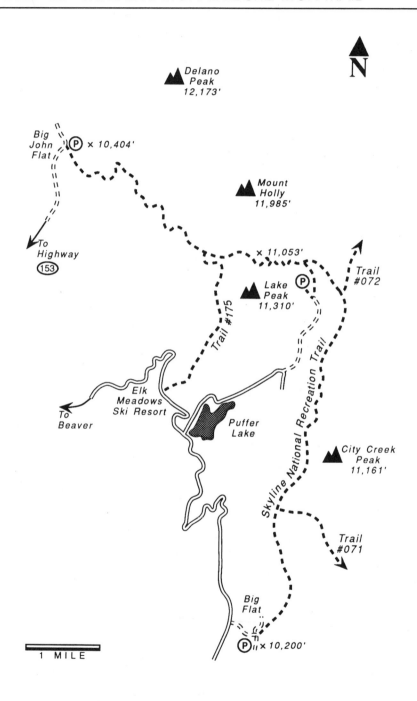

Delano
Peak
12,173'

N

Big
John
Flat ⓟ × 10,404'

Mount
Holly
11,985'

To
Highway
153

× 11,053'

Trail
#072

Trail #175

Lake
Peak ⓟ
11,310'

Skyline National Recreation Trail

Elk
Meadows
Ski Resort

To
Beaver

Puffer
Lake

City Creek
Peak
11,161'

Trail
#071

Big
Flat

1 MILE

ⓟ × 10,200'

top of the mountains near the "skyline".

Closed to all motorized travel, this route is an excellent one for those people who are looking for solitude on foot, mountain bike or horseback. As a whole, the Skyline Trail is rated easy to moderate in difficulty, with only a few short, strenuous sections. The length of the entire trail is between nine and ten miles. All trailheads and junctions along the way are well signed.

The trail crosses elevations ranging from 10,100 feet to 11,100 feet. Mountain peaks seen from the trail range from City Creek Peak (11,161 feet) to Delano Peak (12,173 feet). The Piute Reservoir area and the lowlands to the east of the trail in the Circleville Valley lie at 6,000 feet elevation.

There are three different trailheads on this trail, so you can plan a short half day hike or a point-to-point with a vehicle shuttle. Several trails interconnect with the Skyline for those who want to spend more than just one day.

A good beginning is at the Big Flat trailhead, about twenty-three miles east of Beaver. Take State Highway 153 about twenty miles past Elk meadows Ski and Summer Resort to Puffer Lake. The highway is paved up to Puffer Lake, then turns to gravel. Big Flat is another three miles. The trailhead is located about .25 miles south of the Big Flat Guard Station where the road leaves the timber and enters the Big Flat meadow. There is a sign with directions to the trailhead at this junction. The actual trailhead lies 200 yards east of Highway 153 where there is an unloading ramp for horses.

Skyline Trail #225 heads north past City Creek Peak and auxiliary trails North Fork of City Creek and Bear Hole. After the Bear Hole trail intersection, Skyline turns left (west) up a short, steep section to the Lake Stream trailhead (accessed by Forest Roads #129 and #642 northeast of Puffer Lake). Another steep section takes you past Lake Peak (11,310 feet). The Puffer Lake Trail #175 intersects Skyline from the south another .5 mile farther and is another good choice for a point-to-point trip.

After passing Mount Holly and Delano Peak on your right (north), the trail ends at the Big John Flat trailhead. To access Big John Flat, take State Highway 153 sixteen miles east of Beaver to Forest Road #123. Turn north and drive about five miles to the trailhead on the north end of Big John Flat. — *Fishlake National Forest, Beaver District*

HIKE 43 *FISH LAKE MOUNTAINS*

General description: An overnighter to the Fish Lake Hightop.
General location: Twenty-seven miles south of Salina and thirteen miles northwest of Loa in the Fishlake National Forest.
Maps: Trails Illustrated Fish Lake North and Central Capitol Reef Map, and USGS Fish Lake and Mt. Terrill Quads.
Special attractions: Hiking along a high, glaciated plateau; excellent views of southern Utah from the top.

Mule deer—not necessarily of this stature—are common along Utah's wilderness trails.—John George photo

Best season for hike: Late spring through fall.
For more information: Loa Ranger District, Fishlake National Forest, Box 128, Loa, UT 84747; (801) 836-2811.

The hike: The Fish Lake Hightop—a long, narrow and glaciated plateau—lies just west of Fish Lake, one of the state's largest natural lakes. It offers an excellent overnighter, climbing through aspen, spruce and fir to the plateau at over 11,200 feet.

The recommended twelve-mile route begins at Pelican Overlook, climbs to the Hightop, then traverses north, and descends Tasha Creek to Frying Pan Flat. A car shuttle is required. Of course, an in-and-out hike to the Hightop, returning to Pelican Point, is possible and, indeed, popular.

Take State Highway 25 north from Highway 24 about fourteen miles west of Loa. Drive another twelve miles—the last five with beautiful Fish Lake on your right—and turn left toward Pelican Overlook. The trailhead is about a mile farther at a loop at the end of the road.

To leave a car at the Tasha Creek Campground, drive about three miles beyond the Pelican Overlook turnoff.

Beginning at about 9,100 feet, the trail climbs steadily up Pelican Canyon for

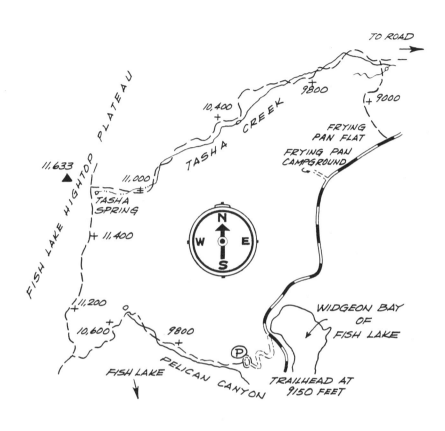

TO ROAD

FISH LAKE HIGHTOP PLATEAU

10,400

9800

9000

TASHA CREEK

FRYING PAN FLAT

FRYING PAN CAMPGROUND

11,633

11,000

TASHA SPRING

N

W   E

S

11,400

11,200

WIDGEON BAY OF FISH LAKE

10,600

9800

FISH LAKE

PELICAN CANYON

TRAILHEAD AT 9150 FEET

ONE MILE

about 2.5 miles before making a steep but short ascent to the plateau. Once on top, the trail makes a gradual, .75-mile climb to a jeep trail used mostly by hunters during the fall.

Turn right (north) and follow the route another 2.5 miles to the Tasha Spring turnoff. You climb gradually among scrubby subalpine fir to over 11,400 feet. There are plenty of campsites on top, but consider using a stove for your cooking rather than burning the little bit of wood you may find.

Views are exceptional from the Hightop. On a clear day you can see the Henry Mountains, the LaSals, the Abajos and the Four Corners area to the east, and the many Great Basin ranges to the west.

From early July to mid-September, you may see domestic sheep on the Hightop, but they are loosely herded and therefore not particularly noticeable.

At the Tasha Spring junction, turn right (east). The spring offers a welcomed water source after several miles along the dry, glaciated plateau.

The 5.5-mile, 2,100-foot descent to the Tasha Creek junction is gradual, and the trail parallels Tasha Creek most of the way.

At the junction, turn right (south), climb the low ridge, and then descend into Frying Pan Flat. The Tasha Creek Campground and Highway 25 are at the southeast end of the flat, 1.5 miles from the junction.

Under the Fishlake National Forest Plan, published in 1986, the entire Hightop, from Tasha Creek north to Daniels Pass, is being managed as a non-motorized recreation area, except during the winter months, when snowmobiles are allowed.—*Dave Hall*

HIKE 44 *BOULDER TOP TRAILS*

General description: Four short trails to Boulder Top, the 11,000 foot plateau that caps Boulder Mountain.
General location: Ten to eighteen miles south of Torrey.
Maps: Trails Illustrated Fish Lake North and Central Capitol Reef Map; and USGS Grover, Lower Bowns, and Deer Creek Lake Quads.
Special attractions: Scenic, sweeping views of southeast Utah; wildlife.
Best season for hike: June through October.
For more information: Teasdale Ranger District, Dixie National Forest, Box 99, Teasdale, UT 84773; (801) 425-3702.

The hike: Boulder Mountain is one of the less publicized wonders of southern Utah. It ascends to over 11,000 feet, starting at Capitol Reef National Park and climbing from pinyon and juniper slickrock canyons, through ponderosa pine forests, aspen hillsides and spruce fir forests, up 500-foot basalt cliffs onto the subalpine meadows and forests of Boulder Top.

The views from the Boulder Mountain Highway (State Highway 12) are spectacular enough to gain it recognition as one of the ten most scenic

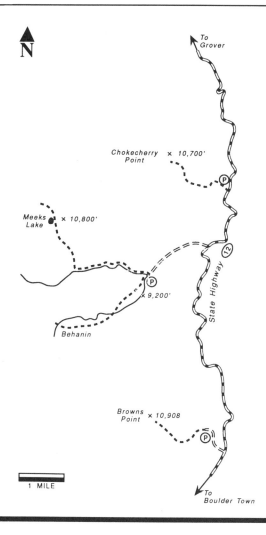

highways in America. The views from the rim of Boulder Top, 2,000 feet higher, are even more spectacular. The LaSal Mountains east of Moab, the Henry Mountains, San Rafael Swell, Navajo Mountain, Monument Valley and even the Kiabab Plateau (north rim of the Grand Canyon) in Arizona can all be seen in the breathtaking panorama.

Four major trails are easily accessed from State Highway 12 and travel short, but steep distances to Boulder Top. The trail to Bowns Point is the shortest at one mile.

Drive about sixteen miles south from Grover (or fourteen miles north of

141

Boulder Town) on State Highway 12. Turn right (west) onto Forest Road #554 for one mile to the Bowns Point trailhead on your left.

The one-mile climb is well worth the effort, as Bowns Point, at the southeast point of Boulder Top, offers the most panoramic views—from Powell Point near Bryce Canyon nearly 180 degrees to the San Rafael Swell. Columbines literally cover the newly reconstructed trail where it ascends the talus slopes below the Top. This new trail replaces a stock driveway a short distance to the north.

Six miles north, the Behanin Trail accesses Behanin Point, offering views of Pleasant Creek Valley. It passes through large aspen groves and an easy crossing of Pleasant Creek. Elk are often seen on this trail.

To reach Behanin Trail, turn west off of Boulder Mountain Highway onto Forest Road #247 at the Forest Service Station (ten miles south of Grover). Almost two miles on an unimproved 4x4 road brings you to the trailhead of Behanin and Meeks Lake trails. Behanin takes off to the left, roughly following Behanin Creek.

Meeks Lake Trail #118 is the right fork and the less steep of the two trails. Following Pleasant Creek, it passes through pure aspen stands where deer and elk are often seen. In early summer, you can enjoy the Pleasant and Meeks creek waterfalls.

The view from Boulder Top.

Two miles farther north on State Highway 12, Chokecherry Point Trail leaves the highway on Forest Road #178. It's a 4x4 trail most of the way, but must be hiked for the last section onto the top of the plateau. This old road was one of the original across points onto Boulder Top used by loggers to access insect-killed spruce trees. One marvels that logging trucks were ever able to travel this steep, rocky stretch.

All but Chokecherry Trail are designated as part of the Great Western Trail, a signed trail travelling the length of Utah. Once on Boulder Top, you have the opportunity to explore the fantastic array of wildflower-strewn meadows, spruce forests and literally hundreds of lakes and ponds contained in the 50,000-acre Top, not to mention the views from the edge of the Top.

Although open to all types of access, don't expect to meet a lot of traffic on these trails. This area is still a truly undiscovered treasure.—*Joe Colwell*

HIKE 45 *FISH CREEK TRAIL*

General description: A day hike to the 11,000-foot Boulder Top with opportunities for world class fishing.
General location: Eight miles south of Torrey.
Maps: Trails Illustrated Fish Lake North and Central Capitol Reef Map, and USGS Blind Lake Quad.
Special attractions: Subalpine country; excellent fishing in mountain lakes.
For more information: Teasdale Ranger District, Dixie National Forest, Box 99, Teasdale, UT 84773; (801) 425-3702.

The hike: The Fish Creek Trail takes you onto Boulder Mountain from its northern edge. The entire 50,000-acre Boulder Top plateau is dotted with a profusion of beautiful little mountain lakes with descriptive names like Bakeskillet, Horseshoe and Halfmoon. It also is home to mountain lakes with some of the best fishing in the world.

Drive south from Torrey on State Highway 12—better known as the Boulder Mountain Highway—for about six miles. Designated as one of the ten most scenic highways in America, it boasts spectacular views along its thirty-two-mile length. Turn right onto Forest Road #179. Follow this dirt road another five miles to a junction with Forest Road #287. The trailhead is on your left (south) just past this junction.

Fish Creek Trail #118 follows a notch in the rim cliffs to climb onto Boulder Top near Beef Meadows. You follow a very steep and rocky 4x4 road about two miles to a junction. The 4x4 road then turns to trail and continues south. After passing through a narrow canyon, the trail skirts an easily missed and unexpected treasure. A small waterfall, nearly dry by mid-summer, cascades down a rocky staircase, draped in moss and wildflowers. Leaving the water-

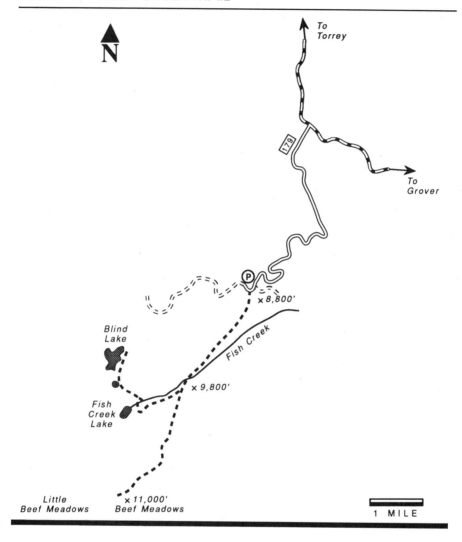

fall, you then finish your climb onto the rocky meadows near Beef and Little Beef meadows.

Take some time to enjoy the breathtaking views and wildflower-carpeted meadows on Boulder Top, then retrace your steps the 2.5 miles back to the trail junction. Turn left (west) and hike a little over a mile to Fish Creek Reservoir (one of the north slope lakes classed by the Utah Division of Wildlife Resources as world class fisheries).

This trail continues northwest past Pear and Blind lakes, also excellent lakes for fishing, and eventually intersects Forest Road #179. In fact, this part of the trail is one of the most popular areas in the national forest because of the fishing. So you're likely to encounter increased motorized traffic. If you crave solitude, it's best to backtrack to the trailhead.—*Joe Colwell*

HIKE 46 *SLICKROCK TRAIL*

General description: A relatively flat day hike at the base of Navajo sandstone cliffs paralleling, but just below Boulder Mountain Scenic Highway.
General location: Ten miles south of Torrey.
Maps: Trails Illustrated Fish Lake North and Central Capitol Reef Map, and USGS Lower Bowns and Grover Quads.
Special attractions: Geology, wildlife, solitude.
Best season for hike: Spring and fall.
For more information: Teasdale Ranger District, Dixie National Forest, Box 99, Teasdale, UT 84773; (801) 425-3702.

The hike: Boulder Mountain is a scenic "island in the desert" that borders the

The black boulders along the Slickrock Trail.

western boundary of Capitol Reef National Park. The fantastic slickrock wilderness of the park gradually ascends onto a flat pinyon and juniper-covered bench before climbing onto the summit of Boulder Top at over 11,000 feet elevation.

The Slickrock Trail follows the original wagon road that once connected Grover to Boulder Town. It follows the base of the Navajo sandstone escarpment—the top of which is the modern State Highway 12 (a designated National Forest Scenic Byway and rated by a national magazine as one of the ten most scenic drives in the United States).

There are numerous access points from Highway 12 to the Slickrock Trail

HIKE 46 *SLICKROCK TRAIL*

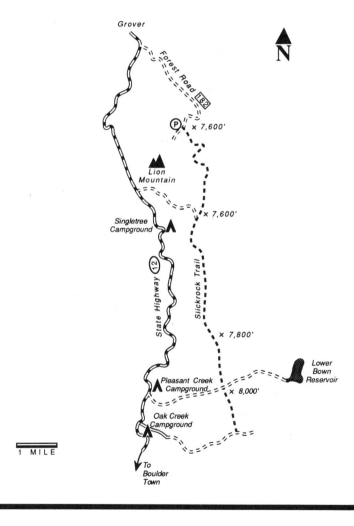

between Grover and Boulder Town. You could choose one of the Forest Service campgrounds along the highway—Oak Creek, Pleasant Creek or Singletree, or the undeveloped campground at Lower Bowns Reservoir, four miles east of the highway on Forest Road #181—to use as a base camp to explore the Slickrock Trail. Or you can hike the entire trail north to south with a vehicle shuttle.

Take State Highway 12 southeast of Grover about .5 mile to its junction with Forest Road #182. Drive two miles on FR #182 to another junction. Both junctions are signed to the Slickrock Trail. Turn right (southwest) at this junction. The road is rough and rocky; you may not be able to drive much farther. The trail takes off to the south a short distance down the road.

The trail maintains a general elevation of about 7,600 feet, but ascends and descends several drainages. It's well-marked with signs and cairns the entire 8.5-mile length. You hike across areas of slickrock Navajo sandstone, old growth ponderosa pine, and pinyon and juniper forests. Interesting geology along the trail includes black basalt boulders sitting in grand profusion on white sandstone.

Enjoyable side trips follow the numerous draws and side canyons crossed by the trail. Water is scarce, but summer thunderstorms may provide small pools in numerous water pockets along the sandstone portions of the trail. Pleasant Creek, Singletree Creek, and Oak Creek are perennial streams, but water should be treated before drinking.—*Joe Colwell*

HIKE 47 *FISH CREEK*

General description: An easy hike up a tributary of the Price River.
General location: Immediately west of Scofield Reservoir, twenty-six miles northwest of Price.
Maps: Northeastern Utah Multipurpose Map, and USGS Scofield Reservoir and C Canyon Quads.
Special attractions: Solitude and good fishing.
Best season for hike: May through September.
For more information: Price Ranger District, Manti-LaSal National Forest, 599 West Price River Drive, Price, UT 84501; (801) 637-2817.

The hike: The Fish Creek Trail is a National Recreation Trail and offers a relatively easy hike, gaining only 700 feet from the trailhead to C Canyon, about six miles in. There is lush river-bottom vegetation and some fine fishing.

Drive south from Provo and up Spanish Fork Canyon on U.S. 89/6. Five miles past Soldier Summit, turn right on State Highway 96 toward Scofield Reservoir. Continue sixteen miles to the town of Scofield. Go to the western-most north-south street in town and follow it north around the west side of the reservoir. After about four miles, an unimproved road branches off to the left

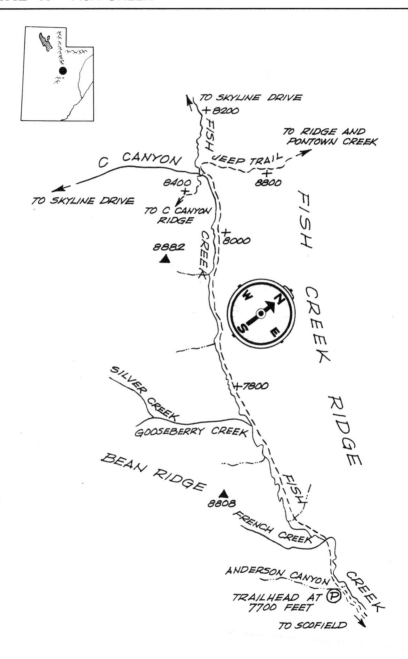

TO SKYLINE DRIVE
+ 8200

TO RIDGE AND
PONTOWN CREEK

C CANYON

FISH JEEP TRAIL

+ 8800

TO SKYLINE DRIVE

8400
+

TO C CANYON
RIDGE

FISH

+ 8000

8882
▲

CREEK

FISH

CREEK

RIDGE

+ 7800

SILVER CREEK

GOOSEBERRY CREEK

BEAN RIDGE

FISH

▲
8808

FRENCH CREEK

CREEK

ANDERSON CANYON

TRAILHEAD AT ⓟ
7700 FEET

TO SCOFIELD

ONE MILE

The beautiful Fish Creek drainage, Manti-LaSal National Forest.—Rick Van Wagenen photo

and heads up the south side of Fish Creek for 1.5 miles before ending at the trailhead. The access road to the campground is not maintained and becomes impassible after a heavy rainstorm.

The view from the trailhead is a good indication of the terrain you'll see traveling up the drainage. The broad, flat canyon bottom is filled with willows, and meandering Fish Creek is often obstructed with beaver dams.

The trail begins on the west side of the campground and winds up the south side of the canyon for .75 mile before reaching French Creek. This first segment of the trail is one of the best on the hike. The trail climbs from 7,700 feet through a cool and shady aspen and fir forest—a relief on a hot summer day.

As you hike, pay attention to the willow-choked stream below. Beaver and deer abound at dusk, and it's sometimes possible to spot a moose, a member of an introduced moose herd. Unfortunately, many of these magnificent animals have been lost to poachers. Also notice the many bird species in the dense willow stands.

At French Creek the trail crosses the stream and continues on the north side of the canyon. From here travel is in direct sun on a hot, dry sagebrush hillside. The trail does not continue up the cooler, forested slope, because genera- tions of fishermen have beaten a path on the north side of the canyon, closer to the creek.

About two miles up the canyon from French Creek, a tributary enters from the southwest. This is the Gooseberry Creek-Silver Creek drainage.

Continue up Fish Creek for 3.5 miles to C Canyon. At this point, a trail running north/south crosses the stream.

The Fish Creek drainage offers a variety of long-distance options if hikers shuttle a car. For instance, at the C Creek drainage you can continue on up C Canyon or explore the upper tributaries of Fish Creek. Skyline Drive is about five miles up either drainage. Alternatively, you can go north from C Creek on a trail 1.5 miles to Fish Creek Ridge and drop down another .75 mile into Pondtown/Bear Creek, traveling downstream about six miles to a dirt road at the mouth of Pondtown Canyon.

The Fish Creek drainage is a 25,560-acre semi-primitive, roadless area. The region has possible reserves of coal, oil and natural gas. There are threats to water quality resulting form ORV use in the upper C Canyon drainage. Proposed plans to transport water from Gooseberry Reservoir to the Manti area would reduce stream flow during the drier summer months.—*Linda and Rick Van Wagenen*

HIKE 48 *LEFT FORK HUNTINGTON CREEK*

General description: A gentle hike along a central Utah trout stream—recommended for day hikes, fishing, and overnight backpacking.

General location: Twenty miles southwest of Price on the Wasatch Plateau.

Maps: Northeastern Utah Multipurpose Map and USGS Candland Moun-tain Quad.

Special attractions: Free-flowing, clear water; wildlife; solitude; a pristine environment; and good trout fishing.

Best season for hike: June through September.

For more information: Price Ranger District, Manti-LaSal National Forest, 599 West Price River Drive, Price, UT 84501; (801) 637-2817.

The hike: The Left Fork Trail is designated a National Recreation Trail. It follows along the right (north) side of the river, gaining about 650 feet in 4.5 miles to a large, broad valley where Scad Valley Creek enters. There are several options from this area—some requiring a car shuttle via dirt roads in the upper drainage.

To reach the trailhead, drive twenty miles south of Price to Huntington on State Highway 10. Turn right on State Highway 31 at a sign indicating Huntington Canyon and Cleveland Reservoir. Continue northwest up Huntington Canyon about eighteen miles. A sign at the fork of the river identifies the campground and trailhead to the left (west). Drive up the Left Fork Road about .5 mile to the end of the campground, and the trailhead.

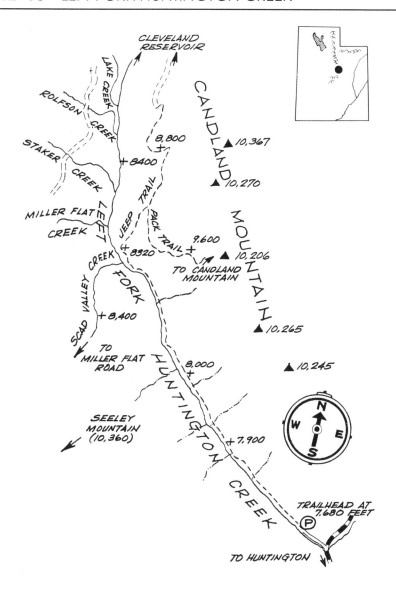

ONE MILE

As you begin the gentle climb, notice Seeley Mountain (10,360 feet) to the west and the several 10,000-foot peaks of Candland Mountain to the north and west. The stream channel flows over sedimentary formations comprising the Wasatch Plateau—interbedded layers of sandstone, shale, and limestone.

After a mile, an intermittent stream enters from the right, and several small springs enter from both sides of the creek as you continue up the drainage.

Four-and-one-half miles from the trailhead, the narrow canyon widens to form a broad valley with sagebrush and some aspen covering the slopes.

Scad Valley Creek enters from the southwest. The creek is small and usually clear with many beaver dams among the willow groves. If you leave the main trail and continue up Scad Valley, you will not find any definite trail, but the going isn't too rough, and you'll enjoy some fine fishing. There are some large cutthroat trout in the creek in spite of its small size. However, muddy water can lead to poor fishing if there have been recent storms.

After three miles and 500 vertical feet, Scad Valley Creek intersects the Miller Flat Road. It is possible to leave a car here.

Another option is to continue up the Left Fork on intermittent trails 3.5 miles to Cleveland Reservoir. The meadows end .5 mile beyond where Scad Valley Creek and the Left Fork meet, and the stream enters a narrow canyon with steep sides. As you travel toward the reservoir, four streams enter the Left Fork from the west: Miller Flat, Staker, Rolfson and Lake Fork. The latter three offer good fishing, and each intersects a dirt road about a mile from the main stream.

Drinking water isn't a problem near the canyon bottoms because many small springs and seeps feed the river. Treat all water to prevent giardiasis.

A third alternative is to continue following the main trail from the valley to its junction with an old jeep road which approaches the creek from the north. After about .75 mile and a gradual 300-foot climb, a pack trail turns to the right (southeast) and climbs 1,600 feet to Candland Mountain.

The predominant life forms of the area are typical of the Canadian and Hudsonian life zones—aspen, Douglas fir, white fir, and spruce-fir forests. The patient and discerning hiker may see mule deer, elk, and beaver, as well as a variety of small mammals and birds. Black bear, mountain lion, coyote, and bobcat also frequent the drainage but are rarely seen. Rainbow and cutthroat trout are the most common species in the stream. However, brown and eastern brook trout inhabit the lower portions of the Huntington.

The Forest Service identified the area as a 31,100-acre semi-primitive roadless area. It was not recommended for wilderness study area classification, despite the fact that it has high scenic value. The drainage has some timber potential, but the greatest threat to the integrity of the landscape is the proven existence of coal field boundaries and the possibility of oil and gas exploration.—*Linda and Rick Van Wagenen*

HIKE 49   SAN RAFAEL RIVER

General description: A day hike or overnighter along the San Rafael River in the Glen Canyon geologic formations.

General location: Sixteen miles southeast of Castle Dale and thirty-five miles northwest of Green River.

Maps: Northeastern and Southeastern Utah Multipurpose Maps and USGS Bottleneck Peak and Sids Mountain Quads.

Special attractions: Interesting geology and riparian vegetation; solitude.

Best season for hike: Spring and fall. Watch for high runoff in late May and flash flood potential in July through September.

For more information: San Rafael Resource Area, Bureau of Land Management, 900 North 700 East, Price, UT 84501; (801) 637-4584.

The hike: Numerous washes and the San Rafael River have cut a path through the thick sandstone layers in the Glen Canyon Series of the San Rafael Swell. Panoramas can be viewed from the top of the Swell as you drive in and out of the region, and unique riparian habitat exists in the washes and canyon bottoms. The seclusion of the region and its unusual beauty offer a unique

HIKE 49   SAN RAFAEL RIVER

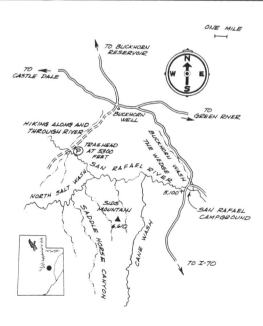

experience.

From the beginning of your hike at the river crossing southwest of Buckhorn Well to the finish at the San Rafael Campground southeast of the well, you will lose less than 200 feet in elevation over about fifteen miles. The canyon walls will tower higher and higher above you as the river cuts deeper into the San Rafael Swell.

Day hikes and "in and out" overnighters are possible from the trailhead. Carry your own water unless you take the proper steps to purify river water. Also, prepare to get wet (a pair of old running shoes or lightweight canvas boots are recommended), since numerous river crossings are necessary. An inner tube or small inflatable raft will aid crossing. Life preservers are recommended for small children.

To reach the upstream river crossing and the beginning of your hike, head east from State Highway 10 on a dirt road two miles north of Castle Dale. (This road meets combined U.S. 6/191 to the east, northwest of Green River.) After about thirteen miles, you reach Buckhorn Well—a tank, pump house, and water trough. From this junction, turn right (south), then take another right (southwest) at the next signed junction.

It's 5.4 miles to the river crossing. You have to pass through two gates along the way; leave the gates as you found them and be sure to respect private property. This road can be rough following bad weather. Contact the Bureau of Land Management (BLM) office in Price for the latest report. Park on the high terrain on the north side of the river.

To shuttle a car to the San Rafael Campground for the complete trip, continue east past Buckhorn Well two miles and turn right toward the river. Descend Buckhorn Wash about nine miles to the river. The campground is on your left just after the crossing.

From the trailhead, follow the river downstream. Notice the river cutting through various geologic layers—specifically, the Carmel (top), Navajo, Kayenta, Wingate, and Chinle formations.

Four miles downstream, North Salt Wash enters from the south. If you have time, this canyon offers interesting exploring. In Saddle Horse Canyon—four miles up North Salt Wash from the San Rafael River—you will find a giant monolith and small wetland areas. Ascents up Sids Mountain can be made from this canyon. Sids Mountain with its high point at 6,610 feet, is 1,200 feet above the river. There are overlooks of Virgin Spring Creek, the Wedge, and, of course, the San Rafael River.

Continuing downstream on the San Rafael another 2.5 miles, you reach Virgin Spring Canyon entering from the south. This canyon also offers interesting possibilities for exploration. The route has a difficult spot after about a mile, and inexperienced hikers might have some trouble here.

Numerous cottonwood groves along the river provide pleasant campsites. Be sure to leave them as you found them, because the area gets more use each year.

Wildlife is abundant along the river. Especially interesting in the San Rafael region are the numerous amphibians, including the woodhouse, red-spotted and spadefoot toads. Also look for the speckled dace (a fish). The toads breed in areas that are not accessible to the dace. The woodhouse and red-spotted toads breed in the same springs, but at different times. Look for the dace in isolated pools up side washes—far from the populations in the river.

Three-and-one-half miles downstream from Virgin Spring Canyon, Good Water Canyon enters from the north. Just around the corner—.5 mile away—Cane Wash joins the San Rafael. This is a long canyon, originating fifteen miles to the south. Its interesting geology and many springs provide a rewarding side excursion.

Soon after Cane Wash, look for an old mining road on the south side of the river. Four miles on this road brings you to the river crossing and the end of your trip.—*Peter Hovingh*

HIKE 50 *LOWER BLACK BOX*

General description: A wet day hike or overnighter through the Lower Black Box of the San Rafael River, within Mexican Mountain Wilderness Study Area.
General location: Fifteen miles west of Green River.
Maps: Southeastern Utah Multipurpose Map and USGS Spotted Wolf Canyon Quad.
Special attractions: Spectacular geology; solitude.
Best season for hike: Early summer and fall.
For more inforrnation: San Rafael Resource Area, Bureau of Land Management, 900 North 700 East, Price, UT 84501; (801) 637-4584.

The hike: The Lower Black Box of the San Rafael River provides one of the more interesting river hikes in the state. The San Rafael area has not received the attention other rivers have. Therefore, chances are you won't be running into many other hikers.

The trip involves about a 4.5-mile hike down to the river, another three miles along the rim on the east side of the river, and then the five-mile hike/wade through the Lower Black Box. The entire trip can be done in a day, but camping at the river is recommended.

Roads to the trailhead are seasonal and can present problems following bad weather. Call the Bureau of Land Management (BLM) to check on conditions. Also, the BLM reports that road signs are occasionally vandalized and are slow to be replaced. Follow your maps carefully.

Be sure to check water conditions. The trip should not be attempted in late spring when water may be cool and very high. Flash floods can be a problem, so get a good weather forecast and take along river survival gear. A trip in early fall is beautiful. Packing in water is recommended, unless proper purification methods are used.

To reach the trailhead, turn east off State Highway 10 about two miles north

The San Rafael River above the Lower Black Box.—Peter Hovingh photo

of Castle Dale. (This dirt road meets combined U.S. 6/191 to the east, northwest of Green River.) After about thirteen miles, you reach Buckhorn Well—a tank, pump house, and water trough. Continue east past Buckhorn Well two miles and turn right toward the river. Descend Buckhorn Wash about nine miles to the San Rafael.

Follow the road south another thirteen miles to Sinkhole Flat and a signed junction. Turn left here. The trailhead can also be more easily accessed from I-70. Take Exit 129 to the northeast 5.5 miles to the signed junction at Sinkhole Flat.

After about two miles, turn left again, passing up the road to Jerrys Flat. About three miles farther along, a ten-mile loop begins around Jackass Benches. Take the right fork of the loop and at 3.6 miles, look for a faint road heading to the east.

This road is in poor condition, so park at the junction. Head east across a wash and then over a pass about .5 mile from your car. From the pass, you descend several hundred feet in about five miles to the river.

A good camping spot exists at the river .5 mile downstream from Sulphur Spring. If you camp here, you can hike upstream along the east side the following morning and then hike down through the Lower Black Box, arriving

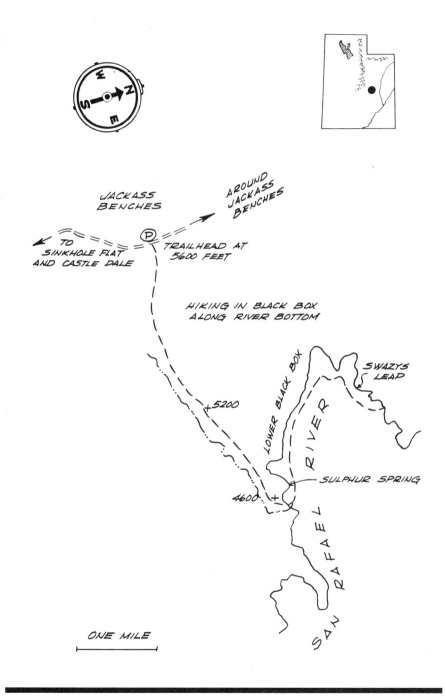

JACKASS BENCHES

AROUND JACKASS BENCHES

TO SINKHOLE FLAT AND CASTLE DALE

TRAILHEAD AT 5600 FEET

HIKING IN BLACK BOX ALONG RIVER BOTTOM

+5200

LOWER BLACK BOX

SWAZYS LEAP

RIVER

SULPHUR SPRING

4600 +

SAN RAFAEL

ONE MILE

back at your camp.

The hike along the east side of the San Rafael is not a difficult one. Cross the river near your camp and head cross-country to the northwest, keeping the river to your left. After about three miles—.5 mile upstream from Swaseys Leap—you are able to descend to the river.

Here, you begin the hike and wade through the Lower Black Box. Take precautions. You should be prepared for several river crossings, some in extremely cold water chest deep or deeper. The first 1.5 miles below Swaseys Leap contain steep boulder drops. Plastic liners in your pack are recommended and an inner tube or small inflatable raft can help with the crossings. Life preservers should be brought along for small children.

The five-mile hike through the Box is spectacular as you cut deeper and deeper into sandstone layers. You will pass under Swaseys Leap, a bridge over the upper end of the canyon. The bridge was used as a crossing for sheep, and several stories have developed around it. One story has it that one of the Swasey brothers acquired his brother's flock of sheep by jumping the gap with his horse and winning a bet. The story is also told that the Wild Bunch, on the run after a bank robbery, eluded a posse by leaping the gap.

Towards the end of the hike, you reach Sulphur Spring, a warm springs along the river. Copper sulfate is forming in one of the springs.

A half mile below Sulphur Spring, you reach your camp. If you spend another night here after your trip through the Box, you may want to hike a few miles downstream the next day. The scenery is spectacular as the river cuts through the San Rafael Reef.—*Peter Hovingh*

HIKE 51 *UPPER BLACK BOX*

General description: A hike/float through the Upper Black Box of the San Rafael River.

General location: Twenty miles west of Green River.

Maps: Northeastern and Southeastern Utah Multipurpose Maps and USGS Devils Hole and Drowned Hole Draw Quads.

Special attractions: Adventure in a striking canyon setting.

Best season for hike: Early summer and fall.

For more information: San Rafael Resource Area, Bureau of Land Management, 900 North 700 East, Price, UT 84501; (801) 637-4584.

The hike: The Black Boxes of the San Rafael River are located on Bureau of Land Management (BLM) administered lands in the northeastern part of the San Rafael Swell. These canyon segments possess spectacular scenery and geology, and provide a unique and challenging adventure. The narrow, deeply incised canyons meander through the Coconino Sandstone, the oldest exposed formation in the Swell.

HIKE 51 *UPPER BLACK BOX*

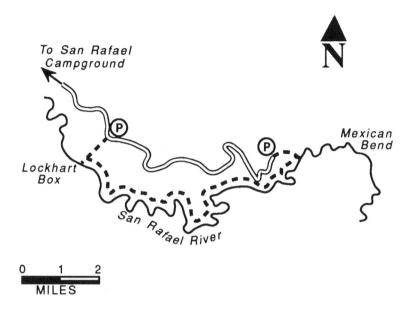

The canyons can be hiked if water flows are less than 100 cfs, however, a lot of floating and wading will still be necessary. Recommended flows for tubing are 100-400 cfs. Lifejackets and innertubes are advised regardless of the flow. You can measure the river's depth mid-stream under the swinging bridge near the San Rafael Campground. To minimize the risks of high water, the maximum depth should not exceed 2.5 feet.

The most popular access point starts near the Lockhart Box. Drive west of Green River on I-70 for about twenty-seven miles. Take Exit 129 to the north about eighteen miles to the San Rafael Campground (please register your trip here). Drive across to the north side of the swinging bridge and continue east for about 7.5 miles to Lockhart Box. A vehicle can be shuttled five miles further to the end of the road, near the takeout point at Mexican Bend.

Allow a minimum of twelve hours to complete the thirteen-mile section from Lockhart Box to Mexican Bend. There are a few benches in the upper portion of the canyon that would be suitable for an overnight bivouac.

From the flats above Lockhart Box, walk in a southwesterly direction for .5 mile along an old stock trail and descend to the river.

The rapids in the Upper Black Box increase in frequency and difficulty as you progress downstream. There are several large boulder fields that require some scrambling. The river disappears into the rocks in some places, requiring scouting or portages. About three-quarters of the way through the canyon there is a large rockfall. Use a twenty-foot section of rope to negotiate this rockfall.

The last few miles are flat water. The canyon ends at Mexican Bend. Exit here and follow the first drainage back to the road and your waiting vehicle.—*BLM, San Rafael Resource Area*

HIKE 52 *THOMPSON CANYON*

General description: An overnighter along the Thompson Canyon stream bed in the Book Cliffs.
General location: Twenty-five miles northeast of Green River.
Maps: Northeastern Utah Multipurpose Map, and USGS Sego Canyon and Bogart Canyon Quads.
Special attractions: Rugged, high elevation canyon country; extraordinary views of the Manti-LaSal Mountains, the Henry Mountains, and the Fish Lake

Bull elk.—John George photo

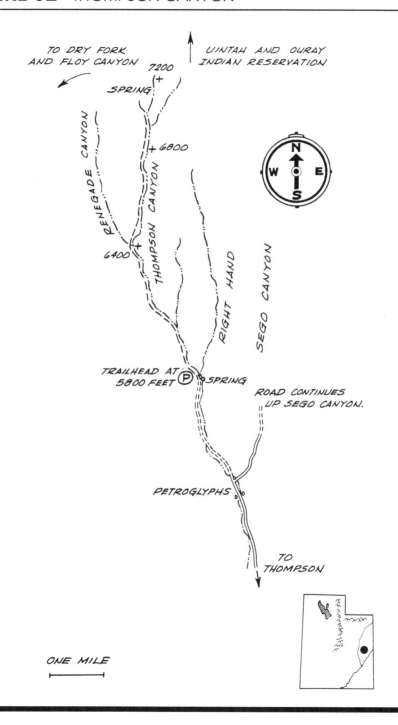

TO DRY FORK
AND FLOY CANYON

UINTAH AND OURAY
INDIAN RESERVATION

7200

SPRING

RENEGADE CANYON

THOMPSON CANYON

6800

6400

RIGHT HAND

SEGO CANYON

TRAILHEAD AT
5800 FEET   (P)   SPRING

ROAD CONTINUES
UP SEGO CANYON.

PETROGLYPHS

TO
THOMPSON

ONE MILE

Mountains.

Best season for hike: Spring or fall.

For more information: Grand Resource Area, Bureau of Land Management, 885 South Sand Flats Road, Moab, UT 84532; (801) 259-8193.

The hike: The Book Cliffs have never been a popular hiking area—a real mystery to those few hikers who have traveled through this rugged and beautiful country. In fact, most people think of the Book Cliffs only as the 800-foot cliff along the route between Price and Green River. The Book Cliffs have much, much more to offer.

The potential wilderness areas identified by the Bureau of Land Management (BLM) in this high plateau country total over 500,000 acres. One of the areas, Desolation Canyon, with more than 300,000 acres, runs the entire length of the world-renowned white water of the Green River's Desolation Canyon.

Thompson Canyon, east of Green River, merely puts you on the doorstep of millions of acres of splendid backcountry. This thirteen-mile overnighter takes you from about 6,000 feet along the creek bottom to the top of Thompson Canyon at over 8,000 feet.

To reach the trailhead, drive east of Green River on I-70. After about twenty-five miles, turn left into the little town of Thompson. Drive through town and into Thompson Canyon on a good, graded road. In about four miles, just after a petroglyph panel on the left, the road splits—the right fork heading up Sego Canyon, the left up Thompson.

Proceed up Thompson Canyon about three miles until the road passes through a sagebrush park with a fence running across it. Look for a parking place here because the road becomes less used a short distance after passing through the fence. (Keep in mind you are on private property in this part of the canyon, so respect the owner's rights.)

A few words of caution are in order for hikers in the Book Cliffs. Summer temperatures can be very warm, and water may not be present in certain areas of the Books. Some water may be too alkaline to drink. Pack enough water for the entire hike.

Also, keep in mind that the Book Cliffs have few maintained hiking trails. Canyon bottoms and ridgelines provide excellent walking terrain, but all hikers should carry the appropriate topographic maps and know how to use them. Experienced hikers have become disoriented in some of the more rugged and dissected areas of the Book Cliffs.

From your car to the upper portions of Thompson Canyon—about five miles— hiking is easy along the stream bed. The sage and pinyon of the lower elevations give way to some conifers in the higher country. Thompson Canyon is not known for abundant Indian ruins, but it does have some petroglyphs.

The canyon bottom has good campsites, but you may also choose to make your way to a ridge top for the evening. The ridge tops provide outstanding vistas, but don't forget to tote some water along with you.

The Book Cliffs are wildlife-rich country. Elk, deer and a healthy population of mountain lions inhabit the area, although your chances of spotting a

Thompson Canyon petroglyphs.—BLM photo

lion are minimal. Desert bighorn sheep have been spotted in Rattlesnake Canyon to the northwest. And you'll probably spot a number of hawks and eagles along the way.

The various finger canyons at the top of Thompson become rugged and steep. You can turn around here, retracing your steps to the trailhead. An option, however, is to hike out of the canyon to the northeast and meet the Sego Canyon road.

Whichever route you choose in Thompson Canyon, consider your hike here merely an introduction to millions of acres of wild and mostly ignored backcountry.—*Bill Hargraves*

HIKE 53 *PINE VALLEY MOUNTAINS*

General description: A moderately difficult two-day loop hike in the Pine Valley Wilderness.
General location: Five miles east of Pine Valley, thirty miles southwest of Cedar City, and twenty miles northeast of St. George.

Maps: Pine Valley Wilderness Map, and USGS Signal Peak and Grass Valley Quads.
Special attractions: Backcountry solitude in rugged country.
Best season for hike: Summer and fall.
For more information: Pine Valley Ranger District, Dixie National Forest, 196 East Tabernacle, St. George, UT 84771; (801) 673-3431.

The hike: The Pine Valley Mountains rise 3,500 feet from the floor of the Colorado Plateau and Great Basin to 10,000-foot peaks forested by virgin Engelmann spruce. Water is one of the most valuable resources in the range. The Pine Valleys are a major source for the Ash Creek, Virgin River, and Santa Clara River drainages. This mountain island surrounded by desert offers wildlife habitat for a large cougar population, mule deer, black bear, golden eagle, and beaver.

The range is located in the extreme southwest corner of the state. From I-15 in Cedar City, take State Highway 56 west about thirty miles to Newcastle. Turn left and drive southwest about nine miles to the junction of State Highway 18 near Enterprise. Turn left and continue another eighteen miles to Central, turning left again. Pine Valley is eight miles down the road. Turn left at the Pine Valley Church and continue the final four miles to the Whipple

Mule deer in velvet.—Harry Engels photo

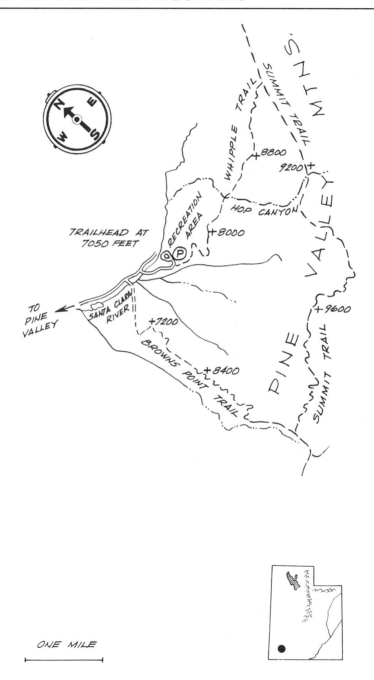

ONE MILE

Trail trailhead in the Pine Valley Campground and Recreation Area.

The loop hike—about fifteen miles total with the last mile on the road returning to the trailhead—involves considerable altitude change and should only be attempted by hikers in good condition.

All drinking water obtained along the trail should be treated to prevent the threat of giardiasis. It's a good idea to fill your water bottles with fresh water available at the recreation area before starting the hike.

From the trailhead just below 7,200 feet the Whipple Trail ascends 3.5 miles to Whipple Valley at 9,200 feet. About halfway along, you cross Hop Canyon, the only water source before Whipple Valley. The 2,000-foot elevation gain only represents the net difference on the topo map. The hike goes up and down quite a bit along the way.

The Whipple Trail is not well blazed but it is still clear enough to follow. Just follow the horse tracks. The trail sign showing directions, destinations, and mileage along the Summit Trail indicates that you have reached Whipple Valley. Whipple Valley holds a lot of water in early summer. A tributary of the Left Fork of the Santa Clara River runs through the middle of the valley, and water stands among the grass and clumps of flowers on the valley floor. The standing water can extend from the tree line at the edge of the valley to the stream banks, so be cautious. All that water early in the year and the iron shoes of a horse or the lugged soles of a hiker's boots can lead to serious trail erosion.

Turn right (south) at the junction. Continue on the Summit Trail .75 mile to South Valley. The Wet Sandy Trail heads east at the southeast corner of the valley, but you should continue on the Summit Trail into the trees.

Cross a stream (Hop Canyon) within a mile. If you find water, stock up. It's seven difficult miles to the Browns Point Trail, your next opportunity for water.

The Summit Trail between South Valley and Browns Point Trail snakes its way up and down a long series of switchbacks that cross a number of ridges—hard on the lungs going up and tough on the knees coming down.

The country here has large aspen, Engelmann spruce, and Douglas fir. Early in the summer, the northern slopes still have snow banks that provide a welcomed handful of moisture. There are blazes all the way, but some of the older ones may be difficult to locate. Occasionally you may have to backtrack 100 feet or so to find one you missed.

The Summit Trail meets Browns Point Trail in Nay Canyon at 9,600 feet. Trail signs with directions and mileage indicate the trail junction.

Turn right (north) into Nay Canyon and take advantage of the water here, as the Browns Point Trail heads up the east side of the canyon and then descends the ridge to the north—away from the creek bed.

From the ridge close to 10,000 feet, you switch back down the ridge about 3,000 feet to the road beyond the Santa Clara River. Again, finding the blazes along this four-mile stretch may be difficult.

The recreation area is in view most of the way down. At the base of the ridge, the trail leaves the wilderness area, meets an old jeep road and continues north .75 mile to the main road. Turn right (east) and hike about a mile to the trailhead.

This hike traverses only a fraction of the 192 miles of trails in the Dixie National Forest. Stop by the ranger station in Pine Valley or the district office in St. George for maps and more information.—*Mark McKeough*

HIKE 54 *KOLOB ARCH*

General description: A long day hike or overnighter into the Kolob Canyons section of Zion National Park.
General location: Eighteen miles southwest of Cedar City.
Maps: Trails Illustrated Zion National Park Map and USGS Kolob Arch Quad.
Special attractions: Dramatic views of the Finger Canyons of the Kolob and massive Kolob Arch; delightful campsites along Timber and La Verkin creeks.
Best season for hike: Late spring through fall.
For more information: Superintendent, Zion National Park, Springdale, UT 84767; (801) 772-3256.

The Kolob Canyons section of Zion National Park, long known for its outstanding scenery, was designated as Zion National Monument in 1937. In 1956 it was added to Zion National Park. John D. Lee lived awhile below the pass bearing his name (where you find the trailhead) following the Mountain Meadows Massacre on September 11, 1857.

The fourteen-mile round trip to Kolob Arch makes a moderate overnight trip or a fairly strenuous day hike. Backcountry permits are required for all overnight trips. Due to heavy use, a zone system restricts the number of campers in the Kolob Arch area. The area between the Kolob Arch and Hop Valley trail junctions shows the heavy impact of too much camping use. Please make your camp away from this area if possible. Permits can be obtained at the Kolob Canyons Visitor Center just off Exit 40 on I-15.

Because the National Park Service is concerned for the safety of hikers and preservation of the natural ecosystem, pets are not permitted on trails. This also makes it easier to see deer and other wildlife. Cougars have been reported in the area and could be dangerous for pets brought illegally on the hike.

Those wishing to cook should bring backpacking stoves—open fires are not permitted. Plan to use one gallon of water per person per day while in the backcountry, particularly during summer months when afternoon temperatures can be over 100 degrees Fahrenheit. Timber and La Verkin creeks are perennial sources of water, so you do not have to carry your entire supply. Just be sure to purify all surface water. And remember that everything packed in should come out with you.

There are several potential problems to consider if you decide to take this trip at other than the "best season." The Kolob Canyon Road is occasionally closed from early November to Easter each year due to snow and loose rocks

Kolob Arch, Zion National Park.—Allen Hagood photo

on the road. This adds seven miles to the hike (3.5 miles each way), because you have to park at the locked gate at the bottom of Hurricane Cliffs and walk to and from the Lee Pass trailhead. High water during spring runoff makes crossing La Verkin Creek difficult and hazardous. Snowstorms during the winter and early spring seasons can complicate your trip by making the steep sections of the trail slippery and/or muddy.

Locate the trailhead by taking Exit 40 (Kolob Canyons) off I-15 about eighteen miles south of Cedar City. Drive east into the park about four miles to Lee Pass (6,065 feet) where parking is provided. The view from here is worth the trip for everyone, but for the backpacker, it is only the beginning.

The trail drops about 500 feet rapidly and reaches Timber Creek in just over a mile. There are good campsites under large cottonwoods along Timber Creek. In the next 2.5 miles, you have commanding views of Timber Top Mountain (8,075 feet) and Shuntavi Butte to the east of the trail.

The route leaves Timber Creek and climbs to a ridge covered with juniper and pinyon pines. The trail gradually descends about 400 feet in the next mile to La Verkin Creek. The decaying corral on your left dates to the days when cattle drives came through here on the way to summer and winter pastures.

This is a good place to enjoy the splashing waters and dramatic views up La Verkin Creek. The towering canyon walls to the northeast culminate in Gregory Butte at 7,705 feet. This feature was named after Herbert E. Gregory, a prominent 20th century geologist of the region. To the southeast are Neagle Ridge and Burnt Mountain (7,669 feet), which was struck by lightning and burned in August, 1978.

From here, it is easy going as you travel upstream (northeast) for the next two miles to the Kolob Arch Trail junction. You pass several good campsites near a stream flowing off the north slopes of Neagle Ridge and Burnt Mountain. As you hike past Burnt Mountain, keep alert for a major canyon opening to the north just past Gregory Butte.

Kolob Arch is nearby, so this is a good place to enjoy the views up and down La Verkin Creek and savor the wilderness beauty. You are in the Kayenta formation (Lower Jurassic) for the entire hike, except for the flood plain alluvium of sand and gravel found along the stream channels. The surrounding cliffs are Navajo sandstone, out of which Kolob Arch has been formed.

Turn left (north) at the Kolob Arch Trail sign. You may wish to follow the trail on the east side of the creek or return to the streambed in a short distance, which some consider easier. For variety, take the alternate route on your return.

About .5 mile from the junction, a small stream comes in from a canyon to the left (west) below Kolob Arch, which can be seen high on the canyon wall above. Because of erosion problems, hiking the side stream and steep slope below the arch is prohibited.

Photography is best in the morning—a good reason to make this an overnight trip. For safety, hikers should camp above the high-water mark in drainages and along rivers.

Kolob Arch is one of the largest freestanding arches on the North American continent. Its span was conservatively measured at 290 to 310 feet by Fred Ayres and A.E. Creswell in 1953. New measurements done in 1984 by two teams measured the span at 310 feet and 292 feet respectively. Accurate measurement is difficult, because the arch is 700 feet above the canyon, and its legs are remnants of the former cliff.

Those who wish to stay longer in this area may want to take side trips to the falls in Beartrap Canyon farther up La Verkin Creek or into Hop Valley to the south. Reach Hop Valley via the Hop Valley Trail junction, .25 mile east of the

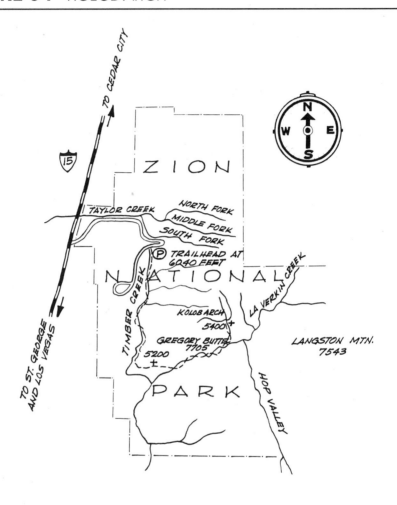

ONE MILE

Kolob Arch junction.

Make sure you are rested and have plenty of drinking water for the return trip to Lee Pass. You must regain 800 feet of elevation you lost coming into the area. Avoid the climb out of Timber Creek on hot summer afternoons, if possible. This south-facing slope can be much hotter than other portions of the hike and is much more enjoyable before noon—another reason to camp out.

Detailed information on other hiking objectives within Zion is available daily all year at the Zion Visitor Center, located a mile north of Springdale or the Kolob Canyons Visitor Center. Uniformed personnel can suggest a variety of trips to fit your interests, skill, and available time for each season of the year.—*Victor Jackson*

HIKE 55 *CANAAN MOUNTAIN*

General description: A moderately demanding loop or traverse hike in a Bureau of Land Management wilderness study area. For the experienced hiker.

General location: South of Zion National Park, thirty-two miles east of St. George.

Maps: Southwestern Utah Multipurpose Map and USGS Springdale West, Springdale East, Smithsonian Butte, and Hildale Quads.

Special attractions: An ecologically intact escarpment 2,000 feet above the surrounding area. It is diverse, isolated, very scenic, and has historical features.

Best season for hike: Early spring to early summer, and fall.

For more information: Dixie Resource Area, Bureau of Land Management, Box 726, St. George, UT 84770; (801) 673-4654.

The hike: Canaan Mountain offers the backcountry enthusiast some of the most scenic and diverse hiking experiences in southern Utah. Hikers should be proficient in backcountry navigation and map-reading, since only the access routes to the mountaintop are readily followed. Features which shouldn't be missed include Water Canyon Arch, Canaan Lake, the historic logging windless, Head of the Pines, and Eagle Crags.

Canaan Mountain boasts terrain similar to Zion National Park, with which it shares a common border. There are only a few trails to the top of the mountain, since 1,800- to 2,200-foot cliffs surround it on three sides. The major trailheads, recently developed by the Bureau of Land Management (BLM), are Squirrel Canyon on the south side of the mountain and Eagle Crags to the north.

The most popular hikes originate at Squirrel Canyon, two miles north of Colorado City, Arizona and traverse the mountain to just south of Rockville,

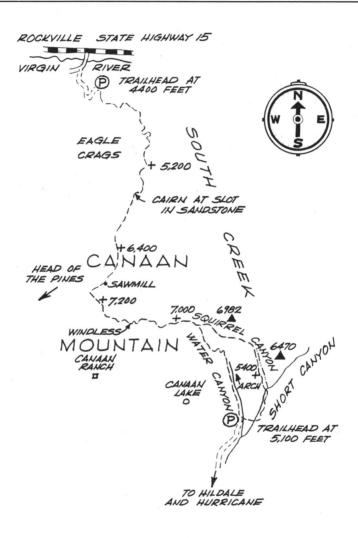

ROCKVILLE   STATE HIGHWAY 15

VIRGIN   RIVER

Ⓟ TRAILHEAD AT 4400 FEET

SOUTH

EAGLE CRAGS

+ 5,200

CAIRN AT SLOT IN SANDSTONE

CREEK

+ 6,400

CANAAN

HEAD OF THE PINES

SAWMILL

+ 7,200

7,000 +   6,982 ▲   SQUIRREL CANYON

WINDLESS

MOUNTAIN

CANAAN RANCH

WATER CANYON

6470 ▲

5400 + ARCH

SHORT CANYON

CANAAN LAKE ○

Ⓟ

TRAILHEAD AT 5,100 FEET

TO HILDALE AND HURRICANE

ONE MILE

Utah (about fifteen miles, depending on the route). From the Squirrel Canyon trailhead, either the Squirrel Canyon Trail or the Water Canyon Trail will take you to the top. You can take a shorter loop hike, starting and finishing at Squirrel Canyon via Water Canyon, or you can spot a car at the Eagle Crags trailhead near Rockville to make the complete hike.

To reach the Squirrel Canyon trailhead, head southeast from Hurricane on State Highway 59 for about twenty-four miles to Hildale, just before the Arizona border. On the northeast end of town, follow a dirt road north 1.5 miles to the trailhead in Short Creek Canyon. There is a small parking lot.

To spot a car on the north end of the mountain, take State Highway 9 to Rockville, south of Zion National Park. At the east end of town, head south on the paved road and cross the Virgin River at the Rockville Bridge. After an eighth mile, the main road swings to the right. Continue straight on a dirt road 1.5 miles to the trailhead. Small signs direct you to the Eagle Crags trailhead.

From the Squirrel Canyon trailhead, begin your hike by skirting to the east around the large bluff and enter Short Creek, heading northeast. Follow Short Creek for about a mile and enter Squirrel Canyon to the northwest.

Once in Squirrel Canyon, you climb 600 feet in a mile before the trail reaches more level terrain on top and joins an old pack trail. Bear to the right of the large expanses of slickrock on the mesa top.

Continue west on the pack trail for another mile. At this point, you have the option of hiking three miles down Water Canyon if you are doing a loop hike. The Water Canyon trail to your left (south) may be difficult to find, so rely on your topo maps. A steep switchback trail has been constructed at the head of the narrow slot canyon. Water Canyon follows a tributary of Short Creek through a nearrow, steep and thickly vegetated canyon bottom, and the trail is difficult to find in places. Don't miss Water Canyon Arch to the east on your way down.

If you choose to remain on top, continue west along the major ridgeline 2.5 miles to the logging windless above the Canaan Ranch. In the 1920s several enterprising loggers lowered rough-sawn ponderosa pine by cable to the benches 2,000 feet below. Remnants of this operation can be seen today.

From the windless, head northwest on the pack trail for 1.5 miles until you reach an old sawmill site in a large grove of aspen and pine. A small spring sometimes provides a cool drink. Follow the trail here, since major cracks or rifts in the Navajo sandstone halt your north-south travel.

Water can be a problem on the mountain. Plan accordingly. Wet-weather springs are plentiful during the spring months, and summer thunder showers provide water in shallow sandstone potholes, but that's about all. The largest of these potholes is Canaan Lake, about 1.5 miles south from the top of the Water Canyon Trail. It provides good camping areas and spectacular views of the Arizona Strip to the south.

Pinyon and ponderosa pine, juniper, aspen, manzanita, Gamble oak, sagebrush, and western wheatgrass are the principal vegetation types on Canaan. Mules ear, sand dropseed, and poa are secondary species.

Maple and fir species are found on cooler sites within large crevices that cut into the heart of the mountain. On the talus slopes below the rims, littleleaf mountain mahogany and juniper are major plant species, with Oregon grape, Gamble oak, and shrubbery maples clinging aggressively to the steep, heavily bouldered terrain.

From the sawmill, work your way downhill to the north. Descending the ridge is an easy hike. Many favorable camping areas exist in the numerous groves of aspen and pine. Looking to the north, you will see the Eagle Crags. They are large sandstone monoliths which provide a ready landmark for descending the north mountain. Zion National Park is also visible to the north.

When you reach the north rim above South Creek—about 5.5 miles from the sawmill—you'll be convinced there is no way down. Take heart. The trail leads through one (marked well with a cairn) of a series of cracks in the sandstone to the talus slopes below. The trail was originally constructed to bring livestock to the mountain from Springdale.

Once through the crack, you traverse a large sagebrush flat and climb the northwest edge of a ridgeline. Continue north for about four miles to the Eagle Crags trailhead and the end of your hike.—*Paul Boos*

HIKE 56 *RATTLESNAKE CREEK AND ASHDOWN GORGE*

General description: A two- to four-day backpack, descending 3,400 feet.
General location: Ten miles east of Cedar City in the Dixie National Forest and Cedar Breaks National Monument.
Maps: Trails Illustrated Dixie National Forest Map and USGS Flanigan Arch Quad.
Special attractions: Views of the Wasatch limestone formation of Cedar Breaks; one of the more accessible routes to the amphitheater of Cedar Breaks.
Best season for hike: Late spring through fall.
For more information: Cedar City Ranger District, Dixie National Forest, Box 627, Cedar City, UT 84721; (801) 586-4462. Also, Superintendent, Cedar Breaks National Monument, Box 749, Cedar City, UT 84720; (801) 586-9451.

The hike: This hike, from the northwest corner of Cedar Breaks National Monument down Rattlesnake Creek and Ashdown Gorge to Highway 14 east of Cedar City, is an exciting and rigorous backpack.

The trail drops 3,400 feet in nine miles and receives only occasional use (mostly during fall hunting seasons). It is not recommended for hikers with little map reading experience. The trail is good only in isolated spots, and you must follow rock cairns and slashes on trees. Be cautious in the gorge due to flash flood potential. Contact the Cedar City Ranger District, Dixie National Forest or Cedar Breaks National Monument for an update on conditions before starting your hike.

The hike to Highway 14 requires a car shuttle, but in-and-out options are also possible from the trailhead.

Rattlesnake and Ashdown creeks usually have water. However, as you near Ashdown Gorge, the water becomes silty. Sheep graze in the Dixie National Forest, and water contamination is possible. Local management agencies advise that you purify all water.

Also consider using your backpacking stove whenever possible and, of course, pack out all trash.

Leave a car at the dirt road which exits north off State Highway 14 about seven miles east of Cedar City. This road exits toward Last Chance Canyon at Martins Flat, then parallels the road and Coal Creek for about 1.5 miles.

The trailhead is on the northern boundary of Cedar Breaks National Monument. From State Highway 143, turn west on a dirt road (signed Rattlesnake Creek - Ashdown Gorge) immediately north of the monument boundary, then drive about a mile and park off the road.

For the first two miles to Stud Flat, the trail is difficult to follow in spots. Follow your map carefully.

From your car, follow a well-trodden trail along the boundary fence to an opening at a small meadow. Cross the meadow, enter another wooded area, and head for the edge of the ridge to the southwest. On the southwest-facing side of the ridge, the trail descends with several switchbacks. Here you catch your first glimpses of the geologic formations of Cedar Breaks National Monument. In the distance to the west is Cedar Valley; the large open meadow at the bottom of the descent is Stud Flat. The rocky cliffs to the south and west of Stud Flat are the narrows of Ashdown Gorge. And the white ridge in the foreground is Snow Ridge.

As you descend the switchbacks and enter an aspen grove, take the first left at the unmarked junction. You will pick up trail markers on trees. Follow around the south edge of the aspen glen. If you like, walk to the southwest .25 mile to the edge of the small ridge and catch another excellent view of Cedar Breaks. You are standing on Adams Barrier, the Monument's northern boundary. As you skirt the south edge of the aspen glen, you again pick up trail tree markers. Notice the evidence of porcupine chewing on several of the aspen.

As the glen opens to a meadow on a small ridge, head to the west to a rock cairn. You once again reach a large, south-facing meadow—still only about a mile from the trailhead. This is a difficult area to locate the trail. Look to the southwest toward Snow Ridge. The trail makes a sharp turn down to the southeast. Continue to the trees on the southeast edge of the meadow. Take your time and look for very large slashes on two trees. The trail heads southeast here but angles to the southwest along the base of Snow Ridge within a few hundred yards.

Follow the trail another mile to Stud Flat—hiking through a wash and then along a ridge top littered with downed timber. Once in Stud Flat, you've descended about 1,550 feet from the trailhead.

From the flat, the trail switches back down the Rattlesnake Creek drainage .75 mile to Tri Story Canyon, then follows the creek. The trail has been severely

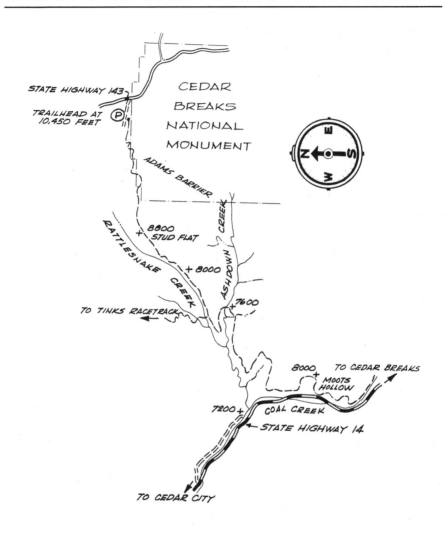

STATE HIGHWAY 143

CEDAR
BREAKS
NATIONAL
MONUMENT

TRAILHEAD AT
10,450 FEET

ADAMS BARRIER

RATTLESNAKE CREEK

8800
STUD FLAT

+ 8000

ASHDOWN CREEK

+ 7600

TO TINKS RACETRACK

8000
MOOTS
HOLLOW

TO CEDAR BREAKS

7200 +
COAL CREEK

STATE HIGHWAY 14

TO CEDAR CITY

ONE MILE

washed out on the east side, so be careful. The trail eventually crosses the creek and continues along the west side (older USGS maps may be in error here).

Follow the creek about 1.5 miles from Tri Story Canyon. When you come to a squared-off, four-foot-high waterfall on Rattlesnake Creek, there is a junction. Turning right (northwest) leads to Tinks Racetrack (not your trail). Take the left fork (southwest), contour around the ridge, then cross over it after .5 mile. The trail swings around to the east and drops into Ashdown Gorge in another .5 mile.

If you head upstream (east) on Ashdown Creek for about four miles, you can explore the fingers of the amphitheater of Cedar Breaks National Monument. This seldom-visited area offers exciting exploring among the sculptured rock formations. However, you will find it impossible to hike to the top of the plateau.

If you decide to hike into this area and camp, Cedar Breaks' rangers ask that you let them know of your plans. They also recommend that you not hike alone in this terrain.

If you have learned that there is no danger of an impending storm, continue your hike by following Ashdown Creek downstream. This spectacular gorge does not descend sharply, losing only about 500 feet from where you enter the creek to its mouth, about 2.5 miles below. You hike in water in several areas, so bring along an old pair of running shoes. (If Ashdown Gorge is inaccessible due to high water, follow the jeep trail along the south side of the gorge, then through Moots Hollow to Highway 14—up the canyon [southeast] from Martins Flat.)

At the mouth of the gorge, Ashdown and Crow creeks meet to form Coal Creek. About .5 mile downstream from the junction, you meet an old jeep trail on the right (north) side of the creek. Follow the roadbed about a mile to Martins Flat on Highway 14.

The Cedar Breaks area has a rich history. Early exploration began in 1851, when Mormons settled in Parowan and Cedar City. In 1852, church leaders explored the headwaters of the Sevier and Virgin rivers, which rise on the Markagunt Plateau, but they made no reports of the cliffs known today as Cedar Breaks.

Both the Wheeler and Powell surveys of 1872 made extensive topographic records of the area, as well as plant, animal, and geologic observations. For more than three decades following these scientific surveys, grazing and timber cutting were principal resource uses.

In 1905, the area was included as a part of the Sevier (now Dixie) National Forest, administered by the Forest Service. It was established as a national monument on August 22, 1933, under the administration of the National Park Service.

Keep in mind that some of the land in lower Ashdown Gorge is privately owned. Your respect for private property will help keep access open to future hikers.—*Nancy Jane Cushing*

View from Sunrise Point, Bryce Canyon National Park.—Heidi
Herendeen photo

HIKE 57 *UNDER-THE-RIM TRAIL*

General description: A 22.5-mile backpack in Bryce Canyon National Park.
General location: Twenty-one miles southeast of Panguitch and fifty miles
east of Cedar City.
Maps: Trails Illustrated Bryce Canyon National Park Map, and USGS Bryce
Point, Tropic Reservoir, and Rainbow Point Quads.
Special attractions: A remote hike through the base of the older sections of
Bryce Canyon; distant panoramic views; abundant wildlife; geologic features;
and marked transitions in vegetation.
Best season for hike: Late spring through fall.
For more inforrnation: Superintendent, Bryce Canyon National Park, Bryce
Canyon, UT 84717; (801) 834-5322.

The hike: Although there are two trailheads for the Under-the-Rim Trail,
Bryce Point and Yovimpa Point, as well as four connecting trails back to the rim

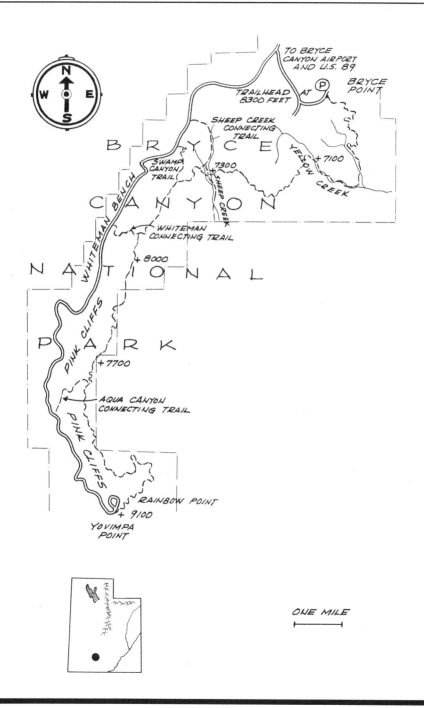

ONE MILE

along the trail's length, Bryce Canyon officials recommend that you hike from north to south, beginning at Bryce Point and finishing the 22.5-mile trail at Yovimpa. Shuttling a car is recommended.

To reach the trailhead, drive south into Bryce Canyon National Park from State Highway 12, southeast of Panguitch and west of Escalante. Drive three miles south along Highway 63 from Highway 12. Stop at the visitor center and ranger station on the right. You must obtain a free backcountry permit. You also have to register for one or more of the nine primitive campsites on the trail. No more than fourteen consecutive days can be spent on the Under-the-Rim Trail.

After stopping here, drive south another 1.5 miles and turn left toward Bryce Point parking area and trailhead. It is another two miles ahead.

To leave a car at Yovimpa Point, drive about 15.5 miles past the Bryce Point turnoff. The Yovimpa Point trailhead is on the right, .25 mile before the loop at the end of the road.

Keep in mind that open fires are not permitted due to fire danger and slow vegetative recovery. Also, domestic animals are not allowed (on or off leash) below the rim. Finally, park officials ask that you carry out all trash. Don't bury it.

The trail at Bryce Point starts at about 8,300 feet. The descent into the canyon is not a continuous one. There is quite a bit of "up and down" hiking as the trail winds around eroding limestone fins and through gullies and ravines. The trail cuts into the Claron Formation (the predominant geologic formation in the park) and the other crossbedded sandstones. The ancient, nearly horizontal strata of the Claron represent Cretaceous geology (sixty million years old) and a time when non-oxidating freshwater lakes covered the Bryce Canyon area. More recently, regional faulting and volcanic activity, as well as the erosional forces of wind, water and freezing temperatures, formed the landscape seen today. The Hat Shop, about 1.5 miles down the trail, is an excellent example of the differential weathering that can occur when these erosional agents work on dissimilar rock types.

Continuing past the Hat Shop, the trail begins a rugged 650-foot descent about 1.5 miles to Yellow Creek. Ponderosa pines give way to Gambel's oak as you pass the first campsite near the creek. You may be able to fill water bottles here, but don't count on it. Carry your own supply and be prepared to treat any water you find.

Depending on the season, cactus blooms may be seen. Similarly impressive is the view back toward the rim where the Pink Cliffs rise to towering heights. About a mile past the junction with Yellow Creek, the trail heads into denser vegetation and topographic diversity.

The Sheep Creek and Swamp Canyon areas—another five miles along—offer good "halfway" points for overnight hikers. Since both camps are only about ten miles from the trailhead, they allow time for exploring washes up toward the cliffs, watching wildlife, or simply enjoying the solitude of the nearby buttes and mesas which run parallel to the rim.

The trail in this area is spectacular. For the adventurous hiker, the side trips up the drainages toward the rim may be rewarding. They yield glimpses of some unrecorded arches and lush spring-loving vegetation, found only where the precious water of this arid region reaches surface levels. Hawks and hummingbirds also flourish in this area. Keep your eyes and ears open. Perhaps you'll spot a Cooper's hawk amidst the trees.

If you're hiking in late summer, thunderstorms are frequent, so avoid isolated trees and viewpoints during storms. Lightning frequently strikes objects along the rim.

From Whiteman Connecting Trail south, the solitude of the area increases. Vegetation becomes denser, giving way to spruce, fir, and groves of aspen. Trail conditions vary from "ball bearing" limestone and wide dry drainages to loose sandy hills. You will find a greater density of seasonal springs and water sources. Toward evening, the native wildlife seek these watering sites. Mule deer may wander right into camp. If you're lucky, you may even spot more secretive mammals. The ring-tailed cat, black bear and cougar have left sign but are seldom seen.

The second half of the trip begins the ascent to the highest point in the park. The climb is rather arduous but well worth the effort, for it provides magnificent vistas back (northwest) toward the rim of the Pink Cliffs and south across the plateaus toward the Grand Canyon. No-Man's Mesa, Coral Pink Sand Dunes, Trumball Mountain, Navajo Mountain, and the proposed Alton coal field area can all be viewed from multiple breaks in the trees and exposed ridges.

The hike concludes by contouring around the Pink Cliffs north of Rainbow Point and then climbing to over 9,000 feet at Yovimpa Point.

If you're not too tired upon ending your hike, or if you allow another day in the park, you may want to hike some of the day trails where you will encounter the pinnacles and formations of the amphitheater for which Bryce is famous.—*Heidi Herendeen*

HIKE 58 *HACKBERRY CANYON*

General description: A relatively easy two- or three-day hike in a Bureau of Land Management wilderness study area.

General location: Forty-two miles northeast of Kanab.

Maps: Southwestern Utah Multipurpose Map, and USGS Slickrock Bench and Calico Peak Quads.

Special attractions: Highly scenic canyon with numerous side canyons to explore; interesting geology; Sam Pollock Arch; and Watson's Cabin, an early homestead.

Best season for hike: Spring or fall.

For more information: Kanab Resource Area, Bureau of Land Management, 318 N. 1st East, Kanab, UT 84741; (801) 644-2672.

HIKE 58 *HACKBERRY CANYON*

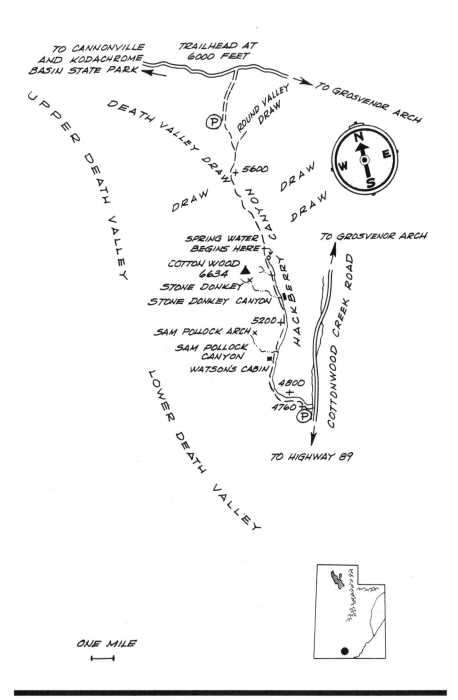

TO CANNONVILLE
AND KODACHROME
BASIN STATE PARK

TRAILHEAD AT
6000 FEET

TO GROSVENOR ARCH

UPPER DEATH VALLEY

DEATH VALLEY DRAW

ROUND VALLEY DRAW

P

+ 5600

DRAW

DRAW

DRAW

CANYON

SPRING WATER
BEGINS HERE

COTTON WOOD
6634

TO GROSVENOR ARCH

STONE DONKEY

STONE DONKEY CANYON

HACKBERRY

COTTONWOOD CREEK ROAD

5200 +

SAM POLLOCK ARCH

SAM POLLOCK
CANYON

WATSON'S CABIN

4800
+

4760 +

P

TO HIGHWAY 89

LOWER DEATH VALLEY

ONE MILE

The hike: Hackberry Canyon offers a variety of scenery as it cuts through the White and Vermilion cliffs. The upper portion of Hackberry is narrow, typical of canyons cut into the Navajo sandstone. Farther south, just before the canyon turns east and cuts through the East Kaibab Monocline (Cockscomb), it forms a valley bounded by the colorful formations making up the Vermillion Cliffs, and also exposes the banded Chinle formation. There are interesting side canyons, and the country above the canyons offers excellent opportunities for exploration. The area receives very little use, which enhances the sense of discovery.

Access is by seasonal roads which may be impassable when wet. From Cannonville on State Highway 12 (about eight miles east of Bryce Canyon National Park), take the Cottonwood Canyon Road southeast about seven miles to the entrance of Kodachrome Basin State Park. Continue east 4.9 miles past Kodachrome Basin and turn right on a low-grade road. Continue about two miles to a wooden corral. Park here to begin your hike.

There is also access from the south via U.S. 89, east of Kanab. Take the Cottonwood Canyon Road north from the highway and continue about twenty-eight miles to the Grosvenor Arch intersection. The trailhead turnoff is on the left 5.1 miles beyond.

Hiking Hackberry's full length requires spotting a vehicle at the mouth of the canyon, located on the Cottonwood Canyon Road 17.5 miles south of the Grosvenor Arch turnoff and 12.5 miles north of U.S. 89.

From the trailhead at about 6,000 feet, you descend to about 4,700 feet at the mouth of the canyon. The canyon begins to narrow immediately at the start of the hike. Vehicles occasionally use Hackberry. Their signs are apparent until reaching Round Valley Draw. After two miles, the canyon becomes very sandy, and evidence of vehicle travel should disappear.

A half-mile after Round Valley Draw, a major side canyon enters from the left (east) and makes a good side hike. There are a number of falls, but you can climb around them. This canyon opens into a large basin with scattered ponderosa pine. It is very scenic and provides access to the rim for a view of the surrounding country. Water first appears in Hackberry about six miles below this canyon, so be prepared to pack water with you.

About a mile below where you first find water is an old livestock trail to the west rim. The trail starts from the top of a high, sandy bench covered with cobbles. The bench is identified by a wire fence.

About a mile farther, again to the west, is the next tributary canyon, Stone Donkey. The name comes from a rock feature north of the canyon. This interesting canyon narrows to a slot a few feet wide toward its upper end. Two storage sheds and a corral mark the mouth of Stone Donkey Canyon.

About a mile and a half below Stone Donkey Canyon there is a large rockfall. In October 1987, a huge slab fell away from the right (west) canyon wall and broke into large fragments that completely filled the canyon. The rockfall temporarily dammed the creek, creating a small lake that extended about 100 yards upstream. The creek has since worked through the debris and drained most of the lake, so it's possible to find a route over the rockfall.

183

As Hackberry Canyon begins to widen another 1.5 miles downstream, the side canyon containing Sam Pollock Arch enters from the right (west). This spectacular arch is about 1.5 miles from Hackberry. You will encounter a twenty-foot waterfall, but you can pick a route around it on the north side.

About .5 mile below Sam Pollock Canyon, also on the west side of Hackberry, is Watson's Cabin, an early homestead. At this point, you have dropped 1,000 feet from the trailhead.

Two miles below, the canyon jogs east and exits the Cockscomb through a gorge about two miles long. You meet the Cottonwood Canyon Road at the end of this narrow section.

Hackberry is on the eastern edge of a wilderness which encompasses the Paria River and a large section of the White Cliffs. It contains many interesting canyons, arches, and rock forms. The scenery is outstanding, and a variety of hiking opportunities are available, ranging in difficulty from easy day hikes to extended trips into more remote areas of the backcountry.—*Bill Booker*

HIKE 59 *PARIA CANYON*

General description: A popular three to six day hike along the Paria River. Alternate routes through Buckskin Gulch tributary are possible.

General location: Thirty-six miles east of Kanab in the Paria Canyon-Vermillion Cliffs Wilderness.

Maps: USGS West Clark Bench, Utah-Arizona; Bridger Point, Utah-Arizona; Wrather Arch, Arizona; Water Pockets, Arizona; Ferry Swale, Arizona; and Lees Ferry, Arizona Quads; and the Bureau of Land Management brochure, "Hikers Guide to Paria Canyon."

Special attractions: Paria Canyon narrows, Buckskin Gulch, Wrather Arch, and prehistoric petroglyph sites.

Best season for hike: Spring or fall. The possibility of flash flooding is greatest in July through early September.

For more information: Bureau of Land Management, Kanab Resource Area, 318 North First East, Kanab, UT 84741; (801) 644-2672.

The hike: Hiking through Paria Canyon has become increasingly popular with visitors to southern Utah and northern Arizona since the early 1970s. In 1969, Paria Canyon was designated as one of the first Bureau of Land Management (BLM) primitive areas in the country. The canyon became part of the Paria Canyon-Vermillion Cliffs Wilderness with the passage of the Arizona Wilderness Act of 1984. Paria Canyon has been written about in various books and magazines, such as *Arizona Highways* and *National Geographic*. Adding to the popularity of the hike is the easy access to the trailheads and the fact that hikers can exit the canyon downstream at the Colorado River. A car shuttle is necessary.

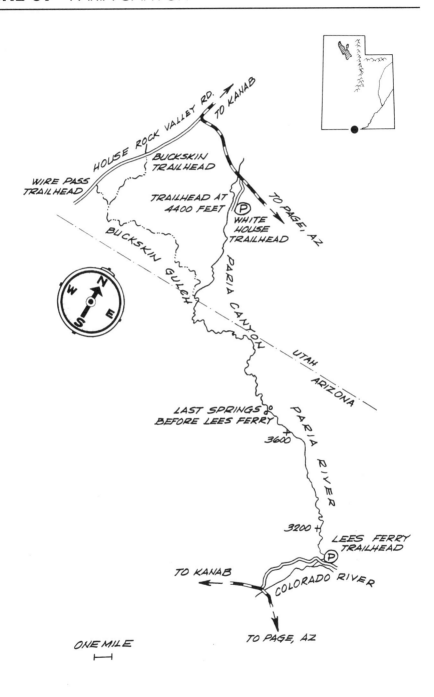

Paria Canyon offers an outstanding hike. For about the first half of its length it cuts through the Navajo sandstone formation. The lower half cuts into progressively older formations, adding variety to the beauty of the canyon.

The most popular hike begins in Utah at the White House trailhead just south of U.S. 89 and ends thirty-seven miles downstream in Arizona at Lees Ferry. A minimum of three days is recommended for the trip, and four to six days are preferable.

The road to the trailhead exits south from U.S. 89 near milepost 21, about forty-four miles east of Kanab and thirty miles west of Page, Arizona. A BLM ranger station—usually occupied during the morning hours in the spring, summer, and fall, Thursday through Monday—is a few hundred yards off the highway. The trailhead is about two miles beyond. The gravel road to the trailhead should not be a problem for most cars.

The hike ends on the Colorado River at Lees Ferry. To spot a car here, take U.S. 89 east from the White House trailhead, cross the Colorado River, and continue on U.S. 89 past Page, Arizona. About twenty-three miles beyond Page, turn right on U.S. 89-A and drive north, recrossing the Colorado River. The road to Lees Ferry turns to the right on the west side of the river. The distance by road from White House to Lees Ferry is about seventy-five miles.

Before entering the canyon, you are required to register with the ranger at the Paria Canyon Ranger Station or at the BLM office in Kanab (either in person or by phone). You must register within twenty-four hours of your hike for safety reasons, since flash floods pose a real danger that may be life-threatening. Current weather forecasts and hiking conditions can be obtained from BLM personnel when you register. The canyon will be closed to hiking if the weather is unfavorable. If the ranger is absent when you arrive for your hike, you may register at the trailheads if the canyon hiking is posted as open on the sign in front of the ranger station. If the canyon is posted as closed, dangerous flash flooding may occur and you must not enter the canyon. Also, hiking completely through the canyon from Lees Ferry upstream to the trailhead is not allowed since weather information will be several days old by the time you reach the narrowest part of the canyon.

Because the hike follows the course of the Paria River, the route is a gradual descent. You lose only about 1,100 feet of elevation in thirty-seven miles.

The BLM brochure for Paria Canyon, when used in conjunction with the USGS topographic maps, is the best source of information on the location of points of interest, mileages, and springs in the canyon. The brochure also includes information on low impact practices for wilderness visitors; wildlife, geology, and history; as well as general information to help you plan your hike.

The first reliable spring is located twelve miles downstream from the trailhead, and the last spring water is available twelve miles upstream from Lees Ferry, with many other good springs located between these two. The smaller seeps often cease to flow when conditions are dry. The Paria River is not recommended for drinking water because upstream sources pollute the river.

Because of flooding throughout the canyons in the Paria Canyon Wilder-

This southern Utah coyote cooperated for hiker-photographer John George.

ness, hiking conditions can change considerably in a short period. Most flash floods are over after a few hours to a day, but the prudent hiker should carry food for an extra day or two in case of flooding. It should be noted that most rescues in the canyon become necessary because parties entered the canyon without registering with the BLM and thus failed to get current hiking and weather conditions.

Because nearly all use of Paria Canyon is concentrated along the narrow corridor of the canyon bottom, rather than being dispersed as in non-canyon wilderness areas, the need to "walk softly" and camp in an environmentally sound manner is even greater here. Litter and human waste have often been found in Paria Canyon, even in its narrowest portions. In order to minimize human impacts, the BLM does not allow campfires within the canyon bottoms, and you are required to pack out all of your trash. Make your latrine on a low river terrace away from the river and any campsite locations. Bury human waste in a six inch deep "cat hole," and remember that your used toilet paper is also part of your trash, and should be packed out (a Ziploc-type bag with a little powdered bleach in it makes an excellent container for used toilet paper).

Hikers should be aware that certain visitor use restrictions become necessary because the BLM must manage Paria Canyon for long-term protection and preservation of the area as wilderness. One of the statements made by people opposed to wilderness designation for other areas is that backpacker impacts are ruining its wilderness character. To some degree this is true. So, when you hike through Paria Canyon, leave the area cleaner than when you found it.

An alternative to hiking down the Paria from the main trailhead is to enter via Buckskin Gulch. This spectacular side canyon in the Navajo Sandstone is one of the ultimate narrow canyon hikes on the Colorado Plateau. The average width of the canyon bottom is less than fifteen feet for over twelve miles of its length, and its confluence with the Paria River is located in the heart of the Paria Canyon narrows. In many places throughout the Buckskin you can touch both walls with your hands.

You can enter the Buckskin at two locations on the House Rock Road, which exits south from U.S. 89 about five miles west of the Paria Ranger Station, immediately west of where the highway cuts through the Cockscomb, near milepost 26. The first trailhead is a little over four miles south of the highway at the Buckskin crossing; the second is four miles farther at Wire Pass. Both trailheads are signed.

Hiking down Buckskin Gulch offers two options: 1) meeting the Paria River and hiking south (downstream) to Lees Ferry, or 2) turning left (upstream) at the Paria and finishing the hike at the White House trailhead.

Hiking through Buckskin Gulch is much more rigorous than hiking the main stream of Paria, and at times it may be impassable. In many places the stream bottom is full of cobbles, and you often encounter deep pools of cold water that must be waded or may require swimming. You may also encounter quicksand. Consult the BLM for current hiking conditions.

The best time for hiking in the Buckskin is May through June, when conditions are driest. Hiking conditions may also be good in October. At other times it is usually too wet and cold, creating the danger of hypothermia. Floods pose a great threat in the Buckskin because it is very narrow and there are few escape routes.

There is a rock jam in the Buckskin with about a thirty foot drop, which may be an obstacle for some people. Ropes are usually not required, as it is possible to find a route to chimney down, but you may want to take along a short piece of rope for lowering packs. Carry plenty of water if you hike through Buckskin Gulch, because none is available.

Hiking through Buckskin Gulch and then up the Paria to the White House trailhead can be done in two days. This route is suggested if you don't have time to hike the entire length of Paria Canyon.

The canyon system here has long been recognized for its outstanding wilderness qualities, resulting in its present designation. As you hike, please leave no trace of your visit within this fragile environment, so that Paria Canyon may be enjoyed by future generations as wilderness.—*Rod Schipper*

HIKE 60 *LOWER MULEY TWIST CANYON*

General description: A day hike with overnight options through part of the Waterpocket Fold.

General location: Twenty-three miles east of Boulder and thirty-eight miles southeast of Torrey in Capitol Reef National Park.

Maps: Trails Illustrated Glen Canyon and Capitol Reef Map, and USGS Wagon Box Mesa and The Post Quads.

Special attractions: A remote, lightly-used wilderness hike in a deep canyon; splendid vistas; and historic identification with Mormon pioneers.

Best season for hike: Spring (early April thorough mid-May) and fall (early October through late November).

For more inforrnation: Superintendent, Capitol Reef National Park, Torrey, UT 84775; (801) 425-3791.

The hike: The Lower Muley Twist hike passes through a representative portion of the 100-mile-long eroded uplift called the Waterpocket Fold, most of which lies within Capitol Reef National Park. Hikers experience a slickrock canyon wilderness while retracing the steps of Mormon pioneers.

There are several possible hikes in the canyon. You may choose an "in and out" day hike starting from the trailhead on the Burr Trail Road, a day or overnight hike from the same trailhead to the Post on the Notom-Bullfrog Road, or an extended overnighter farther into Muley Twist Canyon.

If you choose the overnight option, get a permit at the Highway 24 visitor center in Capitol Reef National Park. Fires are not permitted and you should choose a campsite out of sight and sound of other hikers.

Also, if you choose to begin your hike at the Burr Trail Road and finish at the Post, you can eliminate backtracking or "road stomping" by leaving a car at each.

To reach the trailhead, take the Notom-Bullfrog Road south from State Highway 24 near the east border of Capitol Reef. After about thirty-five miles, turn right (west) on the Burr Trail Road and continue another two miles to the Muley Twist trailhead on the left. The Burr Trail was first used to move cattle across the Waterpocket Fold.

To reach the Post on the right side of the Notom-Bullfrog Road, drive another 2.5 miles past the Burr Trail turnoff. Park here or another .75 mile farther at the end of a short spur road south of the Post.

From the Burr Trail parking area at about 5,600 feet, begin a descent into Lower Muley Twist Canyon. The canyon winds tortuously through its entire length, enough to "twist a mule" pulling a wagon.

Carry water with you, especially in summer. There are no reliable water sources in the area. And during June, July and August, temperatures often rise to over 100 degrees Fahrenheit.

The canyon narrows in some areas while widening in others. For the most

HIKE 60 *LOWER MULEY TWIST CANYON*

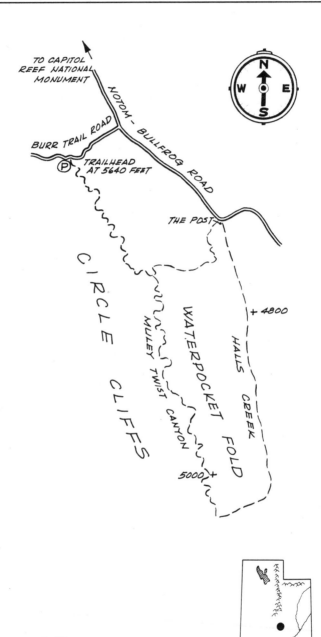

TO CAPITOL
REEF NATIONAL
MONUMENT

NOTOM - BULLFROG ROAD

BURR TRAIL ROAD

TRAILHEAD
AT 5640 FEET

THE POST

+ 4800

CIRCLE CLIFFS

WATERPOCKET FOLD

MULEY TWIST CANYON

HALLS CREEK

5000 +

ONE MILE

Lower Muley Twist in Capitol Reef National Park.—Park Service photo

part, the slickrock canyon walls are white Navajo sandstone that have been colored by streaks of desert varnish and lichens. The red sandstone is from the Kayenta and Wingate formations. It is the Wingate that has been undercut in the canyon, forming "sandstone caves" and high arching overhangs.

About four miles down Muley Twist, after descending approximately 300 feet, you reach the junction of a cutoff trail to the Post on the left (east). Day hikers should not walk much farther south; either backtrack to the trailhead or take the 2.3 mile cutoff to the Post. If you keep going south through Muley Twist, it is eight more miles to Halls Creek, the continuation of Charles Hall's road to the old Colorado River crossing.

In 1880, Charles Hall operated the Hole-in-the-Rock ferry following its creation by Mormon pioneers. Business at the crossing was slow; not many cared to face such an arduous overland journey and nearly impossible descent to the river. Hall found a less hazardous Colorado River crossing and river approach about thirty-five miles up-river from Hole-in-the-Rock at a place today called Halls Crossing. Hall probably also blazed the trail across the Waterpocket Fold to the new crossing.

To reach the crossing, travelers struggled east from Escalante on the Hole-in-the-Rock Trail, then turned into Harris Wash. They then crossed the

Escalante River and ascended a short distance into the narrow canyon of Silver Falls Creek.

After reaching a mesa, the pioneers dropped into a funnel between two cliffs, descending 1,000 feet into a winding, deep canyon, today called Lower Muley Twist Canyon. In 1882, this canyon heard the rumble of wheels and braying of mules as a company moved through the narrow gorge to San Juan County, then a Mormon mission.

Today, little evidence remains of the pioneers' passage, but you can retrace their journey.

Near the end of Muley Twist, the canyon suddenly narrows and heads directly east. As the narrows open, you see sheer cliffs, the east rim of the Strike Valley formed by Halls Creek. Turn left (north) and continue five miles back to the Post, ascending about 300 vertical feet along the way.

The land here is parched and dry. You can hike the creek bed or follow an old jeep road. You pass reminders of use by stockmen over the years—bleached bones of range cattle, cowboy campsites, and trampled wash banks.

If a car has been parked at the Post, your hike is over. For those parked at the Burr Trail Road trailhead, you must decide whether to walk the Notom Road north and then up the Burr Trail Road switchbacks (4.3 miles) to the trailhead or return via the cutoff west and then north up Muley Twist (6.4 miles).— *George Davidson*

HIKE 61 *SWETT CANYON*

General description: A desert canyon hike to Hoskinnini Monument and Lake Powell.

General location: Thirty-seven miles southeast of Hanksville; southeast of the Henry Mountains.

Maps: Trails Illustrated Glen Canyon and Capitol Reef Map, and USGS Mount Holmes Quad.

Special attractions: Spectacular slickrock geology; solitude.

Best season for hike: Spring and fall.

For more inforrnation: Henry Mountains Resource Area, Bureau of Land Management, Box 99, Hanksville, UT 84734; (801) 542-3461.

The hike: The Little Rockies, an unprotected wilderness tucked away in Utah's slickrock country, offer an excellent backpacking experience. The two main peaks, Mt. Holmes (7,930 feet) and Mt. Ellsworth (8,235 feet), twist and spire 3,000 feet above the valley floor to form a rugged outline against the desert sky. The area is part of a 38,700-acre Bureau of Land Management (BLM) wilderness study area.

The 15-mile round trip winds through remote and seldom traveled country. There is little chance you will encounter many other hikers. From the trailhead

HIKE 61 *SWETT CANYON*

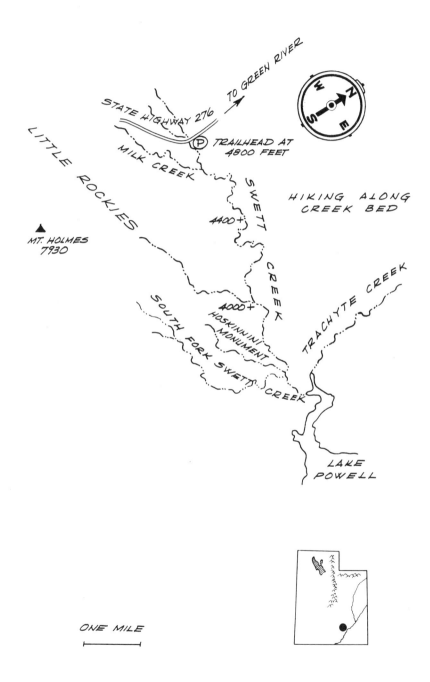

TO GREEN RIVER

STATE HIGHWAY 276

LITTLE ROCKIES

MILK CREEK

P TRAILHEAD AT 4800 FEET

SWETT CREEK

HIKING ALONG CREEK BED

4400+

MT. HOLMES 7930

4000+

HOSKINNINI MONUMENT

SOUTH FORK SWETT CREEK

TRACHYTE CREEK

LAKE POWELL

ONE MILE

at the Highway 276/Swett Creek junction, you descend about 1,100 feet to the shores of Lake Powell.

Access into Swett Creek is from State Highway 276—about fourteen miles south of its junction with State Highway 95. As you drive south on Highway 276, Mt. Holmes is straight ahead. Before the road swings to the southwest, away from and past Mt. Holmes, you cross Swett Creek where a large culvert allows the creek to pass under the road. Park on the east side of the road and begin the hike by passing downstream through the fifteen-foot culvert. The size of this giant culvert incidentally, is an indication of the expected size of the 100-year flood of Swett Creek.

Travel in the narrow canyon is between sandstone walls and over granitic stones and boulders in the streambed. Immense pressures from intrusive volcanic magma called a laccolith formed the Little Rockies and the Henry Mountains directly to the northwest. The laccolith is the source of much of the granitic rock found in the bottom of the river channels.

Because of this granite, sturdy hiking boots are recommended for the canyon. Even though you may get wet, your feet will be more comfortable in boots.

Swett Canyon is usually dry except for isolated pockets of water, which are not dependable. However, during a thunderstorm, the creek turns into a raging torrent, and the hike should never be attempted at this time.

No trail exists through the narrow, winding canyon except for the rocky creek bed. About .5 mile before reaching Lake Powell—seven miles down the canyon—look for Hoskinnini Monument. Hoskinnini was a Navajo chief who lived in Monument Valley and visited the area. The monument is a large rock monolith standing 400 feet high.

Campsites in the canyon are limited, and a good foam pad is advised. Firewood is very scarce, so use your backpacker stove.

As with other canyon hikes, be conscious of the weather. The high, narrow slickrock walls are an excellent channel for flash floods. Contact the BLM's Henry Mountains Resource Area office in Hanksville before making your trip.—*Tim Randle*

HIKE 62 *EGYPT-TWENTYFIVE MILE WASH*

General description: A demanding hike in the Escalante River drainage.
General location: Twenty-six miles southeast of Escalante, primarily in the Glen Canyon National Recreation Area.
Maps: Trails Illustrated Glen Canyon and Capitol Reef Map, and USGS Egypt and Sunset Flat Quads.
Special attractions: Desert hiking in deep, narrow and lush canyons; view of the Escalante canyons from high benches.
Best season for hike: Spring and fall.

Hiking the Escalante River inspires superlatives.—Utah Travel Council photo

For more information: Ranger Station, Glen Canyon National Recreation Area, Box 511, Escalante, UT 84726; (801) 826-4315.

The hike: This loop hike offers a diverse desert canyon hiking experience. The hike can vary in duration, depending on the number and length of side trips taken, but requires a minimum of two long days. The recommended and more leisurely trip, with time for exploring, takes four to five days.

The hike begins on Egypt Bench high above the Escalante River, descending about 1,050 feet into the Escalante River Canyon, continuing downriver to the confluence of Twentyfive Mile Wash. The route then snakes up Twentyfive Mile Wash, exits from the wash to the north, and concludes with a cross-country trek over slickrock back to Egypt Bench.

The loop totals about twenty miles. "In and out" options, rather than the full loop hike, are possible.

Water availability varies considerably from season to season. Check conditions with the National Park Service or the Bureau of Land Management (BLM) office in Escalante when you obtain your free backcountry permit. Boil all surface water, adding iodine or using an appropriate filtering technique.

Several locations along this hike can be extremely hazardous during flash

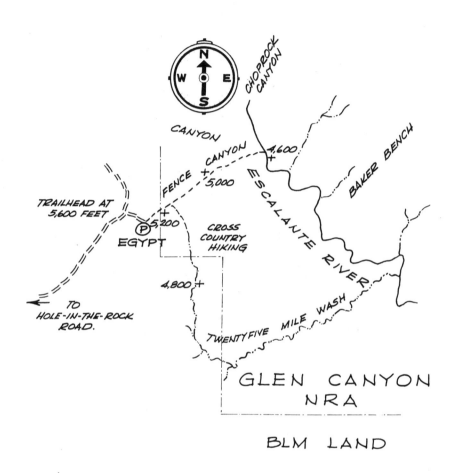

floods, so get an up-to-date forecast, and watch the weather.

You will be hiking in water during much of this trek, so use footwear that stands up to wet conditions, and provides sufficient ankle support. Army surplus "jungle boots" are ideal.

To reach the trailhead, drive east from Escalante on State Highway 12 about five miles to the Hole-in-the-Rock Road. Turn right and drive about twenty miles to the Egypt turnoff on the left. The road crosses the upper portion of Twentyfive Mile Wash within 3.5 miles and continues another six miles to the trailhead. About nine miles from the Hole-in-the-Rock Road, bear right. The trailhead is .5 mile farther. This road is usually passable in vehicles with moderate clearance, but check with the Park Service or BLM for current road conditions.

From the trailhead at about 5,600 feet, descend the bench over slickrock, using a stock trail partially cut into the rock. Head northeast between two short side canyons of the Escalante. Skirt the north rim of Fence Canyon, the more southern of the two canyons. You will be hiking cross-country on slickrock and sand. Just before you reach the junction of these two canyons, the stock trail descends into Fence Canyon. The distance from the trailhead to the junction is about two miles.

Thickly-vegetated Fence Canyon, only a mile long, has a small stream flowing most of the year. The cottonwood-willow vegetation community dominates the wash bottoms.

Hike in the wash bottoms whenever possible. In doing so, human traces are erased during high water. However, camping in wash bottoms can be dangerous.

Fires are not permitted, so use your backpacker stove. Fires cause considerable damage and their remains (ash and charcoal), not to mention rock rings, last for decades.

It is only .5 mile to the mouth of Fence Canyon and the Escalante River. The mouth of the river is at about 4,600 feet—1,000 feet below the trailhead. You descend less than 200 feet over the next five miles before leaving the Escalante at Twentyfive Mile Wash.

Prior to your hike down the Escalante, you might enjoy the side trip upstream about a mile to Choprock, or Widemouth, Canyon. The canyon enters from the right (east). The route offers interesting hiking in narrow, deeply incised canyons. However, do not hike here when bad weather threatens.

Since the hike down the Escalante follows the wash bottom, you will wade in waist deep water at times. The dense vegetation can make passage difficult. Cottonwood, willow, and tamarisk (an exotic) predominate here.

Locate the interesting Anasazi petroglyph panel on the bank of the river about .5 mile downstream from Fence Canyon. Remember, federal law protects all historical and archaeological resources. Do not disturb or deface these treasures in any way.

Continue another .5 mile to an old stock trail leading up and out the left (east) side of the canyon to Baker Bench. This canyon makes an interesting side trip. In only a short distance, you'll get an excellent view below to the

Escalante River.

Twentyfive Mile Wash is another 4.5 miles downstream. Before you reach it, however, there will be fine hiking along the Escalante. There are numerous benches and excellent campsites.

About .5 mile before Twentyfive Mile Wash, a canyon enters from the left (north) side of the Escalante. The river then bends around to the right. Locate Twentyfive Mile Wash entering from the right (west) just beyond the bend.

The lower, two-mile section of Twentyfive Mile Wash is narrow and winding. Watch for a small Anasazi ruin in an inaccessible alcove about fifty feet above the wash bottom.

Twentyfive Mile Wash drains a large area and is subject to flash flooding. The lower portion of this canyon provides little opportunity to climb to higher ground, so use caution.

You might explore some of the small side canyons off the lower portion of Twentyfive Mile Wash. Some of these canyons are deep, shady and lush, and offer interesting photographic opportunities.

About 6 miles up Twentyfive Mile Wash, a side canyon leads into Twentyfive from the right (north). It is the first large canyon upstream (.5 mile) from the Glen Canyon National Recreation Area boundary sign. This route is extremely brushy with deep beaver ponds to wade. A better route is to continue west beyond this side canyon about .75 mile to another place where you can exit Twentyfive Mile Wash on the right (north). Once you have exited Twentyfive Mile, hike cross country over slickrock, using Egypt Bench as your landmark until you reach the stock trail which you used to descend into Fence Canyon.
—*Jay Wells*

HIKE 63 *NAVAJO POINT*

General description: A demanding three-day hike, including a climb to the top of Fiftymile Mountain and cross-country travel.

General location: Forty-eight miles southeast of Escalante in the Glen Canyon National Recreation Area.

Maps: Southeastern Utah Multipurpose Map, and USGS Navajo Point and Sooner Bench Quads.

Special attractions: Spectacular views of the San Juan River canyon, the slickrock expanse but by the lower Escalante River, the maze of canyons and slickrock on the north side of Navajo Mountain, and the Rainbow Plateau.

Best season for hike: Late spring, early summer and fall.

For more inforrnation: Ranger Station, Glen Canyon National Recreation Area, Box 511, Escalante, UT 84726; (801) 826-4315.

The hike: Navajo Point on Fiftymile Mountain offers spectacular views of the Escalante River, San Juan River and the north side of Navajo Mountain— southeast across the former channel of the Colorado River, now Lake Powell.

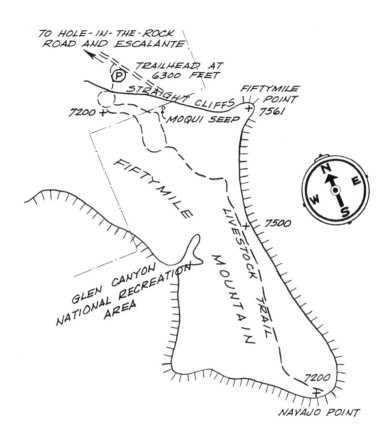

TO HOLE-IN-THE-ROCK
ROAD AND ESCALANTE

TRAILHEAD AT
6300 FEET

STRAIGHT CLIFFS

FIFTYMILE
POINT
7561

7200

MOQUI SEEP

FIFTYMILE

7500

LIVESTOCK TRAIL

GLEN CANYON
NATIONAL RECREATION
AREA

MOUNTAIN

7200

NAVAJO POINT

ONE MILE

Fiftymile Mountain, a major unroaded plateau known in early literature as Wild Horse Mesa, is surrounded by 1,000-foot cliffs and extremely rough canyons. It is part of a 146,000-acre Bureau of Land Management (BLM) wilderness study area.

Solitude predominates on this hike, as it is seldom used by visitors. The lack of reliable or usable water sources requires that hikers plan to carry all the water they need for the entire trip. The hike is recommended for those experienced in desert camping and travel.

You climb to 7,500 feet on the hike, but don't expect cool temperatures in summer. Travel here at this time of year is not recommended.

Pinyon, juniper, and open grass and sagebrush cover the top of the plateau, with aspen in isolated patches, usually at canyon heads. Archaeology in the area is significant because of the density of late Anasazi occupation sites.

Drive five miles east of Escalante on State Highway 12 and turn right on the Hole-in-the-Rock Road. After about forty-eight miles, turn right on the Sooner Slide Road. This is a seasonal road, and the going may be tough for low-clearance vehicles. Drive 4.7 miles up the steep and winding Sooner Slide Road until it forks on top of Fiftymile Bench (the bench below Fiftymile Mountain). Turn left (south) at the fork and continue about 2.2 miles to another fork. Stay to the right here. About 100 feet beyond the fork, an unmarked but visible trail

Lake Powell and Navajo Mountain from Navajo Point.—BLM photo

can be seen on the right heading west towards the Straight Cliffs. Park here to begin your hike to the top of Fiftymile Mountain.

At the base of the cliffs, you'll notice two trails to the top of Fiftymile Mountain. After hiking across the .5 mile flat to the base of the Straight Cliffs, take the newer trail to the north up Fiftymile Mountain. The steep climb to the top is only about .25 mile, but the ascent brings you from 6,500 feet at the base to 7,200 feet where the plateau begins.

Once on Fiftymile Mountain, the trail begins dropping into Trail Hollow Canyon draining to the west. When you come to the main canyon after .25 mile, follow it southeast through a wide flat. At the end of the flat (about .5 mile farther), head east toward the Straight Cliffs. Look for a camp which has been used for years by livestock people. There are remains of a prehistoric dwelling. This is also the location of Moqui Seep. The spring, located below the rim, is the last dependable water, but requires some thrashing through rosebushes and brush to reach it.

The top of Fiftymile Mountain is crisscrossed with numerous stock trails and following the pack trail shown on the Navajo Point quad is difficult in places. It heads south for 1.5 miles, then angles east toward the cliffs in order to cross a large canyon. After skirting the canyon, the trail stays close to the cliffs around a number of other canyons. After 1.5 miles, the trail leaves the rim and continues through pinyon and juniper another two miles to Navajo Point.

The distance from Moqui Seep to Navajo Point is approximately 5.5 miles. But don't be fooled by the topo map. The contour interval on the Navajo 7.5 minute quad is forty feet which makes the terrain look flat on the map; however, there is a lot of relief.

The view from Navajo Point is sometimes spoiled by haze or smog. The National Park Service has built a new marina at Dangling Rope Canyon which will also probably be visible from the point.

Fiftymile Mountain offers a wide variety of hiking experiences. The area has been spared from road building by its remoteness. This wilderness has remained intact, and you will see only minor evidence of human use.—*Bill Booker*

HIKE 64 *MOODY CREEK*

General description: A hike into remote and spectacular side canyons of the Escalante River.

General location: Thirty miles southeast of Boulder in the Glen Canyon National Recreation Area.

Maps: Southeastern Utah Multipurpose Map, and USGS Horse Pasture and Scorpion Gulch Quads.

Special attractions: Solitude; possibility of seeing desert bighorn sheep; and spectacular desert varnish walls.

Best season for hike: Spring and fall.

HIKE 64 *MOODY CREEK*

TO BOULDER

TRAILHEAD
AT ≈ 5000 FEET

+ 4,800

G L E N   CREEK

MIDDLE MOODY CANYON

HIKING ALONG
CREEK BED

SPRING
+ 4,600

C A N Y O N

MOODY

+ 4,800

EAST MOODY CANYON

4,400
+

ESCALANTE RIVER

N R A

ONE MILE

For more inforrnation: Ranger Station, Glen Canyon National Recreation Area, Box 511, Escalante, UT 84726; (801) 826-4315.

The hike: Moody Creek should be attempted only by hikers who are comfortable with and prepared for remote desert backpacking.

Water may be nonexistent except at the Escalante River, and you will probably be the only person for miles around—especially in off-seasons.

In spite of (or possibly because of) its remote nature, the Escalante country receives more and more use each year. Do your part to preserve this unique and fragile wilderness by camping with as little impact as possible.

Reaching the trailhead requires some navigational skills, since travel is on rough Bureau of Land Management (BLM) and Glen Canyon National Recreation Area roads. Signs are occasionally torn down, and new roads may develop, so use your maps carefully.

Drive east of Boulder on the Burr Trail. Turn right (south) onto either the Wolverine Petrified Wood Area Road (nineteen miles east of Boulder) or the unsigned Moody Creek Road (thirty-three miles east of Boulder). These two roads eventually intersect and continue south into Moody Creek. The road descends into the dry wash of Main Moody Canyon and follows it for about three miles, heading south at first. After turning and following the canyon west for about .75 mile, the road leaves the canyon and turns due east. Just after the road leaves the canyon, there is a parking area where the hike begins. Check with Glen Canyon officials on the condition of the roads before making the trip.

The hike begins in a dry, rocky stream bed in spacious upper Moody Creek. There are brilliant cactus blooms during mid-May after a wet spring. Indian paintbrush, red and blue penstemon, purple asters, and evening primrose are among the colorful wildflowers which abound.

About four miles from the parking area, Middle Moody Creek enters the main canyon from the left (east). The Escalante River is about 2.3 miles farther down the canyon.

Canyon walls loom over you during much of the hike to the Escalante, with huge, deep-red Wingate sandstone boulders and rock rubble along the way. You descend about 600 feet from the trailhead to the Escalante.

Notice the many pieces of petrified wood in the stream bed. Keep in mind however, that it is unlawful to collect specimens in the Glen Canyon National Recreation Area.

Excellent campsites exist at the mouth of Moody Creek. Unless recent rains have filled the pools of Moody Creek, the Escalante is your only water source, so purify the water. If you pack in a collapsible one gallon water container, the silted water can settle in it as you make camp.

From this base camp, it is about 1.5 miles downstream to the mouth of East Moody Canyon. Be prepared to do some scrambling on the Escalante River banks as you approach East Moody. If you are hiking in the early morning or evening, notice the splendid canyon wall reflections in the river.

You may see deer along the river, and coyotes, with their special rendition of canyon music, may pierce the evening air.

East Moody is narrow near its mouth, making boulder hopping necessary to hike up the canyon. About two miles from the mouth, observe the skyward-reaching walls covered with desert varnish. The mood changes here with the day's changing light. Reflected light from the opposite wall intensifies the colors and provides some excellent photographic opportunities. Pools from recent rains offer excellent reflection shots.

About three miles farther upstream, the canyon broadens. At the base of the cliff, you may see desert bighorn sheep, introduced by the Division of Wildlife Resources. (The National Park Service requests that you report any sheep sitings to the ranger in Escalante.) Golden eagles and canyon wrens are common. You may also see cougar tracks at some of the water holes, but it will be a unique experience, indeed, if you spot one of these secretive cats.

You could easily spend a lifetime in the remarkable Escalante country without seeing but a portion of its treasures. When you visit this area, respect it—for your own safety and for its continued beauty.—*John George*

HIKE 65 *UPHEAVAL DOME*

General description: A strenuous hike in the Island in the Sky district of Canyonlands National Park.
General location: Twenty-three miles southwest of Moab.
Maps: Trails Illustrated Island in the Sky Canyonlands National Park Map, USGS Upheaval Dome Quad, and Canyonlands National Park Map.
Special attractions: Outstanding views of canyon country, the Green River, and Upheaval Dome.
Best season for hike: Spring and fall.
For more information: Superintendent, Canyonlands National Park, 125 W. 200 S., Moab, UT 84532; (801) 259-7164.

The hike: The Upheaval Dome trip involves hiking in fairly rough terrain. The route offers the only access to the radically distorted and colorful rock interior of Upheaval Dome in Canyonlands National Park.

The round-trip around Upheaval Dome can be done in one day (six to eight hours). Extending the trip to the Green River opens up more magnificent scenery and would make an enjoyable overnighter. This plan, however, is not a good choice in the warm summer months.

To reach the trailhead, take State Highway 313 west from Highway 191 (about ten miles north of Moab). Continue about seventeen miles into Canyonlands National Park. A $3 per vehicle entrance fee is charged from mid-March through October.

The Island in the Sky Visitor Center is two miles farther. The Park Service asks that you pick up a free backcountry permit for overnight trips. Rangers there can advise you as to current trail conditions and regulations. Also, be sure

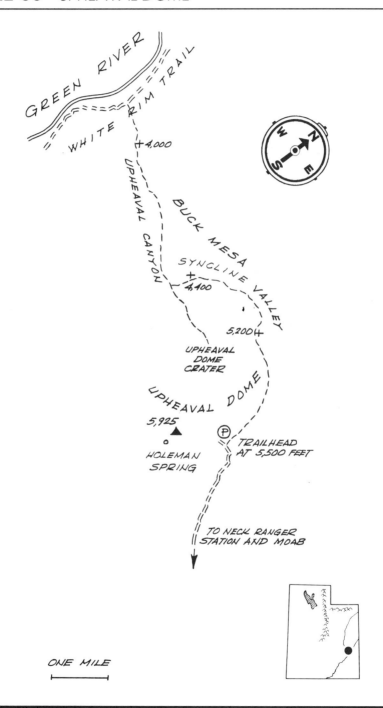

GREEN RIVER

WHITE RIM TRAIL

+ 4,000

UPHEAVAL CANYON

BUCK MESA

SYNCLINE VALLEY

+ 4,100

5,200 +

UPHEAVAL DOME CRATER

UPHEAVAL DOME

5,925 ▲

○ HOLEMAN SPRING

Ⓟ TRAILHEAD AT 5,500 FEET

TO NECK RANGER STATION AND MOAB

ONE MILE

Aerial view of Upheaval Dome, Canyonlands National Park. The Green River is in the background.—Park Service photo

to leave the visitor center with at least one gallon of water per person per day for your hike.

About six miles from the visitor center, turn right (west), driving 5.5 miles farther to the Upheaval Dome parking lot. Pick up a copy of the Crater View Trail Guide at the parking lot. By hiking this .5-mile trail first, you'll have a better understanding of Upheaval Dome and its geology. Returning from the Crater View Trail, take the Syncline Loop Trail in either direction to begin your adventure around Upheaval Dome.

Beginning in a counter-clockwise direction (around the eastern side of the dome), the trail descends 1,300 feet in four miles through Syncline Valley to Upheaval Canyon. At the junction of Syncline Valley and Upheaval Canyon, turn left (upstream in the normally dry wash) and hike about a mile into the interior of the basin at the center of the dome. Here, at about 1,300 feet below the Crater View Trail overlook, you may be able to see other park visitors gazing down upon you.

It's an "other world" experience. Geologists still don't know for sure what caused this medley of rock to dome up in the first place. Possibly, the crater is the result of an impact by an ancient meteorite. Another popular theory states that the layers of rock were forced up by a salt plug pushing from below. In the heat of summer, it's an oven and can be very warm in other seasons as well.

You can reach the Green River three miles downstream via Upheaval Canyon. After an initial 400-foot descent, the canyon opens into a huge desert flatland called Upheaval Bottom. Halfway across the bottom, you intersect the White Rim Road (4x4 road), a 100-mile loop that circles the entire Island in the Sky mesa. Campsites are available here on an advance reservation basis.

Just beyond the road, a wide band of willow, cottonwood, and tamarisk thickets border the river. Buried in the vegetation, but not difficult to find, is an old cowboy line camp corral and cabin. Following the wash will lead you to the river. Remember to treat any water for drinking.

Don't be surprised to see little wildlife and sparse vegetation. The canyon country is a harsh environment and requires large areas of land for its inhabitants to survive. Desert bighorn sheep, mule deer, coyotes, bobcats and the elusive cougar all inhabit this land. Many smaller mammals, birds and reptiles also call this country home. Please report any wildlife sightings to the Park Service.

The return trip around Upheaval Dome along its western side is strenuous. The loose talus slope can cause poor footing and one short section of trail traverses a ledge above a high cliff. The National Park Service has installed railings along the ledge for assistance, but be careful, you're on your own. Allow sufficient time and water to make this trip a safe one.—*Dave May*

HIKE 66 *DARK CANYON*

General description: A forty-mile backpack for experienced hikers.
General location: Twenty-five miles west of Blanding; south of Canyonlands National Park.
Maps: Trails Illustrated Manti-LaSal National Forest Map, and USGS Poison Canyon, Warren Canyon and Black Steer Canyon Quads.
Special attractions: Beautiful forest and desert scenery; Indian ruins; peace and solitude.
Best season for hike: Late spring to early summer, and fall.
For more inforrnation: Monticello Ranger District, Manti-LaSal National Forest, Box 820, Monticello, UT 84535; (801) 587-2041. Also, San Juan Resource Area, Bureau of Land Management, Box 7, Monticello, UT 84535 or call (801) 587-2141.

The hike: This loop hike in the canyons surrounding Dry Mesa—Woodenshoe, Dark, and Peavine canyons—measures about thirty-seven map miles, but with side excursions the trip can easily be extended to twice that. The Dark Canyon area is rich in biological, geological, archaeological, and historical perspectives and remains in a relatively pristine state. The Dark Canyon Wilderness, designated in 1984, encompasses 45,000 acres. The lower portion of Dark

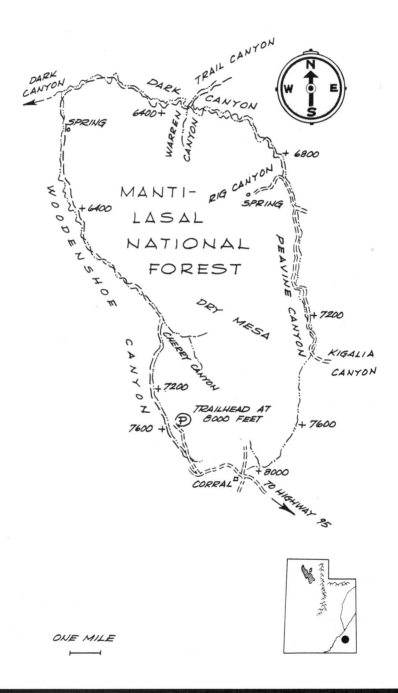

ONE MILE

Canyon is part of the 62,000 acre BLM Dark Canyon Primitive Area.

Hikers in Dark Canyon should be experienced in map reading and able to carry at least a full day's water supply in addition to food and equipment for a five- to seven-day trip. Even in the driest season, water is available about every five miles from springs, seeps, and intermittent streams, but water purification is recommended. The hike is a relatively dry one and can be stressful for persons unaccustomed to desert hiking and summer temperatures reaching 100 degrees Fahrenheit.

Although the hike does not require technical climbing equipment, the route is rugged and undeveloped. Beginning at about 8,500 feet on the plateau and rimrocks of Cedar Mesa sandstone, you descend 2,600 feet to the sandy, dry stream bed in the calcareous layers of the Hermosa formation.

Spring is the best time for making this hike, but hikers make the trip throughout the year. Thunderstorms may be encountered during the summer and early fall, but the canyon bottoms are relatively broad so flash flood danger is not as severe as elsewhere in the canyon country. However, there have been flooding problems in early spring. Some snow accumulates on the plateau in winter but does not present any problems in the canyon.

To reach the trailhead, turn north off State Highway 95 toward Natural Bridges National Monument east of Lake Powell and west of Blanding. After about a mile on the Natural Bridges Road, turn right and follow the graded road up Little Maverick Point and then over Bears Ears Pass. About two miles north of Bears Ears, turn left at a junction.

If you have two cars, leave one about two miles from the junction at a corral near the turnoff north to Twin Springs. This spot is near the head of Peavine Canyon where you will finish the hike. To find the trailhead, drive another two miles and turn right along the east side of upper Woodenshoe Canyon. This road ends within a few miles. Park at the end and scramble down the 300-foot slope to the west into Woodenshoe Canyon.

If you cross the creek bed, you will find an old road on the west side. This road is overgrown, but provides a good route through the upper part of the canyon.

The trail is intermittent for about three miles until you reach a horse path in the drainage. From here on, the hiking is relatively easy, descending gradually along the canyon bottom. About four miles from the trailhead, Cherry Canyon enters from the right (southeast). There is good camping here, and water is plentiful a short distance up Cherry. Hiking among small pools in the stream bed is fascinating.

You can find cliff dwellings about a mile down Woodenshoe beyond the mouth of Cherry Canyon. Three well-preserved petroglyphs are on the walls above the dwellings.

In another mile, an unnamed canyon enters from the east. Look for an arch shaped like a keyhole. There is a large concentration of cliff dwellings in this canyon, and water is also available here.

The tracks of wildlife mix with traces of ancient civilizations. The sandy stream beds reveal tracks of cougar, bear, deer, raccoon, and ring-tailed cat, along with smaller tracks of rodents. Over sixty species of mammals are present in the area. Brilliantly colored lizards sun themselves on rocks, and a variety of birds find an ideal habitat in these canyons.

From "Keyhole Arch Canyon," the sandy stream bed continues northwest with occasional large rocks in wash areas. The canyon walls become steeper and higher. About 2.5 miles down the canyon is a small seep, and approximately three miles farther, you'll see Wates Pond, an excellent camping spot.

The canyon leads due north from Wates Pond. You descend stream-worn steps of bedrock with embedded fossils. Occasionally, the trail wanders away from the stream bed through scrub oak and juniper. The area is strewn with brilliant lithic chips of chert and agate.

About a mile before Woodenshoe Canyon meets Dark Canyon, a spring trickles down from the east canyon wall. Just beyond, Dark Canyon descends to the left (west) toward the Colorado River. That route, however, is for another trip. To complete the loop, turn right (east) into upper Dark Canyon.

From the junction at about 6,100 feet, you climb about 500 feet to the next good campsite—six miles up the canyon, just a mile beyond the spot where Trail Canyon and Warren Canyon enter from the north and south, respectively. Lithic chips, pottery shards, sand dunes and water make for an interesting and comfortable camp.

For the next several miles, you traverse sagebrush flats. At the point where Rig Canyon enters Dark Canyon—about five miles from Trail Canyon—human intrusions (lumber, fences, a road, and a corral) begin to appear. About two miles up Rig Canyon, there is a spring and old oil drilling camp.

Continue southeast past Rig Canyon another mile to Peavine Canyon. Leave upper Dark Canyon here and head southeast on the jeep road into Peavine. In about five miles, the road jogs to the southeast into Kigalia Canyon. Head southwest, on the Peavine Canyon Trail. Peavine Canyon is beautiful with lush vegetation and a good water supply in the upper canyon.

During the final portion of the trip leading to the plateau, read your map carefully. An excellent source of water near the end of the trip provides pools large enough for a dip.

From where you left the jeep road at Kigalia Canyon, it is about five miles to the corrals near the top of Peavine Canyon. Here, you meet the road. If you spotted a car, your hike is over. Otherwise, you must hike about four miles to the trailhead.

This canyon loop around Dry Mesa offers rugged terrain, beautiful scenery, and solitude. Shorter trips in the area are possible, but a week in this splendid backcountry is time not soon forgotten.—*Flo Krall, Ramona Allen, and Bob Stack*

HIKE 67 *FABLE VALLEY*

General description: An in-and-out day trip or overnighter in the Dark Canyon Primitive Area.

General location: Thirty-three miles northwest of Blanding; south of Canyonlands National Park.

Maps: Trails Illustrated Manti-LaSal National Forest Map, and USGS Bowdie Canyon East and Fable Valley Quads.

Special Attractions: Varied scenery; wide range of animal life.

Best season for hike: Late spring to early summer, and fall.

For more information: San Juan Resource Area, Bureau of Land Management, Box 7, Monticello, UT 84535; (801) 587-2141.

The hike: Fable Valley provides a gentle alternative to the steeply walled canyons of the Dark Canyon area just to the south. This open, shallow valley with its sagebrush, grass and sloping sandstone walls makes for pleasant hiking. Fable Valley is part of the Bureau of Land Management's (BLM's) 62,000-acre Dark Canyon Primitive Area. The trail begins just west of the Sweet Alice Hills on Dark Canyon Plateau.

To reach the trailhead, turn north off State Highway 95, toward Natural Bridges National Monument east of Lake Powell and west of Blanding. After about a mile on the Natural Bridges Road, turn right and follow the graded road up Little Maverick Point and then over Bears Ears Pass. About two miles north of the pass, turn right at the junction. Follow Forest Road #88 northeast past Arch Canyon Overlook. Turn left two miles further and head north past The Notch and Duck Lake to the North Long Point Road (Forest Road #91). Turn left here and continue west. Six and a half miles west of the Trail Canyon trailhead, at the junction of Lean-to Point and Fable Valley Pasture, there is a signpost that marks an old road heading north into Fable Valley Canyon. Park here.

Walk two miles to the canyon rim, where you'll find a corral and old stock trail leading to the canyon floor. Once in the bottom, the trail is hard to follow at times, winding in and out of the wash, and staying mostly on the benches above the streambed.

There is a good spring at Fable Spring and a side canyon worth exploring. Generally, water can be found from here intermittently down the rest of the canyon, until the trail rises at a large waterfall. The trail ends at the intersection with a jeep road one mile south of Home Spring, in Beef Basin. Although it passes through a lot of dense brush, this is a fairly easy trail.—*Monticello Ranger District*

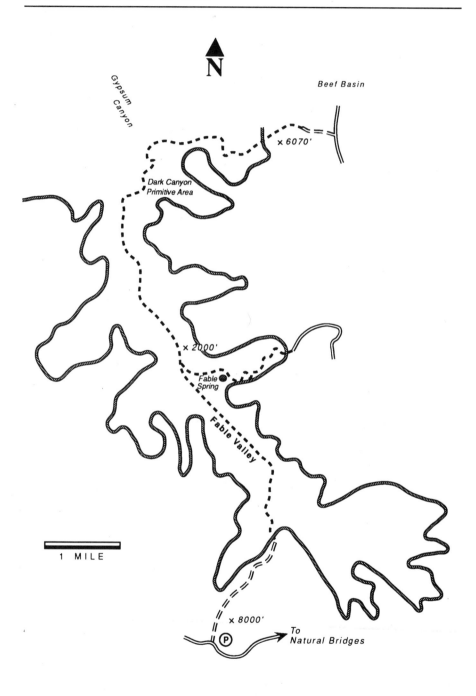

N

Gypsum Canyon

Beef Basin

× 6070'

Dark Canyon
Primitive Area

× 2000'

Fable
Spring

Fable Valley

1 MILE

× 8000'

P   To
Natural Bridges

HIKE 68 *BRIDGES LOOP*

General description: An enjoyable day hike to three natural bridges, with extensive prehistoric Indian ruins and rock art, involving easy walking and no unusual hazards.

General location: Twenty-eight miles west of Blanding in Natural Bridges National Monument.

Maps: Trails Illustrated Manti-LaSal National Forest Map, and USGS Moss Back Butte and Kane Gulch Quads.

Special attractions: Three huge natural sandstone bridges; Anasazi Indian ruins; pictographs and petroglyphs; wide range of vegetation types; and spectacular cliff and canyon scenery.

Best season tor hike: Spring and fall.

For more inforrnation: Superintendent, Natural Bridges National Monument, Box 1, Lake Powell, UT 84533; (801) 259-5174.

The hike: The bridges loop hike—about nine miles—is a superb day trip suitable for experienced hikers and reasonably active families. The unmaintained trail follows White Canyon and Armstrong Canyon past three natural bridges and Anasazi ruins. The only appreciable elevation change involves climbing into and out of the canyons; these stretches are steep but short.

Cars can be left at the Sipapu and Owachomo trailheads. This shuttle shortens the hike by about 2.5 miles. However, if only one car is available, a maintained trail leads from the road above Owachomo Bridge back to Sipapu.

Camping in the monument (except in the developed campground), and overnight parking on Bridge View Drive are prohibited. Nearly all hikers make the loop in a counter-clockwise direction because it is easier. Also, since the loop has an alternate access point near the halfway point (Kachina Bridge), the trip can be easily modified.

From State Highway 95 west of Blanding and southeast of the Hite Bridge, turn north onto State Highway 275 for five miles to Natural Bridges National Monument. Three-quarters of a mile after the visitor center, just inside the monument boundary, is the beginning of eight-mile-long Bridge View Drive. Turn right on the one-way loop and continue about 1.75 miles to the Sipapu Trail. (You pass Sipapu Overlook along the way.)

Follow the trail to the White Canyon stream bed near Sipapu Bridge. This first stretch is only about .5 mile, but you descend about 500 vertical feet in the process. If you looked at the bridge from the overlook or viewpoint before dropping down into the canyon, you will be astonished at how large the bridge is up close. It's a common canyon country and desert phenomenon. Natural features are often larger than they appear to be from a distance. The lack of familiar objects of known size precludes an accurate size estimate by one's mind, and the brain consistently underestimates.

Owachomo Bridge along Armstrong Canyon, Natural Bridges National Monument.—Utah Travel Council photo

The rock of the Natural Bridges area is a crossbedded sandstone known as the Cedar Mesa sandstone. It is of Permian age, more than 225 million years old.

Long after the land here began its slow rise from an ancient sea bed, two small streams formed on the western slopes of Elk Ridge and made meandering channels across the flat land. They gradually entrenched themselves while the land underwent new uplift. As the land continued to rise, the streams cut even deeper channels—known today as White and Armstrong canyons.

Every stream attempts to make a straight channel with an even grade from its source to its mouth. Any obstacles, such as hills or large rock masses, are gradually worn away. Thus, these winding streams constantly tried to straighten their courses. During floods, silt-laden waters were thrown with great force against the walls of the meanders. In several places, a fin of rock around which the stream wound was so thin that over many centuries a hole was gradually bored, and a natural bridge was born. The stream continued to cut its channel and, with the aid of other processes of erosion, to enlarge the opening. Eventually, the old meander was left high and dry as a "fossil" stream bed.

Most of the natural bridges in the United States are in the Four Corners region of the Southwest, where favorable materials and conditions for bridge

HIKE 68 *BRIDGES LOOP*

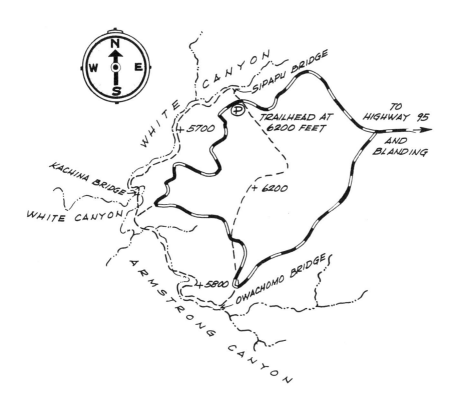

N
W E
S

WHITE CANYON

SIPAPU BRIDGE

+ 5700

TRAILHEAD AT
6200 FEET

TO
HIGHWAY 95

AND
BLANDING

KACHINA BRIDGE

WHITE CANYON

+ 6200

OWACHOMO BRIDGE

+ 5800

ARMSTRONG CANYON

ONE MILE

making exist. Rainbow Bridge, south of here on Lake Powell, is the world's largest.

Leaving Sipapu, walk down the canyon (west and south) in or along the stream bed. There is no developed and maintained trail, so follow the drainage.

Not far from Sipapu, on a broad ledge sheltered by an alcove on the right, Horsecollar Ruins is worth a stop. It is an Anasazi village, abandoned 800 or more years ago but still in good shape. Remember, these sites are irreplaceable. Don't enter the structures, climb on them, rub the mortar, or wiggle rocks. The Park Service and BLM have found that "innocent vandalism" damages more of these ancient treasures than malicious effort. That's because only a few nuts want to destroy them, but thousands of us want to touch them. The result is less dramatic, but inevitably the same—destruction of the art and architecture left by the previous owner of this real estate.

About two miles downstream from Sipapu, Kachina Bridge spans the canyon in massive grandeur. More Anasazi ruins are on the right just beyond the bridge, and rock art is on the near abutments. Most of the ancient dwellings are in positions exposed to the winter sun but sheltered from the hottest summer sun, a very effective use of passive solar energy.

Immediately beyond Kachina, White Canyon bears right (west) and, on the left (east), Armstrong Canyon enters. Head up Armstrong Canyon. There's usually a nice pool at the foot of a dry falls near the mouth of Armstrong. It's a great place to frolic in the cool water, but it's also in plain view of a heavily-visited overlook on the canyon rim. You may want to be discreet.

Continue up Armstrong Canyon about three miles, following the stream bed, until you get to Owachomo natural bridge. This very old, thin, and delicate bridge does not span Armstrong Canyon; it parallels it. Owachomo's evolution has been very different from that of the other bridges. Although unlikely, it is possible to walk right by Owachomo without seeing it. A very short distance up the canyon, hikers encounter a fairly large pool at the junction of Armstrong and Tuwa canyons. Tuwa enters from the left (east). Depending on the quantity and temperature of the water in the pool, it can be a very pleasant swimming hole. If you get to the pool without seeing Owachomo, however, you've gone a little too far.

At Owachomo Bridge, climb the short but steep trail north up to the park road on the mesa top. Cross the road and continue on the trail about two miles back to the Sipapu trailhead. This portion of the hike travels through the "pygmy forest" of pinyon and juniper, typical of most of the area for miles around. On spring trips you may encounter wildflowers. At any season, birds, small animals, and occasional deer can be seen. Be meticulous about staying on the trail. A very delicate soil/lichen/plant community covers much of the area. Walking across a patch of this cryptogamic crust can create a long-lasting disturbance.—*Dave May*

HIKE 69 GRAND GULCH

General description: A three-day to two-week hike in an outstanding desert canyon.

General location: Twenty-five miles southwest of Blanding in the Grand Gulch Primitive Area.

Maps: Trails Illustrated Grand Gulch Map, and USGS Kane Gulch, Cedar Mesa North, Pollys Pasture, Red House Spring, and Slickhorn Canyon West Quads.

Special attractions: A unique and fragile combination of archaeology and wilderness.

Best season for hike: Spring and fall.

For more information: San Juan Resource Area, Bureau of Land Management, Box 7, Monicello, UT 84535; (801) 587-2141.

Grand Gulch is much more than a hike; it is a trip through 2,000 years of history. The Anasazi civilization flourished here, and signs of their architectural skills are common as you hike along the creek, dwarfed by massive sandstone walls.

The Bureau of Land Management (BLM) established Grand Gulch as a primitive area in 1970. Since then, the hike has been extremely popular, and annual use figures have risen dramatically. The BLM has begun directing traffic to some of the nearby canyons to minimize the impacts in Grand Gulch. Responsible backcountry ethics are increasingly important as more and more hikers discover the area.

Grand Gulch has three main trailheads—Kane Gulch, Bullet Canyon, and Collins Spring. Kane Gulch, near the top of the canyon, is the most popular. Grand Gulch joins Kane Gulch about four miles from the trailhead and then winds about fifty miles to the San Juan River. Bullet Canyon enters from the east about a third of the way down, and the drainage from Collins Spring enters from the northwest about two-thirds down the gulch. Ask the BLM for more information on these two additional trailheads.

Few hikers actually hike all the way to the San Juan River and back out again. But with the trailhead options and the considerable length of Grand Gulch, trips of a few nights up to two weeks are possible. Most hikers enter at Kane Gulch, hike for a day or two, and then retrace their steps.

To reach the Kane Gulch trailhead, take State Highway 261 off State Highway 95 east of Natural Bridges National Monument and west of Blanding. Drive about four miles and turn right on the road into the Kane Gulch Ranger Station.

The station is usually open between March 1 and November 15. Get a backcountry permit here, as well as information on protecting the area.

The Kane Gulch Trail follows Kane Wash from the ranger station. Beginning at about 6,400 feet, the trail descends along a wash bottom for about a mile and

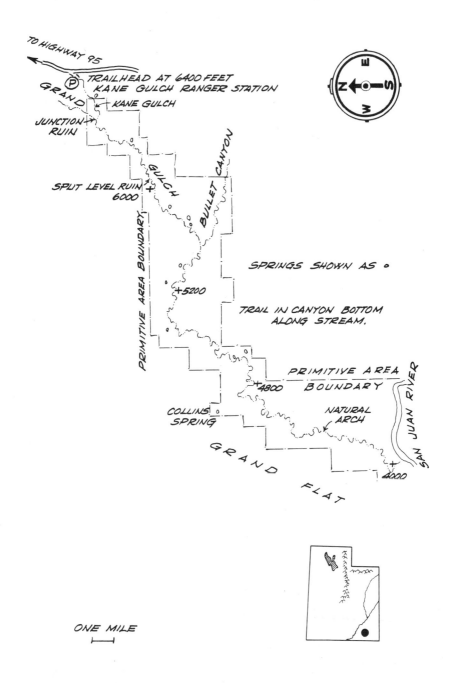

TO HIGHWAY 95

TRAILHEAD AT 6400 FEET
KANE GULCH RANGER STATION

KANE GULCH

GRAND

JUNCTION
RUIN

SPLIT LEVEL RUIN
6000

GULCH

BULLET CANYON

+5200

SPRINGS SHOWN AS ○

TRAIL IN CANYON BOTTOM
ALONG STREAM.

PRIMITIVE AREA BOUNDARY

PRIMITIVE AREA
BOUNDARY

+4800

COLLINS
SPRING

NATURAL
ARCH

SAN JUAN RIVER

GRAND FLAT

+4000

ONE MILE

then enters the canyon bottom—following the right (northwest) side. Work your way along ledges and around large boulders and pour offs. Richard Wetherill, exploring in the late nineteenth century, used this trail first, and ranchers later improved it to move cattle.

After hiking about 4.5 miles and descending 500 feet, you arrive at Junction Ruins, the largest in the canyon. This beautiful spot at the junction of Kane and Grand gulches has several fine campsites beneath large cottonwoods. If you decide to stay here for the night—as do many hikers—you will want to explore the area after making camp.

Many ruins are nearby. You may learn from the BLM that recent impacts have caused considerable damage. Although the Antiquities Act and the Archaeological Resources Protection Act of 1979 (see page 9) protect artifacts, they have been routinely carried out of Grand Gulch over the years, diminishing the value of this outdoor museum. Still, you will find the area fascinating. You can do your small part by not climbing over ruins. Also, avoid walking in the midden heaps (areas used for trash disposal by ancient occupants of the ruin).

Water can be found in many areas of the Gulch. However, drought, flooding, and the time of year can affect runoff or eliminate water sources. Check with the BLM's San Juan Resource Area Office or with the ranger at Kane Gulch before beginning your hike. Increased visitation in Grand Gulch threatens the water quality. Boiling water or treating with iodine is recommended to prevent the threat of *Giardia* (see page 16).

Below Junction Ruins, Grand Gulch meanders toward the San Juan, among cottonwoods and the geological formations of the Cedar Mesa sandstone. Many of the south-facing alcoves contain Anasazi ruins. Some are near the canyon bottom; others are high in seemingly unreachable niches. Of particular interest are Turkey Pen and Split Level ruins, but you will also enjoy discovering many of the unnamed ruins in the numerous side canyons. You can spend days in these side canyons, and the distance you eventually hike down Grand Gulch will depend on the amount of exploring you do.

Several books record the history and archaeology of Grand Gulch. The first documented exploration and extensive excavation of the canyon occurred in 1891-93 by Charles McCloyd and Charles Cary Graham. They entered Bullet Canyon, then called Graham Canyon, from the rim and left their signatures in several locations, using charcoal or a lead bullet as a writing tool (see Anasazi of Falls Creek by Helen Sloan Daniels).

Richard Wetherill was the next to enter Bullet Canyon as part of the Hyde expedition during 1894-95. He made a second trip in 1897 (see Anasazi by Richard Wetherill).

An excellent book on Grand Gulch, as well as other canyons in the area, is Wind in the Rock by Ann Zwinger. It is a perfect introduction to Grand Gulch.

Pot hunting and collecting have occurred through the years. In 1970, when Grand Gulch was declared a primitive area, this activity became rampant, and the ranger program was initiated in 1973. Pot hunting and vandalism still occur, and you can help by reporting any violations to the BLM.

As you hike in Grand Gulch, you may see several wildlife species. The ideal cover, water conditions, and lack of domestic grazing means an abundance of towhees, woodpeckers, owls, and hawks. The ringtail cat is becoming a frequent visitor at camps. Fox, bats and an occasional mountain lion or mule deer make wildlife observation exciting.—*Fred Blackburn*

HIKE 70 *FISH CREEK AND OWL CREEK LOOP*

General description: A fifteen- to twenty-five-mile loop hike in spectacular desert canyons.
General location: Twenty miles southwest of Blanding.
Maps: Southeastern Utah Multipurpose Map, and USGS Bluff, Cedar Mesa, and Bears Ears Quads.
Special attractions: Nevill's Arch; two unnamed arches; Anasazi sites; and solitude.
Best season for hike: Spring and fall.
For more information: San Juan Resource Area, Bureau of Land Management, Box 7, Monticello, UT 84535; (801) 587-2141.

The hike: This wonderful canyon hike is becoming a popular backpack for hikers of all ages. The area is experiencing increased visitation as a result of overcrowding in Grand Gulch—just to the west on the other side of State Highway 261. The Bureau of Land Management (BLM) has begun developing and publicizing the Fish and Owl complex as an "overflow" area for Grand Gulch.

Keep this in mind while you hike. More hikers, of course, mean more impact on the land. Do your part by "walking softly"—keep a clean camp, use your backpacker stove, respect the privacy of other hikers, and, above all, do not climb on Anasazi ruins. The BLM is finding that innocent but frequent hiker impacts on these ruins can do as much harm as isolated cases of malicious damage.

Fish Creek and Owl Creek offer an environment quite different from Grand Gulch. While pinyon, juniper, and yucca vegetate the gravel and dirt bottoms in Grand Gulch, hiking in Fish and Owl is along a slickrock stream bed in the upper canyon areas and along sand-cemented gravel near the junction. Vegetation ranges from yucca, prickly pear, pinyon, and juniper to the spectacular ponderosa pine and manzanita groves in upper Fish Creek.

From State Highway 95 east of Natural Bridges National Monument and west of Blanding, drive south on State Highway 261. In about 4 miles, you pass the Kane Gulch Ranger Station on your right. Drive another 1.5 miles and turn left on a graded road. After about five miles on this road, you arrive at the trailhead at a reclaimed drill hole.

The loop hike can be done in either direction, but the trailhead is closer to

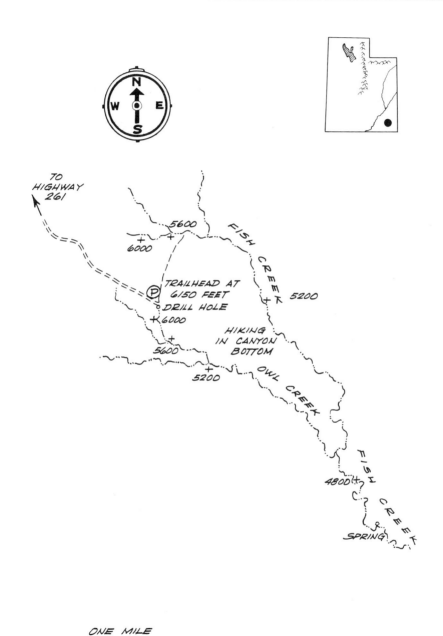

TO
HIGHWAY
261

5600
+
6000

FISH CREEK

TRAILHEAD AT
6150 FEET
DRILL HOLE
+6000

5200
+

5600
+

5200
+

HIKING
IN CANYON
BOTTOM

OWL CREEK

FISH CREEK

4800'+

SPRING

ONE MILE

Owl Creek, and BLM cairns lead .25 mile south to this canyon, so most hikers enter Owl Creek and exit through Fish Creek to the north.

The 6.5-mile hike from the trailhead to the Fish and Owl junction descends about 1,400 feet. At the junction, you begin regaining this elevation. It is another nine miles back to your car.

Follow the BLM cairns to Owl Canyon. You will shinny down sandstone, pass a small Anasazi site, and become immersed in the canyon. Two pour offs have to be navigated before you reach fresh water at the first canyon split—about 1.5 miles from the rim.

At both pour offs, cairns mark a path on the left side. At the bottom of the second is a good campsite for the first night. A spring is here, as well as several side canyons worthy of exploration.

Except for the pools, Owl Creek is usually dry between this spot and the middle of Fish Creek, about nine miles away. Plan accordingly for this dry stretch ahead. (It can be wetter during spring melt.)

Upon reaching the Fish and Owl junction, turn left (north) and begin winding up Fish Creek. This beautiful canyon has 400-foot walls dotted with many Anasazi sites, with hiking primarily on ledged slickrock, creating many pools.

About six miles up Fish Creek is a major junction. Take the left (west) fork and continue .5 mile to a spring. A good campsite exists here, not far from the trail out of the canyon to the top. This is a good place to camp for a day or two in order to explore the upper reaches of Fish Creek. Here, towering ponderosa pines reach for the canyon rim, and dense patches of manzanita carpet what little terrain is not slickrock.

If you encounter rain, by all means go hiking, but as with other canyon hikes, check with a local resource area office for an extended forecast. Avoid hiking in narrow canyons if the weather looks bad and don't camp in a wash bottom. However, if you're prepared for it, a storm in canyon country can be a delightful experience. The canyons turn silver as countless cascading rivulets pour over the rims, down slickrock walls, and into the stream bed.

The climb out begins at the spring on the south wall of Fish Creek's Left Fork. The steep, 600-foot climb requires a slow, steady pace. There are no dangerous exposures, and at the top, several places just under the rim allow you to climb out. Take one of these routes and then locate the well-used trail at the canyon edge which heads south 1.5 miles to your car at the trailhead.

The Fish Creek and Owl Creek area is now part of a 50,000-acre BLM wilderness study area. After you hike, you may want to write a letter to your congressmen, the BLM, and the Utah Wilderness Association in favor of wilderness designation.—*Bruce Hucko.*

HIKE 71 ARCH CANYON

General description: A little-known canyon on Bureau of Land Management and Forest Service land suitable for two to four day backpacking trips.
General Location: Thirteen miles southwest of Blanding.
Maps: Trails Illustrated Manti-LaSal National Forest Map, and USGS South Long Point and Hotel Rock Quads.
Special attractions: Easy access by car; many Anasazi ruins; and solitude.
Best season for hike: Late spring and early fall.
For more information: For the lower canyon, San Juan Resource Area Bureau of Land Management, Box 7, Monticello UT 84535; (801) 587-2141. For the upper canyon, Monticello Ranger District, Manti-LaSal National Forest, Box 820, Monticello, UT 84535; (801) 587-2041.

The hike: The high, forested massif of the Abajo Mountains is drained by numerous canyons, many of which are not only fascinating to explore but difficult to reach by road. For this reason, the area offers more solitude than other, better-known parts of Utah's redrock country. In addition, spring snow melt in the mountains above ensures a steady flow of water in many canyons, making desert backpacking less of a chore than usual. The Anasazi Indians found the area ideal, and most south-facing alcoves contain evidence of their culture, from petroglyphs and three-bushel granaries to multi-leveled apartments and kivas. You can help preserve these sites by not climbing on walls or camping in alcoves with ruins. Of course, all artifacts are protected by state and federal antiquities acts.

Arch Canyon, on Bureau of Land Management (BLM) and Forest Service land due east of Natural Bridges and west of Blanding, receives little use compared with the better-known Grand Gulch and Dark Canyon primitive areas. Yet it offers outstanding scenery and numerous ruins; also, it is comparatively easy to get to by car.

To reach the entrance to Arch Canyon, take State Highway 95 south from Hanksville, cross Lake Powell at Hite Marina, and continue toward the entrance to Natural Bridges National Monument, forty-three miles from Lake Powell. Continue east on Highway 95 for nineteen miles through pinyon and juniper forest until the road dips rapidly toward the floor of Comb Wash. You'll see Comb Ridge straight ahead, apparently blocking your way. It's a rock wall several hundred feet high and about twenty miles long. Just before the highway crosses the wash on a steel bridge, take a dirt road to the left and drive up the left side of the wash for about five miles, passing a corral and ranch buildings—still in use, incidentally. About 200 yards beyond the ranch, the road turns east to cross the wash. Park here, in a grove of giant cottonwoods. About 100 yards upstream, Arch Canyon Creek issues from a slot in a steep sandstone slope on your left.

Arch Canyon is about thirteen miles long, climbing gradually from 5,000

Backpacker entering Arch Canyon.—John Tallmadge photo

feet at the trailhead to 8,000 feet at its upper reaches, northeast of Bears Ears. Several tributaries of four to six miles make the hiking possibilities quite varied. A number of deep pools in the stream make for good swimming and wading early in the summer, and several tiny waterfalls occur where rock strata come together. Campsites are easy to find all along the canyon. Few fire scars exist here, so use discretion when choosing a spot for your kitchen. A backpacking stove is recommended.

The water in Arch Canyon has been reported good by some hikers, but due to wildlife and domestic grazing upstream, treatment is recommended. Also, deer flies can be numerous in the summer. Take along a good insect repellent, even during late spring.

Arch Canyon has a floor of red, sandy soil that supports a heavy growth of sagebrush, yucca, pinyon pine, juniper, cactus, and wildflowers. Most of these bloom in May and June, when there is plenty of water in the ground.

Enter the canyon through its narrow outlet in the sandstone wall and be sure to close the stock gate behind you. Immediately inside the entrance is a cluster of ruins which the BLM has tried to protect from trampling by cattle with a chain link fence. Fortunately, the destruction only extends this far—the rest of the canyon has been left alone, and grazing does not appear to be heavy.

After 2.5 miles of gentle hiking, the first tributary canyon enters from the

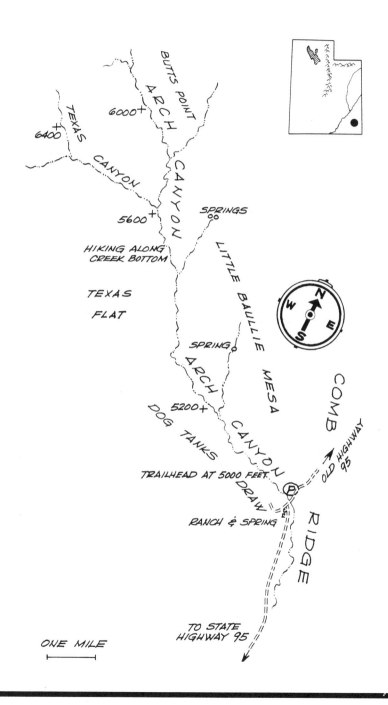

BUTTS POINT

ARCH CANYON

TEXAS
6400 +

6000 +

TEXAS CANYON

5600 +

SPRINGS

HIKING ALONG
CREEK BOTTOM

LITTLE BAULLIE MESA

TEXAS

FLAT

SPRING

ARCH

5200 +

CANYON

DOG TANKS

DRAW

TRAILHEAD AT 5000 FEET

P

OLD HIGHWAY 95

COMB RIDGE

RANCH & SPRING

TO STATE
HIGHWAY 95

ONE MILE

right (north). Near its head, about 1.5 miles upstream, is a spring and a ruin. The next tributary also enters from the right, another 3.5 miles farther up the main canyon. As you approach, the walls become steeper and higher, with more precipitous and photogenic rock formations. In late spring, wildflowers abound along here, particularly the sego lily, lupine, penstemon, and desert paintbrush, not to mention the extravagant pincushion, claret cup, and prickly pear cactus. This second tributary also contains a cliff dwelling and a spring near its head—1.5 miles to the north.

At the mouth of the second tributary, you will have climbed 500 feet from the trailhead.

One-and-one-half miles farther, after entering the Manti-LaSal National Forest, Texas Canyon joins Arch Canyon from the left (west) in a beautiful grove of ponderosa pine. Several excellent camping spots exist nearby, and directly opposite, on the canyon's northeast wall, is a massive circular arch which catches the full light of the evening sun. While the rock behind the arch remains in shadow, the arch seems to swell up out of the canyon wall, as if it had just been cast in molten gold.

Texas Canyon heads due west for two miles and then forks. It has many exciting rock formations and is well-worth exploring. Arch Canyon also forks into Butts Canyon about a mile above its junction with Texas. Both branches have numerous steep alcoves and castellated buttresses which offer interesting possibilities for climbs and photographs. You could easily spend a week in the Arch Canyon system and never waste a minute.

Arch Canyon is part of a BLM wilderness study area. Until *(and unless)* it is officially designated as wilderness, you may encounter occasional ORV use on the rough jeep road which extends several miles into the canyon.—*John Tallmadge*

HIKE 72 *MULE CANYON*

General description: An easily accessible day hike or overnighter in a canyon of the Grand Gulch Plateau.

General location: Eighteen miles southwest of Blanding.

Maps: Trails Illustrated Manti-LaSal National Forest Map, and USGS South Long Point and Hotel Rock Quads.

Special attractions: Quiet canyon hiking; Anasazi ruins; and archaeoastronomy sites.

Best season for hike: Spring and fall.

For more information: San Juan Resource Area, Bureau of Land Management, Box 7, Monticello, UT 84535; (801) 587-2141.

The hike: Mule Canyon offers an easily accessible canyon trip. Hikers of all ages enjoy the Cedar Mesa sandstone, Indian ruins, and solitude. You can hike in Mule Canyon during any season, although caution is advised in winter due

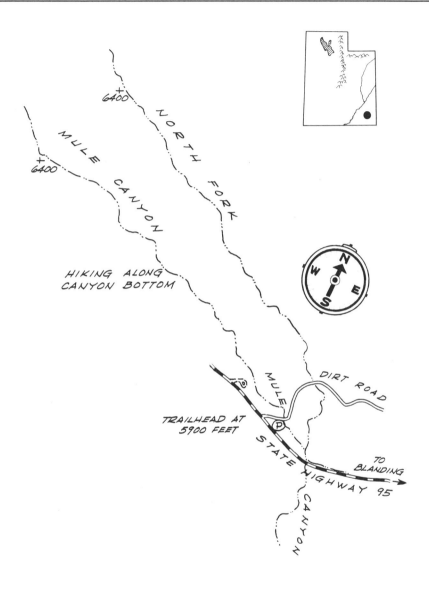

NORTH FORK

6400

MULE CANYON

6400

HIKING ALONG
CANYON BOTTOM

N
W E
S

DIRT ROAD

MULE

TRAILHEAD AT
5900 FEET

P

TO
BLANDING

STATE HIGHWAY 95

CANYON

ONE MILE

to potentially icy conditions. Access may also be limited during this season.

State Highway 95 crosses Mule Canyon west of Blanding, just south of where Mule and the North Fork join. Day hikes and overnighters are excellent in both of these canyons. Mule Canyon carves its way south of Highway 95; however, deep pour offs (dry waterfalls) make hiking more difficult here.

To reach the trailhead, take State Highway 95 to a dirt road (old Highway 95) which exits to the north about twenty-three miles west of Blanding. This road is about .5 mile east of a stabilized roadside ruin called Mule Canyon Ruins and a mile west of the Highway 95/Mule Canyon junction.

In .5 mile, this dirt road crosses Mule Canyon. Park here to begin your hike. The North Fork of Mule Canyon, also an excellent hike, is .75 mile farther up the road. You may want to try this hike another time.

The canyons in this upper stretch are ideal for a family outing, winding through the pinkish white sandstone of the Cedar Mesa and highlighted by relict Douglas fir and ponderosa pine.

From the trailhead at about 6 000 feet, the canyon meanders approximately seven miles to 7,600 feet. Occasionally, a cliff dwelling shows among the trees. Splendid opportunities exist here to appreciate the crafts of the late Pueblo II and III Anasazi cultures, although pottery shards, flint, and other artifacts have been carried off by hikers who ignored the value of the outdoor museum. Remember that all artifacts are protected by federal law (see page 9); do your part by leaving artifacts where you find them.

The many beautiful seeps along the canyon walls support patches of red monkey-flower, shooting star, columbine, and the rare canyon orchid.

You may see mule deer, as the canyon serves as a migratory area, and occasionally predators. Watch for birds of prey soaring above the canyon.

Many of the cliff dwellings have a long "defensive wall" with holes pointing toward different directions of the canyon. These ports, according to some archaeoastronomers, may have been built with the solstices in mind.

One site in the canyon may be connected with present Zuni puberty rites. As the sun sets during the summer solstice, it shines through a port and sends a beam of light below a petroglyph representing a woman. A Zuni legend says, "A light shown through the port, impregnated the woman and the twins were born."

These sites combine rock art, building structure, and modern Zuni ethnography for a fascinating new aspect to Anasazi culture.—*Fred Blackburn*

HIKE 73 *MARCHING MEN AND TOWER ARCH*

General description: An easy hike into a wonderland of sandstone formations.
General location: Sixteen miles northwest of Moab in the northwest corner of Arches National Park.

Petroglyphs, Arches National Park.—John George photo

Maps: Trails Illustrated Arches National Park Map and USGS Klondike Bluffs.
Special attractions: Uniquely eroded sandstone "marching men"; Tower Arch; and an historical inscription left by the man who first suggested that this area be preserved.
Best season for hike: Fall through spring.
For more information: Superintendent, Arches National Park, P.O. Box 907, Moab, UT 84532; (801) 259-8161.

The hike: Arches National Park offers a number of "major attractions" served by developed trails, but each of these destinations also has opportunities for informal side trips or extensions. Additionally, many very pleasant places are not served by trails but are still easily accessible. If you get to wandering around off of the trails, you're likely to want to make a habit of it.

This is rugged-looking country; but it is also very delicate terrain. Irresponsible hikers can leave long-lasting scars. Use your backpacker stove and camp in a manner so that those coming behind you will not know you were here. Avoid wandering through patches of microbiotic crust—low-lying, nonflowering plants. Follow the little drainage routes through this crust.

The hike to Marching Men and Tower Arch is an easy 5.5-mile loop hike over Klondike Bluffs and into an area of slickrock and beautifully eroded

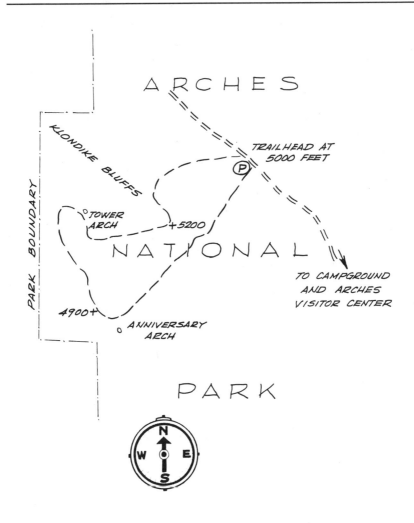

A R C H E S

KLONDIKE BLUFFS

PARK BOUNDARY

TRAILHEAD AT
5000 FEET

P

TOWER
ARCH

+5200

N A T I O N A L

TO CAMPGROUND
AND ARCHES
VISITOR CENTER

4900+

ANNIVERSARY
ARCH

P A R K

N
W E
S

ONE MILE

sandstone. The elevation changes less than 300 feet. Most of the route is on four-wheel or two-wheel drive dirt roads; however, traffic is minimal.

Along the way is a row of towering monoliths called the Marching Men, an impressive stone arch, an historic inscription, and much more. Usually, hikers make the trip to see Tower Arch, but that's just an excuse to get into this fabulous backcountry.

To reach the trailhead, enter Arches National Park near Moab from U.S. 191. Stop at the visitor center just off the highway and pick up a backcountry permit if you plan an overnighter (the Klondike Bluffs area is closed to camping from January 1 to July 15 each year, to protect critical wildlife habitat). Also, check on road conditions to Klondike Bluffs.

Drive about seventeen miles into the park to the Salt Valley dirt road—on your left after driving through most of the park. The Salt Valley Road is generally passable to two-wheel drive vehicles. However, heavy rains can make the road impassable to any vehicle, so be certain to ask at the visitor center about road conditions. Follow this road for 7.7 miles to a junction, where a sign points you to the left and to the Klondike Bluffs parking area, 1.3 miles farther.

A developed, maintained trail leads from the parking area over the east end of the Bluffs, passes through a maze of elaborately eroded sandstone figures, and passes Tower Arch after about 1.2 miles.

Tower Arch spans an opening over forty feet high and about ninety feet long. A nearby sandstone "tower" is the reason for the name. The rock in which this arch—and others in the park—has formed was deposited as sand about 150 million years ago during the Jurassic period. This 300-foot layer, called the Entrada sandstone, is believed to have been laid down mainly by wind. Its characteristics suggest that it accumulated in a vast coastal desert. In time it was buried by new layers and hardened to rock.

The rock then uplifted, twisted, and severely cracked several times. Later, after erosion stripped away the overlying layers, the sandstone was exposed to weathering, and the formation of arches began. Water entering cracks in the sandstone dissolved some of the cementing material, and running water and wind removed the loose sand. Cracks widened into narrow canyons separated by fins. More rapid weathering of softer areas in some of these vertical walls resulted in undercutting. The quarrying by water and frost persisted, perforating the fins, enlarging the perforations (or windows), and smoothing their contours until large, graceful arches were the final creation.

One of the Tower Arch abutments bears a 1922 carved inscription recording the presence of Alex Ringhoffer and his family in the area. Ringhoffer was a prospector so impressed by the Tower Arch area (which he called Devils Garden) that he recommended to the Rio Grande Railroad that they develop it as a tourist attraction. Ringhoffer's suggestion led to a series of events that resulted in President Hoover's 1929 proclamation establishing Arches National Monument. The original proclamation covered two small areas, one of them being Devils Garden. The area Ringhoffer called Devils Garden, however, was not included. Confusion during the late 1920's resulted in inadvertent transfer of the name to another location and to the exclusion of the originally-pro- posed site from the monument. It was forty years before Ringhoffer's Devils Garden was added to the monument, and by that time (1969), it was called Klondike Bluffs.

From Tower Arch, the trail continues north for .25 mile. At this point, you join the four-wheel drive road that continues three miles back to the Salt Valley Road. Here, you are about 1.3 miles from your parked vehicle. Walking this stretch of road is generally enjoyable; traffic is very light and you're likely to have it to yourself.

Tower Arch is the usual attraction for most hikers, but the entire Klondike Bluffs area is a great place for fascinating exploring. "Unstructured" wandering amid eroded sandstone rock gardens, discovery of slickrock potholes—teeming with unusual critters—and observations of diverse vegetation can be an exercise in serendipity.

Watch for wildlife. The species here are characteristic of the sparse pinyon-juniper forest communities of the Great Basin Desert. Larger mammals, such as deer, coyotes, and foxes, are present but are most active at night. You may, however, see birds, ground squirrels, kangaroo rats, rabbits, and small reptiles.

The hike is a perfect introduction to the Arches backcountry. After completing it, you'll want to begin plans for your next trip.—*Dave May*

HIKE 74 *NEGRO BILL CANYON*

General description: A delightful day hike in a slickrock canyon.
General location: Three miles north of Moab.
Maps: Trails Illustrated Arches National Park Map, and USGS Moab and Rill Creek Quads.
Special attractions: Peaceful canyon hiking; Morning Glory Arch.
Best season for hike: Spring and fall.
For more inforrnation: Grand Resource Area, Bureau of Land Management, 885 S. Sand Flats Road, Moab UT 84532; (801) 259-8193.

The hike: This lovely little canyon has been one of the most controversial sites in southeastern Utah, an early battleground of the Sagebrush Rebellion. It is a fine place for beginning hikers, with Morning Glory Arch in the canyon's main section only two miles from the trailhead.

Drive two miles northwest of Moab on U.S. 191 and turn right on State Highway 128, just south of the Colorado River. Follow the meanders of the river for about three miles to the mouth of Negro Bill Canyon on the right.

Park in the dirt parking lot. The hike begins on the off-road vehicle tracks (which continue for about a mile) at about 4,000 feet. The canyon climbs gradually from here.

The road follows the canyon bottom, sometimes in the stream bed. Occa-

HIKE 74 *NEGRO BILL CANYON*

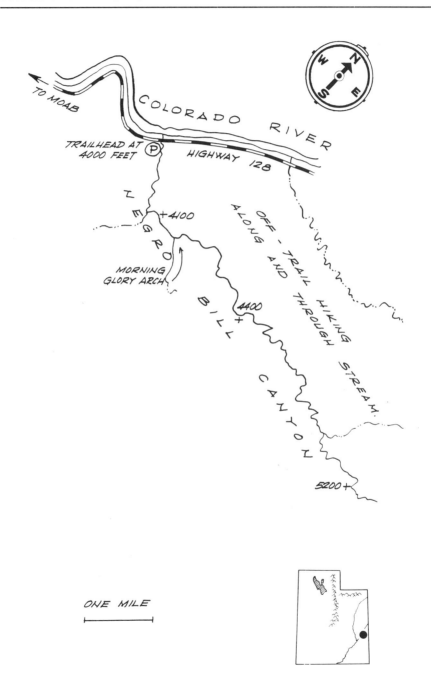

TO MOAB

COLORADO RIVER

TRAILHEAD AT
4000 FEET Ⓟ HIGHWAY 128

NEGRO +4100

MORNING
GLORY ARCH

OFF - TRAIL HIKING
ALONG AND THROUGH STREAM.

BILL 4400 +

CANYON

5200 +

ONE MILE

Negro Bill Canyon outside Moab has been the site of intense land management battles.—Joe Bauman photo

sionally, you can hop this perennial stream, but expect some crossings where you have to wade.

Pink and gray cliffs rise above the talus slopes, from which sprout abundant vegetation. Not far from the trailhead, a pink boulder sits in the middle of the stream, just up from a small waterfall. Along this section, the cliff faces are close together, smooth or rippled, streaked and rough, often gouged by deep cracks or caves. They are laced with bands of bushes.

Wildlife is abundant. You may see garter snakes and frogs along the stream; lizards are everywhere, and hawks soar above the pink sandstone walls and knobs. Look for big tea-green crayfish in some of the stream's larger pools.

About .5 mile from the trailhead, look for a beautiful alcove in the left (north) wall. In the fall, the thick vegetation is spectacular. The alcove has a sandy floor and sheer cliffs that glow salmon and orange. You can almost always find a shady nook in this spot.

At a large spine of rocks, a little more than a mile into the canyon, a major side canyon enters from the right (south). This canyon has some interesting hiking, although thick vegetation makes the going tough in spots. You encounter rough slickrock terrain, requiring scrambling at times. The trail parallels cliffs, drops into water pockets and crosses boulder-strewn stretches. You may find an enormous cottonwood tree in a box canyon in this area.

Continuing up Negro Bill, the jeep trail ends just beyond the first side canyon. In another mile, nestled in a side canyon to the right, look for Morning Glory Natural Bridge, a 243-foot long rock span, set back against the cliff above a spring and a small pool. It is hard to distinguish from the rock wall until you are almost under it.

In June 1979, Negro Bill Canyon was the center of a land management battle. Local anti-environmental and anti-federal activists—part of the Sagebrush Rebellion—used a county bulldozer to demolish a modest dirt barrier the Bureau of Land Management (BLM) had built to keep vehicles from damaging the canyon while it was being considered for possible wilderness status. The BLM replaced the barrier in mid-July, 1979.

A week later, angry Grand County commissioners held a formal meeting and declared that the road up the canyon belonged to the county. The same day, county officials used the bulldozer again to plow through the new barrier. Then the county reportedly spread gravel on the lower part of the road to "improve it," making it an improved way and thus not suitable for a roadless area.

The federal government filed suit in U.S. District Court over the incident. The result was a negotiated settlement; Grand County dropped its claim to .25 mile of road at the canyon mouth, and the BLM agreed to maintain the road for public access.—*Joe Bauman*

HIKE 75 *BEHIND THE ROCKS*

General description: Off-trail hiking among eroded sandstone fins in a Bureau of Land Management wilderness study area.
General location: Immediately southwest of Moab.
Maps: Southeastern Utah Multipurpose Map and USGS Moab Quad.
Special attractions: Solitude, spectacular geology, and prehistoric ruins.
Best season for hike: Spring and fall.
For more information: Grand Resource Area, Bureau of Land Management, 885 S. Sand Flats Road, Moab, UT 84532; (801) 259-8193.

The hike: Most hikers who have spent any time in southeastern Utah's canyon country have stopped in Moab. Usually, however, the time spent here is for food and refueling before heading on to distant backcountry haunts. Few hikers realize that within sight of Moab's main street is one of the premier hiking spots around.

As you drive through Moab, notice the 1000-foot sandstone wall to the southwest. This wall guards a Bureau of Land Management (BLM) wilderness study area of more than 12,000 acres. The area, called Behind the Rocks, offers fascinating hiking among eroded sandstone fins. In fact, the name might be a bit misleading, because as you hike through Behind the Rocks, you feel like you're actually in the rocks. Or, as one hiker described the experience in comments to the BLM supporting wilderness, it is like you are "in between the slices of a loaf of fresh bread."

Behind the Rocks has no maintained trails through it, but access is good due to a few jeep roads and trails for mineral development. Once you've climbed above Moab and the Colorado River, you're pretty much on your own to explore the geologic and archaeologic treasures here. In spite of proximity to Moab, a strong case for wilderness has been made because of the solitude provided by the many sandstone fins. After the climb to the top, you'll feel totally isolated, even though Moab is but a few miles away.

The Navajo sandstone fins are an eighth to a quarter mile long, a few hundred feet thick, and several hundred feet high. Once you get back among them, you'll find virtually unlimited opportunities for exploration. Fin canyons often end in pour offs that cannot be climbed without ropes. Be cautious—it is relatively easy to become disoriented and lost in this maze of rock. If you do become lost, remember that the fins are oriented in an east-west direction. Follow the fins to the west and you reach the overlook to the Colorado River; to the east, you find the upper end of Spanish Valley near Moab.

Water is either unreliable or unavailable in most of this country, so plan on carrying it in with you. And while overnighters are certainly possible, most hikers make day trips into Behind the Rocks.

The easiest access to the area is via the Moab Rim Trail. Turn west off U.S. 191 in Moab onto Kane Creek Boulevard. This road is located on the south end of town—about .5 mile from Center Street. After going under the power lines that cross the Colorado River, travel about a mile. Look for a small turnoff on the left side of the road, .1 mile beyond the first cattleguard. It appears that the road goes nowhere; but if you look closely, you see it running along the redrock ledge. After hiking for a short distance, you begin to see the rubber marks of the jeepers. The road becomes more obvious on top, and you come to a 700-foot overlook of Moab. There's plenty of exploring from here. If you follow the jeep road southeast, you connect with the Hidden Valley Trail, which originates at Angel Rock Road, three miles south of Moab on U.S. Highway 191.

Another access along Kane Creek Boulevard is on the Pritchett Canyon jeep road—3.1 miles from the power lines just outside of Moab. You can hike up the jeep trail and then head north in among the fins. About a mile up Pritchett Canyon, a drainage heads to the left (north). You will encounter several pools which must be crossed and a rope is helpful; but the country is spectacular and you may locate a large, unnamed arch.

Whichever route you take, there is fascinating hiking and exploring here. Human disturbance is minimal once you get off the jeep roads, and you will find plenty of solitude.—*Glen Lathrop*

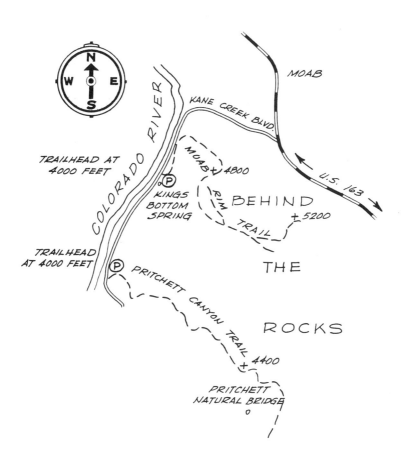

Appendix I
Local conservation organizations

Utah Wilderness Association
455 E. 400 South, #306
Salt Lake City, UT 84111
(801) 359-1337

Utah Wilderness Coalition
P.O. Box 11446
Salt Lake City, UT 84147
(801) 532-5959

Utah Wildlife Federation
P.O. Box 15636
Salt Lake City, UT 84115
(801) 264-4981

Utah Environment Center
637 E. 400 South
Salt Lake City, UT 84111
(801) 322-0220

Sierra Club, Utah Chapter
177 E. 900 South
Salt Lake City, UT 84108
(801) 363-9621

Wasatch Mountain Club
888 S. 200 East
Salt Lake City, UT 84106
(801) 363-7150

Appendix II
Federal and state agencies

Federal Land Management Agencies

U.S. Forest Service

U.S. Dept. of Agriculture
Forest Service
Intermountain Region
324 25th Street
Ogden, UT 84401
(801) 625-5182

Ashley National Forest
353 N. Vernal Avenue
Vernal, UT 84078
(801) 789-1181

Flaming Gorge Ranger District
P.O. Box 278
Manila, UT 84046
(801) 784-3445

Vernal Ranger District
353 N. Vernal Avenue
Vernal, UT 84078
(801) 789-1181

Roosevelt Ranger District
244 West Highway 40
Box 333-6
Roosevelt, UT 84066
(801) 722-5018

Duchesne Ranger District
85 West Main
P.O. Box 1
Duchesne, UT 84021
(801) 738-2482

Dixie National Forest
82 North 100 East
P.O. Box 0580
Cedar City, UT 84721-0580
(801) 865-3700

Pine Valley Ranger District
196 East Tabernacle St., Rm. 40
P.O. Box 2288
St. George, UT 84771-2288
(801) 673-3431

Cedar City Ranger District
82 North 100 East
P.O. Box 0627
Cedar City, UT 84721-0627
(801) 865-3200

Powell Ranger District
225 East Center
P.O. Box 80
Panquitch, UT 84759
(801) 676-8815

Escalante Ranger District
270 West Main
P.O. Box 246
Escalante, UT 84726
(801) 826-4221

Teasdale Ranger District
138 E. Main
P.O. Box 99
Teasdale, UT 84773
(801) 425-3702

Fishlake National Forest
115 East 900 North
Richfield, UT 84701
(801) 896-9233

Fillmore Ranger District
390 South Main
P.O. Box 265
Fillmore, UT 84631
(801) 743-5721

Loa Ranger District
150 South Main
P.O. Box 128
Loa, UT 8474
(801) 836-2811

Beaver Ranger District
190 North 100 East
P.O. Box E
Beaver, UT 84713
(801) 438-2436

Richfield Ranger District
115 East 900 North
Richfield, UT 84701
(801) 896-9233

Uinta National Forest
88 West 100 North
P.O. Box 1428
Provo, UT 84603
(801) 377-5780

Heber Ranger District
125 East 100 North
P.O. Box 190
Heber City, UT 84032
(801) 654-0470

Pleasant Grove Ranger District
390 North 100 East
P.O. Box 228
Pleasant Grove, UT 84062
(801) 785-3563

Spanish Fork Ranger District
44 West 400 North
Spanish Fork, UT 84660
(801) 798-3571

Wasatch-Cache National Forest
8230 Federal Building
125 South State Street
Salt Lake City, UT 84138
(801) 524-5030

Salt Lake Ranger District
6944 South 3000 East
Salt Lake City, UT 84121
(801) 524-5042

Kamas Ranger District
50 East Center Street
P.O. Box 68
Kamas, UT 84036
(801) 783-4338

Evanston Ranger District
1565 Hwy. 150, Suite A
P.O. Box 1880
Evanston, WY 82931-1880
(307) 789-3194

Mountain View Ranger District
Lone Tree Road, Hwy. 44
P.O. Box 129
Mountain View, WY 82939
(307) 782-6555

Ogden Ranger District
507 25th Street
P.O. Box 1433
Odgen, UT 84401
(801) 625-5110

Logan Ranger District
860 N. 1200 E.
Logan, UT 84321
(801) 753-2772

National Park Service (NPS)

Arches National Park
P.O. Box 907
Moab, UT 84532
(801) 259-8161

Bryce Canyon National Park
Bryce Canyon, UT 84717
(801) 834-5322

Canyonlands National Park
125 W. 200 South
Moab, UT 84532
(801) 259-7164

Capitol Reef National Park
Torrey, UT 84775-0015
(801) 425-3791

Cedar Breaks National Monument
P.O. Box 749
Cedar City, UT 84720
(801) 586-9451

Dinosaur National Monument
P.O. Box 210
Dinosaur, CO 81610
(303) 374-2216

Glen Canyon National Recreation
   Area
P.O. Box 1507
Page, AZ 86040
(602) 645-2471

Natural Bridges National
   Monument
P.O. Box 1
Lake Powell, UT 84533
(801) 259-5174

Rainbow Bridge Nat. Monument
P.O. Box 1507
Page, AZ 86040
(602) 645-2471

Timpanogos Cave National
   Monument
Route 3, Box 200
American Fork, UT 84003
(801) 756-0351

Zion National Park
Springdale, UT 84767
(801) 772-3256

State Offices and Land Management Agencies

Governor's Office
210 State Capitol
Salt Lake City, UT 84114
(801) 538-1000

Department of Natural Resources
1636 W. North Temple
Salt Lake City, UT 84116
(801) 538-7200

Division of Wildlife Resources
1596 W. North Temple
Salt Lake City, UT 84116
(801) 538-4700

Division of Parks and Recreation
1636 W. North Temple
Salt Lake City, UT 84116
(801) 538-7220

Division of State Lands and Forestry
3 Triad Center, Suite 400
Salt Lake City, UT 84180
(801) 538-5508

Bureau of Land Management

Bureau of Land Management
Utah State Office
324 South State, Suite 301
Salt Lake City, UT 84111-2303

Salt Lake District
2370 South 2300 West,
Salt Lake City, UT 84119
(801) 977-4300

Bear River Resource Area
2370 South 2300 West,
Salt Lake City, UT 84119
(801) 977-4300

Pony Express Resource Area
2370 South 2300 West
Salt Lake City, UT 84119
(801) 977-4300

Cedar City District
176 East D.L. Sargent Drive
Cedar City, UT 84720
(801) 586-2401

Beaver River Resource Area
444 South Main #C-3
Cedar City, UT 84720
(801) 586-2458

Dixie Resource Area
225 North Bluff
St. George, UT 84770
(801) 673-4654

Escalante Resource Area
Escalante, UT 84726
(801) 826-4291

Kanab Resource Area
318 North First East
P.O. Box 459
Kanab, UT 84741
(801) 644-2672

Richfield District
150 East 900 North
P.O. Box 768
Richfield, UT 84701
(801) 896-8221

House Range Resource Area
P.O. Box 778
Fillmore, UT 84631
(801) 743-6811

Warm Springs Resource Area
P.O. Box 778
Fillmore, UT 84631
(801) 743-6811

Sevier River Resource Area
180 North 100 East
Richfield, UT 84701
(801) 896-8228

Henry Mountains Resource Area
P.O. Box 99
Hanksville, UT 84734
(801) 542-3461

Moab District
82 East Dogwood
P.O. Box 970
Moab, UT 84532
(801) 259-6111

Grand Resource Area
885 S. Sand Flats Road
P.O. Box M
Moab, UT 84532
(801) 259-8193

Price River Resource Area
900 North 7th East
Price, UT 84501
(801) 637-4584

San Rafael Resource Area
900 North 7th East
Price, UT 84501
(801) 637-4584

San Juan Resource Area
435 North Main
Monticello, UT 84535
(801) 587-2141

Vernal District
170 South 500 East
P.O. Box F
Vernal, UT 84078
(801) 789-1362

Diamond Mountain Resource Area
170 South 500 East
P.O. Box F
Vernal, UT 84078
(801) 789-1362

Book Cliffs Resource Area
170 South 500 East
P.O. Box F
Vernal, UT 84078
(801) 789-1362

Appendix III
Finding Maps

Maps published by the United States Geological Survey (USGS), Trails Illustrated and the Utah Travel Council are recommended as supplements to those in this guide.

The USGS maps are detailed 7.5 minute quads and are available from many commercial outlets throughout the state. Topos and state map indexes are available directly from the U.S. Geological Survey, Box 25286, Federal Center, Denver, CO 80225. Older 15 minute quads are no longer published and may be permanently out of stock. You may also find the USGS 1:100,000 series useful as an overview of an area. These maps are based on 1980 aerial photos.

Trails Illustrated, a Colorado-based recreational map publisher, produces an excellent line of maps covering many of Utah's most popular backcountry destinations and all its national parks. Each map is based on photo reproductions of USGS topographic maps, which are then updated and customized on an annual or biennial basis. The waterproof maps are available at sporting goods stores, book stores, forest service district offices, or can be ordered directly from Trails Illustrated, P.O. Box 3610, Evergreen, CO 80439-3425, 1-800-962-1643.

The Utah Travel Council publishes a set of 5 multi-purpose maps, which are helpful in navigating to the trailhead, since they offer a broader picture of the area. They are available from the Utah Travel Council, Council Hall/Capitol Hill, Salt Lake City 84114, (801) 538-1030.

Other map outlets:
• The Forest Service publishes maps for each of the six national forests in the state. These maps are available at national forest and ranger district offices. Check also for more detailed maps at the district offices.
• The Bureau of Land Management offers useful maps for some popular hiking areas. Check with a district or resource area office before making your hike to see if maps are available.
• The National Park Service has maps—generally as part of a brochure—for each of the parks. Stop in at a ranger station on the way to the trailhead.
• The Division of Wildlife Resources publishes *Lakes of the High Uintas*, a helpful series of booklets describing the fishing potential in most of the Uinta lakes. Maps are included. They are available from the Division of Wildlife Resources, 1596 West North Temple, Salt Lake City 84116 and from some regional offices.
• AAA Engineering publishes two maps—Uinta Lakes West and Uinta Lakes East—which, like the Wildlife Resources booklets, are for the backpacking angler. These maps can be purchased from Wildlife Resources and from some sporting goods stores.

Out here–there's no one to ask directions

. . . except your **FALCON**GUIDE.

FALCONGUIDES is a series of recreation guidebooks designed to help you safely enjoy the great outdoors. Each title features up-to-date maps, photos, and detailed information on access, hazards, side trips, special attractions, and more. The 6 x 9" softcover format makes every book an ideal travel companion as you discover the scenic wonders around you.

FALCONGUIDES... leading the way!

HIKING NOTES